SWORDS and PLOUGHSHARES

Harry and Lillian Cole circa 1948 with their children Paul, Doreen, Gwen, Godfrey, Christopher and Maurice – see Chapter 7

SWORDS
and
PLOUGHSHARES

Codford during the Twentieth Century

Romy Wyeth

GEMINI

Published in 2007 by Gemini
Chitterne Road
Codford
Warminster
BA12 0PG

Origination by Ex Libris Press
St Helier, Jersey

Printed by Cromwell Press
Trowbridge, Wiltshire

Cover design by Brian Marshall

© 2007 Romy Wyeth

ISBN 978-0-9515199-7-4

*This book is dedicated to Maurice and Godfrey Cole
with deep affection and gratitude*

CONTENTS

Hippy convoy on A36 leading to Ivy Cottages, Codford, 1980s. Photo Stefan Trojak.

Acknowledgements

This book owes a great deal to many people for their generosity with copyright permissions, information, personal stories, old postcards and family photos. I am especially grateful to the following:

Andrew Davis & the Lackham College of Agriculture & Rural Life for permission to use Susie Notley's story of her childhood in Codford St Mary; Charlie MacDonald for information about 'Kitchener's Keelies'; John Hatherley for his father's letters; the Commonwealth War Graves Commission; Georgie Kemp, Terry Crawford & Rod Priddle; the Cole family-Maurice, Godfrey, Doreen & Gwen for permission to publish Harry Cole's History of Codford; to David Frostick and Rita Chapman for their stories; David Greenacre, Lt Col Charles Stephens & Lance Sgt Mark Morgan of the Welsh Guards; John Tilbury-Grenadier Guards; Mike Taylor; Mike Prince; the Swansea & West Glamorgan Branch of the Welsh Guards; Craig Fuller- Aviation Archaeological Investigation & Research, Ian Hodgkiss, Gareth Jones & David Williams; Christopher Green & Tim Woods; Ann & John Bennett; Denis & Geoff Bissell; David Last; Stefan Trojak, Doreen & Ken Axtell, Col. Jerry Hunter, Andrew Garratt, Owen Pearce, Maurice Colson; Reverend Ian Duff. Finally to Roger Jones for designing and typesetting *Swords and Ploughshares* and Brian Marshall for photographs, cover design and maps.

Soldiers in the ford, World War I

Introduction

Codford lies in the heart of the Wylye Valley and at the edge of Salisbury Plain in Wiltshire. During the whole of the twentieth century the small community was defined by agriculture and the military. 'Swords and Ploughshares' is a collection of stories that trace the twin themes of farming folk and soldiers through the twentieth century. The book tells the story of two remarkable men, following an Australian soldier from England to the trenches of the Somme and hospital's in France and London and a London orphan who became an Olympic wrestler and, at the time of his death, the oldest living commando. The complete Codford history from WWI to the 1960's as written by Harry Cole and Susie Notley's nineteenth century childhood are intermingled with tales from the Highland Light Infantry, of Rex Whistler, of guardsmen and their tanks and of the search for the Codford Spitfire. I hope you enjoy reading the book as much as I have enjoyed writing it.

Romy Wyeth
May 2007

Joel 3 v 10
Beat your plowshares into swords and your pruning hooks into spears: let the weak say, I am strong.

Micah 4 v 3
And he shall judge among many people, and rebuke strong nations afar off: and they shall beat their swords into plowshares, and their spears into pruning hooks: nation shall not lift up sword against nation, neither shall they learn war anymore.

1

Susie Notley's Nineteenth Century Childhood

Caroline Notley known as Susie was born in the Wiltshire of Victorian England on 2nd November 1884 and lived her whole life in the Wylye Valley. Susie spent her childhood at Church Farm, now East Farm, growing up in what today is East Farm House. The family moved to Upton Lovell after her father's death, first to Manor House and then after her mother died in 1940, to The Gables. By the time she died on 25th November 1972 aged 88 her world had encompassed the reigns of six sovereigns, two global conflicts, the loss of the British Empire and the beginning of space exploration. The lost world of a rural lifestyle at the end of the nineteenth century is vividly captured by Susie in her book *My Childhood Days at Codford St Mary*:

My childhood days were very happy in that dear little old thatched house nestling at the foot of the Wiltshire Downs, where years ago Father came as a boy of 10 with his Father and Mother. There were five of us, four girls and a boy, also Aimee the little girl who died when she was a baby. I was very nervous as a child, in fact Martha who was a servant to father before he married[1] used to say as a baby when she had me in her arms and the carthorses came in from work I used to quite jump from the noise they made.

When there was a dinner party Martha who was married to Tom House a shepherd used to come back and help the housemaid wait at table and Mrs Harry House, who also lived in Malmpit, used to come back and help Pollie the cook we had for 48 years. I think was quite tiny when one day I went out in the kitchen and Mrs Harry House had arrived and as the custom was in those days she curtsied to me and I curtsied back thinking it was the right thing to do.

Pollie's real name was Mary Ann Cox, so some times we used to call her Mrs Cox, and she used to love to get us children in the kitchen and give us sugar on bread and butter, much to the disgust of our nurse. Pollie's Mother came to see her one day and I remember her saying to Mother in the kitchen, if you can do anything with Mary Ann, we can't, you keep her. It was strange too; when we could get her to have a holiday she said when she came back, "Oh its lovely to be home again."

Mother used to get one of Brockway's daughters in to help and she used to play games with us. Eliza the eldest used to say that I was difficult to get to sleep but she was always successful. Sometimes when I got older I was put in the box room to sleep, you reached it by going through Father and Mother's bedroom. I could not have been very old then, as there was a trap door there, which opened to, the back kitchen below where there was a long narrow table carved, a refectory table like the monks used I think.

Well at 6.30 in the morning when Pollie had got the big open fire going with the huger logs burning, she would put a kitchen chair which had lost its back so it was like a stool and lift me down, I wonder we did not both collapse. Then I would sit on the stool by the kitchen fire and nurse one of the many white cats we had. Then for breakfast Pollie would get out the grid iron and put the home grown rashers of bacon on over the red coals and they used to smell very good and taste better. When there was game about they used to be cooked in front of the open fire as Father would not have any meat cooked in the oven. There was a very large dripping pan and a long thing like a spear which could take six partridges at a time, then we children used to climb on the stool and wind up the jack to keep them going over and over. The jack had to be wound up continually. Half a pound of butter to baste a hare, its back covered with rashers of bacon. We lived well in those days I can tell you. It was a good kitchen for beetles and crickets if you came down in the night the floor would be black with them and the crickets chirping in the fireplace; we used to bait traps with sugar to catch the beetles. Then Brockway [who was Father's groom for over 30 years] used to brew the beer for the men; there was a huge copper in the back kitchen and he had a long pole with which he stirred it, I did not like the smell of that much.

Sometimes we used to go with Brockway to hunt eggs round the rick yard that was great fun, very enjoyable. If the weather was wet we went across the yard to the barn where huge bags of sheep's wool were stored, and we played on them until we burst the bags, then there was trouble.

We used to keep bees and one day I got one in my hair and it stung my head; the next day my face was all swollen up and I was such a sight, and Dr could not understand it. In latter years when we had to move to Upton Lovell, Mother said we would leave the bees behind, as I think they worried her too much when she was gardening.

Every year the taskers came for the hoeing of the turnips, Pearce and his sons, Isaac, Frank and Arthur, they were quite nice men.

The home field leading from our gardens up to the downs was lovely, many walnut trees, some of them had double walnuts, and we used to see these dear little brown squirrels skipping about the branches. There were several yew trees dating back I should think from the time when the hermit lived there in a cave, mentioned in the memorials of Codford St Mary, they used to speak of yew trees being there, one was hollow inside and there we used to play houses.

Then in the spring we picked lovely white violets with a beautiful scent up there and later, on the cleeve we had cowslips, fine ones too. Basil and Cyril Aston [the Rector's boys] used to come and play jailers in the rick yard with us and sometimes Dora and Lionel Dear, the two youngest of a family of eleven living at the Beeches, Codford St Peter, their father was wool-stapler.

Father used to hunt four or five times a week, sometimes to the meet of Lord Portman's hounds in Dorset, then Brockway used to go with his second horse. When the hounds met at our place we had a holiday from lessons and walked on the downs following as best we could.

I remember once an old gentleman [Mr Collins] came for the day from Trowbridge to do some fishing,; when he got back at night his two sisters asked him how he had got on, he only said what struck him most was our good cider Father gave him and the little girl with the black eyes; of course mine are brown, but I often wonder if that was how I derived my nickname as Father and Uncle Stephen always called me Susan.

When Kitty was 10 years old she had diphtheria; she and I had bad throats so were sleeping together in the spare room, and the next morning Dr Wilcox said she had diphtheria, he did not worry about me, but said to Nellie "Get that little white one away", so she went to stay with Mr Tom Harding and his housekeeper at Ashton Gifford, Codford St Peter. I think she was plucky to go as she was only six years old. Mr Harding bought her a doll and some barley sugar from Warminster and she went to church with him on Sundays. I think the staff were very good to her, he kept three maids. Kitty had a relapse Christmas Day but she finally recovered

I stayed at home and we went for walks with the governess. Miss Hopkins was the first we had, she was rather lively, and the Rev. Macleane at Codford St Peter had three pupils, Cruikshank, Tighe and one other, we used to meet these three when we were out for walks, very entertaining for us children. Sometimes we walked to Sherrington where there were watercress beds and an old woman kept a sweet shop where we used to buy peppermint bulls-eyes, we each used to take one and see who could make theirs last longest. Then there was the day Nellie fell in the river going over the wooded bridge, Miss Hopkins and I were out for a walk, she pulled her out and we had to return home for her to get dry clothes.

The next governess we had was Miss Highman; I was so fond of her, but when she was vexed with me I always knew as she called me Carrie, otherwise it was Susie. I was very fond of drawing and painting though I was never much good at it. Then she used to take me out sketching and one day we went down in the meadow and sketched and painted the old hatch house.

Mother had a friend Maude Ellis who came from London once a year to stay with us. I think her father was brother to Sir Whittaker Ellis who was Lord Mayor of London and who married Mother's Aunt, we always called her cousin Maude; she was a very good sort and always called a spade a spade. She used to try and find the most comfortable rick on the farm and sit there and do her work. She used to say when you send me cowslips in the spring be sure and put in some grass for the cat.

One haymaking time our cousin Kathleen Webb came to stay with us and

Father had just had a field of grass cut near the rickyard, he said to us three, you can go and pick out the docks out of the grass and put them in heaps of one hundred each and Mr Cottle [the bailiff he was] will give you a penny a hundred for them. I think we thought we were going to be quite rich but to our dismay Mr Cottle told us 120 went to a hundred, rather a come down for us.

I remember when the women in their sunbonnets used to go out in the fields to work and Father used to say when he came in for a meal, he must get back to the women or they would be fighting.

In the autumn when the blackberries were ripe we used to have the donkey cart and take our tea onto the downs by the second cover, where there were very fine ones, we used to light a fire to boil the kettle and have a picnic, that was quite an outing for us. Then one day we used to go down in the meadows to get sloes for Mother to make sloe gin, at least they were bullaces, a bigger thing than a sloe. Then at Christmas time the clothes we had grown out of Mother used to tie up in parcels for the children whose father's worked on the farm and we used to take them round. One Christmas Dr and Mrs Ward gave a children's party, with a lovely Christmas tree, I got a sweet little Japanese teapot filled with chocolates.

When quite small I remember Mr Walter Wightwick coming back from Bath races, he had a coconut which he said I could have if I could get it through the banisters, of course I could not, but I expect he eventually gave it to me. He was a brother of the Misses Wightwicks who lived at Codford St Peter, their father was the rector there some years ago. Rev. Wightwick had a long family and he told Mother's Father at Langford, when he heard Mother was engaged, that he wished someone would come along and take one of his daughters.

Then there was a man in the village who used to mend our shoes, he grew the most lovely dark red roses I have ever seen, and a good scent too, not like some of the new ones. Mother used to try and have a buttonhole for Father when he was going out, he was particularly fond of auriculars and there was a lovely bed of them just outside the garden door.

The lawn between our house and the church was never consecrated or buried in as they said no one would live in our house if they did, so we used to play croquet there, but when Mr Aston rang the church bells for his daily services, which he did morning and evening, we had to pack up. It was only after we left Codford that the Bishop had it consecrated and took possession. There used to be an old dame's school in the corner of the churchyard before our time, but Father used to say the children so annoyed grandfather Anthony Notley that he used to chase them with a stick.

Mr Aston prepared me for confirmation with the house parlour-maid we had then. The service was to have been held at St Mary's but the hounds were meeting at our place, so they put the confirmation at St Peter's [not nearly such a lovable church] in fact I think Father should have put off the hounds as our service was much more important. Lionel Dear was confirmed at the same time by Bishop Wordsworth of Salisbury on 8th March 1899.

October 4th was Castle Fair. Father used to bring his friends back to dinner, Mr Hending, the Stratton's, Arthur Jeffries etc. and we always had a brace of pheasants and a huge joint of beef, the dinner was at three o'clock. Mother had a very nice piano in the dining room [the little room Father liked so much as one of the windows looked on to the farm.] Well it was a Collard and Collard piano which father bought for Mother when they were married, he paid 100 guineas for it at the London Exhibition, we only came across the receipt a year or so ago. Mother used to sing to us in the evenings and for Sundays she had a lot of Blockley's sacred songs which were very good. A Mr Harrison used to come from Milsoms in Bath to tune it, he used to come on the train and Brockway would meet him with the pony and trap at Codford Station. Mother left the piano to me so we still have it and still have a tuner from Milsoms. I meant to say in those days the decanter of sherry and biscuits were put out to satisfy Mr Harrison, but now Mr Mitchell who comes has to be satisfied with tea.

Aunt Emily [Mother's sister] used to come and stay with us, she used to bring us a bottle of lovely cushion sweets, I never see them now they must belong to the olden days but they were very nice. She also said she would give a prize to the one who picked the best bunch of wild flowers, so we went up to Long Hedge as that was where we got so many lovely ones. I do not remember who got the prize or what it was.

Queen Victoria's diamond jubilee was celebrated in Codford, someone wanted the two Codfords to join but Father said Peter and Mary never did agree, so they should be separate. We had a big feast in the cart house which was a large building in the rickyard. Then we went into one of the home fields for sports. Father ran in a race for elderly men and won something I think but passed it to the next man. Nellie planted a tree in St Mary's churchyard and finally we went up to Long Hedge and on to the Downs where Kittie, Nellie and I set a bonfire alight. Mrs Ashton the Rector's wife lost her way and landed in a field of turnips. One of our many white cats had kittens in jubilee year, we named them Victoria, Regina and Jubilee. I had Victoria, Kitty and Nellie the other two. Victoria used to climb the kitchen door and unfasten the latch when she wanted to come in. We used to buy jam tarts in the village and then beg Pollie to let us have some cream, that was when we played houses.

David Cooper and Fred Love, who lived in the cottages over Cheapside oxbarn, used to plough with the oxen; they were slow moving the oxen but very good. When any of the men on the farm were ill we children used to take them a hot Sunday dinner, which I think they must have much enjoyed.

We had three more governesses, Miss McElvey, Miss Randall and last of all before we went to school, Miss Saxby, she taught us Latin which I thought much more interesting than German which we had to learn at Badminton House.

I wonder our house never caught fire as the sparks used to come out of that big kitchen chimney in the morning and drop on the thatch, the farm men going to work used to notice it. Also there was an engine in the rickyard close to one of the barns for grinding the meal for the animals, and sparks used to come out of that chimney and them barn was thatched too. Rather strange and very sad too that many years later, long after we had left, Jack Stratton had electric installed in all the buildings as well as the house, fire started in the barn with a strong wind blowing in the direction of the house and burnt it out except for the walls and a bit of the garden end, the thatch was wired on an it took a long time to get it off. The church too was full of smoke, they were afraid that was going too, but they saved that I am glad to say. However Jack had the walls built up as near as possible, but they could not do that bit jutting out which was the little dining room.

A lovely church Codford St Mary and is now beautifully kept inside and out. We always went to the services twice on Sundays and enjoyed them. Father was churchwarden for 48 years, he died in June 1904 and we put up a Tablet to him in the church.

In December 1905 we moved to the Manor House, Upton Lovel. Of course I was past childhood then, I had had my 21st birthday, but I remember the day we moved, we had tea in the drawing room by the light of two candles. It was a big house with nine underground cellars, and when father bought it for Mother she said she did not want to live at Upton Lovel, but she really got fond of it. When Mother died in 1940 and we had to turn out of the Manor House we learned that "The Gables" was up for sale, so we bought it and have never regretted it.

Notes

Susie's parents met when 15 year-old Carrie Swayne was seen walking on the Downs with her governess by the young farmer who immediately told his sister he had seen his future wife.

Sources

A Wylye Valley Childhood was first published by the Wiltshire Life Society. The WLS no longer exists, copyright in now with The Lackham Museum of Agriculture & Rural Life Trust. The book is now out of print; thanks to the Trust and to Andrew Davis for permission to reproduce Susie Notley's life in Codford.

Codford Station

Hutted Camp

FSC Camp

2

Kitchener's Keelies

The Service Battalions of the Highland Light Infantry made up of the 15th [Glasgow Tramways], the 16th [Boys Brigade] and the 17th [Glasgow Commercials] were jointly known as Kitchener's Keelies. The Battalion Notes in the HLI magazine THE OUTPOST:

"We arrived at Codford Station in the early hours of the morning of Wednesday, 10th August, and marched through the village and passed many camps to our own, Camp No.11.

Here we are pleasantly situated on a hillside with an extensive view of Salisbury Plain, a prairie-like expanse of undulating arable land, carrying a fine crop of wheat and oats.

Since our arrival we have been engaged in Battalion and Brigade Training, interspersed with Bayonet Fighting and Physical Drill, Musketry Exercises and Miniature Range practice. Distances on the Plain are about as misleading as on the sea. The parts not under cultivation (sheep pastures) give plenty of scope for our manoeuvres.

On Sunday, 8th August, Col. Morton and Capt. Neilson left Totley to proceed to France in order to study the Army in the Field. The Battalion turned out to wish them good luck. They arrived back at Codford on the 13th, and were very heartily welcomed back by the Battalion."

Another less than appreciative impression commented:

"Oh, what about Codford? Codford? Oh, it's a village on the Plain, a very plain village- one pub and dozens of gypsy show booths, and dozens of huts for swaddies. What's a swaddie? A swaddie is a soldier. He doesn't get a straw heap to doss on. He spreads his little thin blankets on the wood floor, says his prayer, thinks of the job he used to have and his decent salary, wishes he were at the Front where all the comforts must necessarily be dispensed with, and, while wondering if starvation diet is the reward of real, staunch patriotism, falls asleep to dream about bob luncheons in the Carlton Restaurant in St Vincent Street in Old Mungo. This is 'some' Plain, and 2,000 yards looks like 1,000, for so spacious are the fields and so undulating the country that distance is deceptive.

However, it is rumoured we are not long for this airt, and as the Colonel has returned from a visit to the Front and has twigged a good place for a good battalion of good boys, we are going on a journey to a far off better land, as the hymn says." AYE

The diverse comments on the sparse rations, the conditions and the lack of female companionship 'enjoyed' by the troops in the land of the Sassenachs were a regular feature on THE OUTPOST:

"It is said that our boys at the Front are very well fed. Send us there at once. We're hungry."

"The Bible say's 'man shall not live by bread alone,' but we jolly well have to."

"While under canvas we could always depend on finding a little grass in our grub, but that didn't make it pate de foie gras."

"We have been advised not to drink the camp water. Is this some deep scheme to make us visit the wet canteen? Bad Bacchus and bad beer."

" It's a good job the potatoes have jackets that fit them for it takes the tailor three weeks to alter one of ours."

"Salisbury Plain, from the hill on which our bedless huts stand, seems plain Salisbury. We do miss the frills and flounces and the misses."

"A deputation is to be sent to Prees to ask some of the fair maids there to come to the Codford YMCA. No Cod! That's fishy!"

Soldiers and villagers at the ford

The Pilgrims Progress

Oft in the halcyon days of youth,
Unshaved, untutored, and uncouth,
I took it as the simple truth,
I loved no one but
Nora.

But I had spoken all too soon,
For when I found myself at Troon,
In uniform, I loved to spoon,
With one whose name was
Flora.

At Prees my heart was all aflame,
(Though I confess it with some shame)
For one whose figure was her fame,
The blithe and buxom
Milly.

But Age can wither, Custom stale,
And so, arrived at Wensleydale,
I struck upon another trail,
And sauntered out with
Lily.

Sheffield saw me once again,
Afflicted by an amorous strain,
And there I did my best to feign
A simple love for
Peggy

And now interned at Salisbury Plain,
I sing myself the old refrain,
'He who loves all, loves in vain'
And consequently I remain,
Your ever loveless
Reggie

In September the suggestion that a Dramatic Club be formed was mooted:

"Battalion Entertainers. The long, dreich winter nights will soon be with us again and some one has requested the raising of a Dramatic Club amongst us. We think this is a good idea, and we submit that a committee be formed to carry it out. We do not lack talent, and there is no doubt about our being forced to amuse ourselves as best we can, as Codford cannot cater for the requirements of so many men. Let us have every form of interesting amusement possible, and 'muckie,' 'banker,' 'nap,' and other forms of more or less reprehensible pastime will die a natural death. There is nothing like ennui to make men travel the primrose path, so it is up to us to do our bit to kill the tedium of the long dark evenings now rapidly approaching. Friends at home will do well to let us have any music they can spare, also books and novels, and that gramophone which has lain on the shelf since the boys rallied to the Colours.

An extract "The 15ᵗʰ Battalion History of the Glasgow Tramways Battalion" chronicles the Codford period on their journey into battle on the Western Front:

"Salisbury Plain, most famous of British Military encampments, was the war station of the 32ⁿᵈ Division. It was reached from Strensall by the Division on August 5, 1915. The 15ᵗʰ H.L.I. found themselves in a world of huts, tents, limbers, cookhouses, horse lines, old fences and new fences, dusty brown parks which were traffic beaten as hard as tarmac, all sorts and sizes of personnel and material. Their camp was on the face of a hill. On one side of the climbing road were the men's huts, served by duckboards that chuckled in mud every time it rained- and that was often enough- and on the other side the officers' mess and headquarters. Nearby were the Brigade headquarters and stables, the latter a plague spot that bred flies as a swamp breeds mosquitoes. Buzzing hordes of flies, house flies, horse flies, dung flies, invaded the huts and messes and teased the very sleep out of men. The troops were forced to improvise fly-catchers! Huts festooned with strips of dead and dying flies. Ugh! There were rats, too, which came from a black sluggish stream behind the officers' quarters- but they were not so troublesome as the flies….In spite of the vermin and the bleakness of camp little complaint was made, for there was an over-riding satisfaction that the Battalion, at last, after many months of impatience, had reached the heart of the military organism, was now thoroughly in it.

The final stages of training began very early in September. The routine was stern, but there was the joy of supreme physical fitness which had come to them after a year of clean, active and disciplined life and the pleasure of growing proficiency in a craft which their ancestors plied and to which their descendents are indebted. 'Camp will be left at 2 in the afternoon and the Battalion will proceed to Stockton, Conyger Burn and the Bake.' There is a strange fascination about the place names here that make word-careless men run the musical syllables over the tongue for the pleasure of it. The men, when on these last, long tramps carried packs, full equipment, a blanket in which to curl up at nights, towel and soap with which to wash beside friendly

Mules in camp

Flooding 1915 junction of Chitterne Road and High Street

The Mud Guard

Warminster Road, Codford St Peter

burns, and water slung in bottles to drink when no hospitable farm was struck. The ranks were hardening. Few men arrived back in camp without cheerfulness and good humour, even after a heavy march, and the searching regimen sent only a few weaklings limping to the medical board to be classified as fit only for home or garrison service. The record was superb compared with that of some of the other battalions of the brigade. The Glasgow tramwaymen rose superior even to the vile boots with which they were issued, badly made and stiff as plasterboards.

Over there! The minds of officers and men kept harping on that string. Over there…and what then? Persistent rumours of departure stirred the impatient Battalion and became chief currency of conversation. These were substantially confirmed by the issue to the companies, on October 11, of Army Form B103- the Active Service Casualty form. Mobilisation stores began to fill up. The Signalling Officer was seen regularly in and out of the mob. stores carrying reels of wire. The Transport Officer went daily with his wagons to Warminster and returned always laden. Orders arrived to fire the trained man's course- and the shooting was so much improved that the Battalion rose from fourth to second place in the returns,. Special courses for this and that and everything else drained the unit of officers. A shrapnel-wounded officer of the Inniskillings appeared and gave tips on trench technique in a series of lectures. Hurried visits were made by officers to Salisbury, and even to London, to buy the latest in puttees and waterproof leggings. At last emerged the sure omen of near-departure- the despatch of the remnant of the Battalion that was due to leave. Then a final development at which all the company commanders suffered chagrin. The munition factory took away scores of men laboriously trained as signallers, bombers, range-finders, and so on- a great hardship, as some of the very best men in the Battalion were gone, men not only apt and skilful, but also hardened to discipline and the march. Their places were taken by a raw draft. Ah, well…."

The October Battalion Notes in THE OUTPOST continue the Kitchener's Keelies Codford experience:

" It is just twelve months since we made our triumphal entry into Troon, that famous city on the Firth of Clyde reputed for the boundless magnanimity of its billet mistresses, the fabulously fathomless luxury of its feather beds, the beauty of its Chippendale, the tone of its pianos, and-the kitten on the rug.

October sees us still at Codford, and STILL going to the Front- sometime and somewhere. Rumour springs eternal; in the human breast.

Our 'Nights-out' are as common as ever, and just as enjoyable. On Divisional operations by day and by night we have been allowed to serve out between one and two rounds of 'blank' per man, the remaining 75 per cent of our ammunition being carried, not in the 1st line Transport- for we cannot risk losing it- but in the Company Reserve.

We have been very busy lately at our digging area, near the renowned fortress known as Yarnbury Castle. A sketch of the trenches has just come to hand, showing the names allotted to each portion. Two of the communication trenches on our front are named

'Half-Moon Street' and 'Park Lane;' the last-named clearly shows the high position we have obtained in the ranks of the aristocracy.

We take this opportunity of welcoming the Battalion's first draft from the Depot Company at Gailes. Our strength has been augmented by four officers and 101 men. The latter so far have had a special programme of work preparatory to firing Parts I and II of the Musketry Course. They are a very promising lot.

About half the Battalion went to Bath on 2nd October, ostensibly to play the City at soccer, but, in reality, to take part in a recruiting rally. In the latter, as in the former, our efforts were crowned with success, though our ardour was perhaps somewhat dampened on the march, in spite of the knowledge that the people of Bath have seldom, if ever, before seen the 'Scotties' on parade.

The six days' leave is now at an end, no doubt much to the regret of many. Free railway warrants are very handy in these days, when the railway companies are so lenient. 'To Glasgow, by the shortest route,' appeared on the warrants. The 'shortest route' was via Sheffield, or perhaps London, or perhaps Whitchurch. Anyhow the warrant was very handy.

Did we say we have spent another month and are no further on? No rifles- but we have at last got a machine gun. The section has already fired on the range and has done exceedingly well, each member not only qualifying, but going also reaching the necessary standard to obtain registration as a 'first class gunner.'

The Battalion stretcher-bearers are making good progress under our popular medical officer.

We congratulate D Company on their most excellent concert held on the 14th inst. In the YMCA Hut, and hope that others of the kind will be arranged and carried through on equally successful lines.

We notice in Orders (WE always read Orders) that the revolver range has been allotted to the Battalion on Fridays, but where are the revolvers? Packed away with the service rifles?"

Yarnbury Castle today is no longer considered part of Codford; it is closer to the twin villages of Wylye and Deptford approximately three miles along the A303. In "The Shell Guide to British Archaeology" by Jacquetta Hawkes Yarnbury Castle is described as an iron age hill fort dating from the 1st century BC with an earlier circular enclosure inside, and evidence possibly of Roman use outside the fort in a small triangular enclosure. A famous sheep fair was held there in the days of the great Wessex novelist Thomas Hardy, a tradition discontinued in 1916.

A map in THE OUTPOST, drawn by L/Corp Chapman and dated November 2, 1915, shows the Yarnbury trench system. The 15th HLI were to the left and the 17th to the right of the system, the HLI 15th HQ and the 17th Company HQ's were to the rear, while the 'A' Comp 15th was a little further forward. The Front Line was situated some 150 yards away from the enemy's trenches. There were five machine gun positions, one of them covered and, very importantly, ten latrines. The trench system to and from the Front Line was mostly one way, obviously in a combat situation men rushing forward or retreating within

Yarnbury Castle

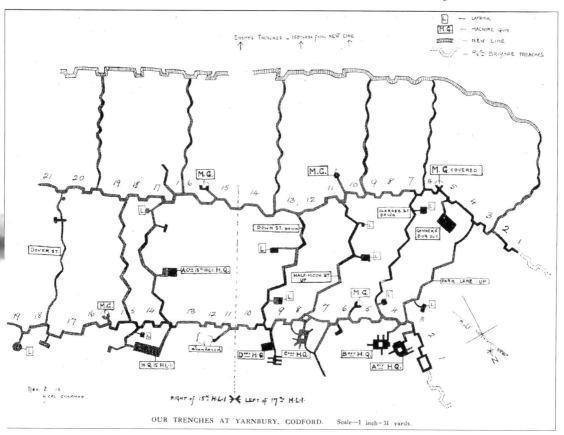

Yarnbury Trenches

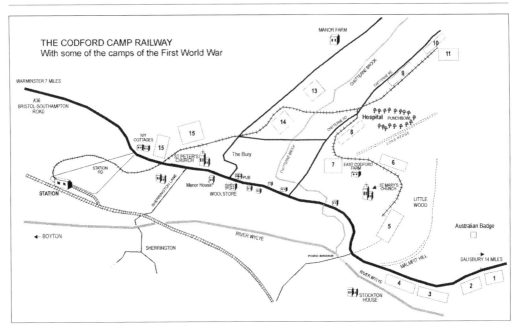

Codford Camp Railway

The Empire Cinema in the Woolstore

the enclosed space of the trench would be dangerous and hamper activities, so men went forward along one route and to the rear by another. They also named many of their routes, Down & Clarges Streets were down, Half-Moon Street & Park Lane was up and Dover Street appears to have been two way.

On Sunday 26th October 1915 Codford was the venue for the largest cross-country race that had ever been held in the South of England. It was a purely military event organised jointly by the Southern Counties Cross-Country Association and the 32nd Division. The race was open to all units in the 32nd Division with each Battalion allowed to enter four teams of twenty men, one from each company. The time of the 10th man was taken as the time of the team, the team that took the shortest time being declared the winner. Fifty-two teams entered the race making a field of 1,040 runners. There were 13 heats with five-minute intervals between, each heat consisting of four teams.

THE OUTPOST report of 32nd Division Sports records:

"The weather was ideal for distance running, and the course, of close on five miles, over the undulating Salisbury Plain, proved quite a severe test. The 17th soon showed that they were going to be hard to beat for the Battalion Trophy, which went to the Battalion with the lowest average time.

C Company had registered 29 mins., 48 secs., B Company, 30 mins., 1 sec., and D Company 30 mins.,32secs.,and as A Company had still to run and from whom much was expected by its immediate supporters, the chance of the Cup coming to the Battalion was indeed rosy. As A Company did not disappoint and their tenth man finished in the splendid time of 28mins., 43 secs. This ultimately proved the fastest time of the race, and was nearly a minute better than the fastest time of the next team, who turned out to be the 16th Northumberland Fusiliers. It is curious to note that the team which finished second to A Company in the heat was 16th N.F. in the good time of 29 mins. 22 secs. This goes to show that A Company's performance was all the more meritorious. Not a little credit for A Company's win is reflected on L.Corpl. G.W. Deans, who attended assiduously to the team during its short training spell, and captained them to perfection on the day of the race. The Battalion's gross time was 1hr. 58 mins. 24secs., and their average per team , 29 mins. 36 secs. The 17th N.F. were second in Battalion times with 2 hrs 1 min.57secs. per team.

This was a veritable day of triumph for the 17th. For they took away with them the first prizes for Company teams, and also the beautiful Battalion Trophy. It was no mean performance when one considers that close on 90% of the opposing teams were English and from a harrier district.

Too much praise cannot be bestowed on A Company; even Mr Otway, Secretary of the SCCCA, who has a long experience of distance running in the Southern Counties of England, said it was a remarkable performance. The names of the team which brought honour to the Battalion and also to Glasgow, are as follows:

Sergt. T. Richie	Sixth
Corpl. J.M'William	Fourth
L. Corpl. G.W. Deans	Eighth
Private R. Craig	Seventh
Private N. Currie	Second
Private W. Hyslop	Fifth
Private J. Kerr	Third
Private R. Morrison	Tenth
Private J.M.Rogerson	First
Private H.F.Scott	Ninth

The last team to finish ten men took 36 mins. 43 secs.; the first being 28 mins.43 secs."

The 'History of the 15th H.L.I'. takes up the story of their final days in Codford:

"Where's that limber? Hurry up that limber." The Transport Officer, giving voice, cantered up the column, the charger's hooves padding heavily on the soft surface, the offside lamps on the stationary wagons gilded silken flanks and haunches. It was 4.15 on a November morning- November 22, 1915- dark and starless on the hill road that cut through the camp of the 15th H.L.I. on Salisbury Plain. The great Plain exuded warm, clinging miasmas that flung a golden nimbus around the face of every limber's lamp. The 15th H.L.I.'s transport was restively awaiting orders to leave for Codford Station to entrain for France. "Where's that limber.....that limber?" Was it, the drivers stoically wondered, the same old mythical limber? Or had someone genuinely blundered this time? The voice of the T.O. was more than usually urgent.

Perhaps Number Four had had to go back for his whip again?; they should put that whip on a lanyard round his neck! Maybe that wall-eyed brute of a mule that broke Number Five's finger had put him in a ditch. There shouldn't have been a wait; the loading had been done the night before- and sharply done too. On the Major's own testimony. Ach well, what was the use of guessing. They'd have to wait anyway, for there was always something to wait for; if not one thing then another. Good job it wasn't cold.

What are we waiting for now? The sergeant has disappeared into a lit doorway across the duckboards- the only relieving gleam in the oppressive murk, except the dull glow of the cookhouse fire's lately in use to boil a couple of dixies of tea for the early-going transport; it is impossible to see the bulk of the nearby huts where the foot-sloggers of an infantry battalion, not to follow for a day yet, are fast asleep in warm brown and grey blankets....Where's that sanguinary sergeant got to?....At last the sergeant, as if in answer to common prayer, emerges and hurries impressively to the column. "All correct, Sir," they hear him say. They take a firmer grip on the reins. " Number one section, forward." There is a straining of leather, the metallic shoes of the horse and mule scrabble on the camber of the road, the limbers lurch and groan and wheels turn grittily. The movement is taken up in sequence down the column,

Members of the Cycling Club outside The George

View from the Royal Engineers Camp

with a heying and a hoying. The morning resounds presently with rhythmic rumblings, the jingle and clop-clop of the cavalcade as it moves down the hill, hissing brakes applied, towards the crossroads.

The Battalion transport, the advance guard of the 15th Light Highland Division, one of the New Army Units, has left Codford for France. Two miles distant, somewhere in this sticky fudge of a morning, is the railway station and the waiting train with Southampton as its destination. Tomorrow the main body will go the Folkestone route. Keeping to the left of the road, lamp wicks dancing with the rude vibration, drivers and their mates huddled on the dickey seats, the column clatters on....

It was early morning of the next day, November 23, 191, and scarcely light. The main body of the 15th H.L.I. was following its transport on the way to France in trains now speeding to Folkestone. It was not quite a full battalion- not taking into account the defections brought about by the claims of the munitions factories- for a bombing accident just prior to departure had caused a change to be made in the command of companies. Captain D.K. Michie, commanding C Company had been struck in the leg by a splinter at bombing practice and, much to his disappointment, had been compelled to enter hospital and to defer his departure to France. The command of C Company had been assumed by Captain Hume of B Company, and Captain Craig, second-in-command of B Company had succeeded to that command….."

Unfortunately 'The History of the 16th H.L.I.' mentions its time in Codford with brevity:

"On to Doncaster for musketry training, which was only secured to every man through the most careful co-ordination, so short was the supply of rifles. For the second time the Battalion encamped on a great sporting enclosure- this time it was Doncaster Racecourse. The next venue was Codford St Mary, on Salisbury Plain- the final disposition before embarkation- the last whetstone of the sword. The significant message from the King arrived to herald the embarkation orders that quickly followed. The preparations for the great moment had almost struck, including the issue to the Battalion of the new balmoral that replaced the old glengarry.

The valley- as the future – was shrouded in mist on the morning of November 23, 1915, as the Battalion swung down the road to the railway station where the Colonels wife stood to wish her husband's command godspeed. And so to Folkestone- the transports awaited starkly in the roads by twelve black, low-hulled destroyers-and France."

We learn of the 17th Highland Light Infantry from 'The Glasgow Commercials Battalion History'

"Three months were spent at Codford- months of rigorous training, of long interesting divisional manoeuvres, and general hardening. The men learned to dig trenches quickly and well, for they had to spend nights in them.; to march many miles without complaint, and fight at the end of the hardest day's march; to use Lewis guns, not as amateurs with a strange toy, but as men whose lives depended upon their speed and ability. The mysteries of transport, and the value of a timetable were revealed.

Needless to say these days of field exercises were not lacking in some amusing incidents which seem to dog the footsteps of peace condition manoeuvres and which act as very welcome episodes amid the hard work which such training involves. Towards the close of one of the periodic manoeuvres carried out by the Seventeenth under the critical eye of an Inspecting General a bugle had sounded and the manoeuvres had ceased. Officers grouped together and men lay on their backs and talked. The General turned to one of the Battalion officers who were beginning to assemble around him, and said, "What was that call?" He often did such things as this to test knowledge of detail. "The Stand Fast," said the officer to whom the question was addressed. "Oh! Come! Come!" said the General, "Now what was it?" he further questioned a Company Commander. No reply came. Then he turned to the Second in Command, "Now, Major, what was it? Tell him." "The Stand Fast, sir," said the Major. "Really," said the General, "you gentlemen must learn the elementary things in soldiering. Bugler, tell these gentlemen what that call was." "The Stand Fast, sir," replied the bugler. The General hurried on with the conference.

At Codford the Battalion had its first taste of army biscuit and bully-beef. From Monday to Thursday manoeuvres were held; on Friday, 'clean up,' and on Saturday, after the Colonel's inspection, the luckier ones went to Bath and Bristol for the day, or to London or Bournemouth for the week-end. Friday was pay day-'Seven Shillings me lucky lad", and after pay-out, the reading of the Army Act or a Lecture on bayonet fighting or tactics. Games flourished. The Battalion football team played and defeated Bath City, and met the other Battalions of the Division at Rugby Football, and invariably won. On the ranges with rifle and Lewis gun, the Battalion maintained its place as the Battalion in the Division.

At last word was received that the Battalion would cross to France on November 22. Only fifty per cent got week-end leave- there was no time for more. Training was over. Few will forget the brave skirl of the pipes as the Battalion swung home in the morning from Yarnbury Castle , file after file silhouetted against the orange and gold of the rising sun. Always, when the wind blows fresh and sweet in the morning, those who are left of those happy times will think of Codford, the 'jumping off place' of the Seventeenth for France.

The following message of God-speed and goodwill was received by the Battalion as part of the 32nd Division before setting out:

17TH SERVICE BATTALION HIGHLAND LIGHT INFANTRY.
BRIGADE ORDER NO 1285, OF 19TH NOVEMBER, 1915.
MESSAGE FROM HIS MAJESTY THE KING

'Officers, Non-Commissioned Officers and Men of the 32nd Division, on the eve of your departure for Active Service I send you my heartfelt good wishes.

It is a bitter disappointment to me, owing to an unfortunate accident, I am unable to see the Division on Parade before it leaves England; but I can assure you that my thoughts are with you all.

Your period of training has been long and arduous, but the time has now come for you to prove on the Field of Battle the results of your instruction.

From the good accounts that I have received of the Division, I am confident that the high traditions of the British Army are safe in your hands, and that with your comrades now in the Field you will maintain the unceasing efforts necessary to bring the War to a victorious ending.

Goodbye and God-speed."

To the above the following reply was sent:

"First convey to His Majesty the heartfelt thanks of all ranks of the 32nd Division for His gracious message and their determination to justify His expectations.

The Division deeply regrets the accident which has deprived it of the honour of a visit from His Majesty, and humbly offers its best wishes for His Majesty's speedy and complete recovery."

On Sunday, 21st November, 1915, the Battalion paraded in full strength, 1,032 all ranks, at their hutments, Codford. A minute and final inspection was made, and everything pronounced in order. A memorable feature of this parade was the head-gear, Balmoral bonnets of the war service pattern being worn for the first time. Next morning the Battalion left Codford in three parties for Southampton, and without any delay embarked on two transports for Le Havre, the remainder of the Division going via Bologne. It was a perfect crossing, no wind, bright moonlight and everyone in the best of spirits.

At 7am on the 23rd, and marched off at once to the Rest Camp, three miles away, great interest being displayed in the few German prisoners working on the docks. On arrival the Battalion found it was under canvas, no floor-boards and plenty of mud- a first taste of real discomfort. Moreover the day was raw, with a suspicion of snow, and no one was sorry when it was announced that the Camp was being left first thing in the morning. That evening a few of the Officers visited the town itself, and others went out on a first reconnaissance to discover the route to the station and the Ration Depot.

The next day, after drawing two days rations as well as 'Iron Rations,' the Battalion left for the 'Front,' –'A,' 'B,' and 'C' Companies going off at 1.15pm, and 'D' Company following a few hours later."

An inquisitive old lady in Codford Station, who must have been dreaming about mutineers, approached a squad of Munitions Board soldiers and asked what they were. "We're munitioneers," she was told. "How dreadful! Are they taking you away to be shot? Fact!

Tales from 'The Outpost': Codford August-November 1915

'The Last Bustard' by Sergeant Mark Drummond

"A sad but interesting event in the world of British Ornithology took place on the summit of a fine rounded hill called Codford East Down, about half a mile above the one-time camp of the 17th Highland Light Infantry.

Codford Circle

A great number of our members used to walk up to Codford Circle, the remains of the Brito-Roman hill-fort which crown the top of this Down, and enjoy the extensive view in all directions over the wide-spreading undulations of Salisbury Plain. But they may not have been aware that local records point to the little isolated clump of bushes on the north-eastern edge of the rampart as the spot where the last British specimen of the Great Bustard was shot by a prowling poacher in the year 1872.

This magnificent member of quail family was by a long way the largest and finest of all the indigenous British game birds. It grew to a size considerably larger that a large turkey, and was justly esteemed from Roman times as the choicest table delicacy that the game-list of Britain could provide.

What a splendid sight it must have been, up to the early nineteenth century, to behold whole flocks of these noble birds as they raced over the Yorkshire Wolds or the broad plains of Wiltshire, which were their last refuges. Although capable of great velocity in flight, when once on the wing, the Bustard had considerable difficulty in rising, and it trusted mostly to its running powers for safety.

But the primeval law of 'the survival of the fittest' told in its case as in countless other instances. Its Latin class-name, Otis Tarda, the slow bird, tells us that, just like the Moa of New Zealand, the Dodo, and the Great Auk, all extinct now, the Great Bustard was deficient in the special requirement of modern times- speed. Its great size rendered concealment difficult, and it thus became a sure prey to its relentless persecutors.

Harried on every hand by that spirit of insensate destructiveness which passes among certain people in the name of sport, hunted by trained hawks and coursed by greyhounds, driven into cunningly-spread nets, caught in snares and shot at every opportunity by greedy pot hunters, its numbers steadily diminished, and by the middle of the century the species was practically extinct, except on the lonely Downs north and west of Stonehenge, where a few wary individuals, by incessant vigilance, managed to eke out a precarious existence.

Parliamentary restrictions might possible have protected and saved these birds and their progeny to our own day, but the early Victorian legislators were too deeply engrossed in the consideration of money-making schemes, corn-law squabbles, and trade disputes to spare a thought for such a subject as the preservation of the grandest of our game-birds.

There is a stuffed example in Salisbury Museum marked 'killed on Chitterne Down near Maddington, in 1871,' which for a time was believed to be the very last of the race. But old villagers of Codford tell that in the following year, as a local 'gunner' [I cannot call him a sportsman- may his name be lost in deserved oblivion], was passing in the grey of the autumn morning round the rampart of Codford Circle, a fine male bustard raced from the clump of bushes out across the Circle, only to fall under the double discharge of heavy shot from the ready duck-gun.

Travellers tell us that the Great Bustard is to be seen yet in flocks in Asia Minor, Armenia, and Mesopotamia, and in considerable numbers on the extensive rolling plains of Hungary and the boundless steppes of Central and Southern Russia. Occasionally, one is brought to the Zoological Gardens, London, but the great Bustard is a native of the free, open plains and soon dies in captivity.

What a regrettable ornithological loss it is that the King of our British Game-birds has vanished from our island, never to return."

Alive and Kicking

We had just finished Friday's dinner, and Jack and I were standing idly at the canteen door, gargling our throats with Young's famous mouthwash. "There go the week-enders," said Jack, in tones that implied that he begrudged the fellows their holiday because he was left behind. "Why the Dickens can't those who start their six days leave on a Sunday get off today and therefore start their leave at home?" I grumbled. Jack looked too fed up for words, but he managed to put whole volumes of meaning into hi s laconic "Hell!" With a gesture of despair he produced his cigarette case and, forgetting himself for once under the stress of his emotions, he was in the act of offering me a fag when one of the Battalion Rolls-Fords stopped in front of us with a jerk and the Colonel's Orderly yelled on us to jump in. I had just time to remark that nothing on earth would persuade me to accept a commission until my leave was over, when the car drew up at the Orderly room door, where the Colonel was awaiting our arrival with evident anxiety. He motioned us to the Chesterfield couch and brought over his Habana-Kabalistica-Grandiosos. We made some fatuous remarks about the weather, and would have proceeded to the discussion of the European situation , but the Colonel looked at his watch and said, "You men can catch the 3-12 home if you hurry."

Hurry! You should have seen the blank space we left in that Orderly Room as we streaked to the hut. E grabbed a few necessaries, answered quite unintelligibly the questions thrown at us by our comrades, and, to use a colloquialism, 'bunked' for the train. The people we passed on the road, particularly the semi-somnolent sentries, rubbed their eyes, looked again at the place where they had seen us, and, seeing nothing, decided they had been mistaken.

In Codford St Mary we suffered a physical shock, a set-back to our mad career, for, on turning a corner without slowing down, in one of those magnificent swerves of ours, we found ourselves lying on our backs, staring up into the vast blue of the empyrean and wondering vaguely WHY? Jack was the first to sit up, and when he did I heard him ejaculate, "Oh! Gee! One-Two-Three-Four-" "Counting the stars I enquired, sympathetically, as I sat up. Then I knew, for I was looking straight at the identification plate on the back of a rather dirty motor-car [O.G.12345] which was standing at the side of the road. "Well, what are you going to do about it?" Jack asked. I answered by raising myself from my lowly position, collecting my thoughts and gathering my possessions together, and turning the former over in my mind, I stowed the latter in my tonneau. We asked the individual who was polishing the driving seat with his trousers if he would take us to the station. He demurred at first, but when we promised him largesse he acquiesced and turned towards his house to wash his hands and don his coat. We were exasperated, for we didn't wish to miss the train. I started up the engine and Jack, in his characteristic fashion, collared the driver low and threw him into the driving seat. Ordering him to go 'hell-for- leather,' we jumped in as the car moved off.

As we were whizzing through Codford St Peter I recognised the back view of one of our Subalterns hurrying towards the station in front of us. I knew he would lose the train, so without further thought I opened the door and leant out, and just as the car was passing him, I grabbed the shoulder strap of his Sam Browne belt and yanked him on board. We got to the station as the whistle blew, and, having satisfied the exorbitant demands of Jehu, we made for the train as it was moving out. The picture of us three boarding the train in step and time made the porter and the red-cap sit up and take notice.

Our Mascot

Margus is a goat – only a young thing, by the way, being not more than one month old when he was duly attested and added to the strength of the Battalion at Prees Camp.

Up to that time we had nothing in the shape of a pet, at least nothing to speak of, barring, of course, various pug dogs, poms and other nondescript pups and rolling-stone poodles which used to come nosing around us when route-marching in the neighbourhood of Troon.

Of course it was inevitable that we should have to face the awful truth sooner or later. A mascot had to be found. Well, it was found, and Margus came into the personnel of the 17th.

What a poor, shrinking, timid creature he was at first! Of course he was somewhat larger than the proverbial fourpenny rabbit, but not much. He was only a baby and seemed to feel his position very keenly. Night after night he cried out his troubles to the dark sky above him, his poor infantile bleat mingling with those vague and indefinable rustlings and nocturnal murmurings that otherwise go to break the peaceful silence of the evenings earthly sleep. We fancy he wanted his mammy, but it was no use, She was far too far away to send an answering call. Gradually he became more resigned to his fate, and the moonlight bleats died down, soon to cease forever.

After a month or so, he began to feel his feet, and confidence asserted itself. He suddenly realised that the bhoys were trying to make friends with him, and thereupon he cast off all reserve. Life in camp was going to be alright after all, and why not make the best of things.

So we see him roaming about our tents and huts at will, no one checking him. Like a youngster, inquisitive, and every bit as precocious, he got used to taking all for granted.

However, he had passed time so far, in the camp, and never been out of its confines. One day his wandering spirit got the better of him.

It happened that the Battalion was just leaving the parade ground for manoeuvres. Margus looked on, and then- well he thought he was going to be deserted. Something seemed to overcome him, and, with a rush, he joined the column, to the surprise of all. Very soon he found himself at the head.

Proudly he trotted in front, not caring very much about keeping in step with the rest. He was there, and that was enough for him.

Every now and then he would ease up, and those behind found great difficulty in keeping their number tens off his straggling tootsies.

About three miles out, Margus began to show very obvious signs of approaching exhaustion. His head, which had for so long been proudly held high, now began to droop. Soon his tongue started to loll about in his mouth, his breath coming and going in labouring gasps. Poor beggar! E had let himself in for something totally unbargained for. Bravely and gamely he tried to stick it, but the pace was too hot, and as we approached the top of a hill, he gave it up as a bad job.

Word was sent back how things stood, and two of us were deputed to escort him back to camp. I was one of the two. Never again will I tackle such a job. In future a board fitted with wheels should be taken when Margus sets out on a route march. Nursing a boisterous baby is a picnic compared with looking after a juvenile goat, as the two of us found out to our sorrow.

At first we looked at each other and smiled. We thought we had 'struck oil.' Margus's bump of awkwardness and obstinacy is developed to an alarming degree, almost pitch to perfection. If we had known we should have taken him to a phrenologist to have his head read. However, we were too late in thinking about it, and - well, there you are!

To continue- the Battalion soon left us far behind. This had the most disquieting effect on the goat. He gave vent to a succession of heartbreaking bleats, and looked like dying of grief. He thought he had been left in the lurch.

From that moment our doom was sealed, and our work began. We tried to lead him along the road, but there was 'nothing doing.' He simply wouldn't have it at any price. His idea was to go the other way. We held a confab as we could see trouble brewing.

As there seemed no prospect of him changing his mind, we lifted him up and carried him in our arms.

Now, Margus is no light weight, and twenty or thirty paces was enough at a time. Then we changed ends as at football. Thus we progressed for half-a- mile or so, eventually reaching that picturesque village of Chitterne St Mary.

As we might have foreseen, complications arose. The villagers were there in force, babbling about the 'fine body of men' that had just passed by.

They started to cheer us when they saw how matters stood. We felt embarrassed, so we put Margus down. He immediately walked into a garden. Some kiddies who were playing there made a rush into the house. The good lady came out with a basin of milk, which she offered to our pet. We tried to make him drink, but it turned out to be a horse-to-the well job. He turned away with a lordly sniff, so we desisted. Then we tried him with apples. This was abortive. There was nothing now but cajolery. We might have known the result. Nothing, as usual. We thought we had better move on. We turned away, and walked down the road, thinking he might follow. He looked on with a disdainful air, so we had to think of something else. A few minutes passed and he ambled on, much to our relief, but our troubles were far from being at an end. He started making calls at various houses along the road, introducing himself to all and sundry with the born assurance of a lance-private. This was disconcerting to us, for our difficulty was magnified. Our duty was apparent, so once more he found himself being borne along in our arms.

This couldn't endure forever, but we stuck to our task until we got clear of the village. Then we set him down on the roadside, and fell out for a rest- a well deserved rest, we thought.

Some kiddies came along, and once more the pantomime started. We swore inwardly. The blithering goat ran into a field, so we had to follow. We caught him, and once more set off for camp. Just then he seemed to see the gravity of the situation, and our hearts lifted when, on setting him down on his feet, he peacefully followed our rear. We started to trot and found him coming behind like a frisky two-year old. This was comforting.

Our joy was short-lived, however, for a couple of horsemen came cantering along the road. We passed the time of day, had a few words about our charge, and they passed on. Margus had evidently been doing some hard thinking at this juncture, and must have come to the conclusion that they had brought him an invitation or something of the sort. We might have known, but never gave it a thought, and it was only when we saw the goat pelting away in front of us that we had visions of more trouble. We set off in hot pursuit, but the distance between steadily increased, and for fully a mile we were kept going. The goat was now almost out of sight, but we could still hear his bleating voice calling us.

The horsemen seemed to be aware of our distress, for they slowed down, and waited until we arrived on the scene. We grabbed Margus with a grip of iron and held him until his new made friends trotted well out of sight. Then we sat down and rested our weary legs.

By this time we had covered almost half the distance to camp, but felt as if we had marched twenty miles. Besides our packs were beginning to feel like huge chunks of lead. We took them off, and flung ourselves in the grass like logs. We were done, but Margus was brimming over with sparkling vitality. He seemed to be in the pink.

Soon we got our breath under control, and once more the ground felt the tramp of our armoured barges. Things were all right for a while, and we should have got back in good time, but once more we struck a bad patch.

We were just rounding a bend in the road when we caught sight of a battalion manoeuvring on the hillsides. Margus got his eyes glued on them too, and must have had an idea that he was near home. He set off at a gallop, we, hard on his heels. Up the hillside he went and very soon he was among the chaps who were lying about there in extended order.

When he saw us coming he cleared off, always keeping a good distance away from us. For the better part of half an hour the chase continued, but human intelligence and cunning triumphed in the end, and once more Margus found himself a prisoner.

We were now confronted with the difficulty of getting him away from the scene of our labours. We now knew what to expect, and so took every precaution. We carried him, this seemed to be the easiest way of getting him to camp in safety.

On the way back we had the good fortune to meet one of the boys who knew more about Margus than we did. The goat recognised him at once, and the burden on our hearts was lifted. We put the cause of all our troubles down, and he followed us like Mary's little lamb. We could see brilliant prospects of getting him home now.

The rest of our journey passed without further incident, to our relief. Margus was landed safely, and he commenced to eat grass.

A.N.R.

3

The Plague Ships of the Great War

In the early summer of 1916, Codford was chosen by the New Zealand Expeditionary Force, as a Command Depot, a camp especially devoted to the reception of unfit men from the infantry or general base depots. The Codford Hospital, situated beneath the Wiltshire Downs at the edge of the village in an area known as the Punchbowl, originally the responsibility of the Royal Army Medical Corps, was taken over by the New Zealand Medical Corps in July of that year. Casualties from the Western Front would be tended at either Walton on Thames or Brockenhurst, convalesce at Hornchurch, then after a brief period of leave, arrive in Codford to take part in a fitness regime which would decide their future destination. They would either go back to the trenches, be allocated to base camp duties or a return across the ocean to the Land of the Long White Cloud whence they came.

In 1920, Charles Thomas Perfect published the book ' Hornchurch During the Great War: an illustrated account of local activities and experiences.' In it he says:

'Soon after the advent of the New Zealand Division in France at the end of April or the beginning of May, 1916, and after their first entry into action on the western front, a large number of wounded, and the usual toll of sick, began to filter through to England.

It was then realised that Hornchurch was far too small for the purpose of a Command Depot, and that, moreover, it was necessary to establish a Convalescent Hospital there. Such 'details,' therefore, as had been at Hornchurch were now moved en bloc to Codford, Salisbury Plain, a certain percentage of the personnel being left behind to form the staff of the New Zealand Convalescent Hospital. This transition took place on 6 July, 1916.'

'New Zealand Medical Services in the Great War 1914-18' vividly depicts the problems faced by the medical personnel in England; dealing not with war wounds, not only with accidents and ailments, but with self inflicted [venereal] diseases and early twentieth century plagues [virulent strains of influenza, bronchitis, measles and meningitis.]

'With the arrival of the training battalions from Egypt, it became necessary to open a new unit for the infantry base, its Commandant, Lt.-Col. Smyth, ADC, NZSC, took over Sling Camp on Salisbury Plain or infantry – training unit. It was also decided to form a command depot for New Zealand troops at Codford. The Imperial Government had early found that a general base depot was unsuited to the requirements of category

A camp being built along Chitterne Road

Robin Selby served in the Wellington Infantry Regiment and was in Codford twice in 1916 and 1917 after being wounded in France

men, whose training must differ considerably from that of fit men. The British Command Depots were originally medical units under the control of a medical officer, the inmates were provided with special treatment, by physico-therapeutic measures, massage, electrical treatment, mechano-therapy, special baths, and graduated physical exercises; the course designed as a stepping stone from convalescent hospital to infantry training depot. Later, these units were commanded by a combatant officer, with a senior medical officer assisting. Lt.-Col. Brown, DSO, NZMC, took command at Codford Camp where the New Zealand Command Depot was established. Captain Aubyn, NZMC, the first SMO, was succeeded by Lt.-Col. Peerless, late RMO Canterbury Battalion in Gallipoli. The standing board transferred 467 category men to this camp, the 'A' class men, including the dysentery convalescents who had been detained for tests, were sent to Sling by Army Council instructions.

No. 3 New Zealand General Hospital was formed at Codford by taking over an RAMC Hospital in the Command Depot; it had some 330 beds available, and by September was partly manned. Lt.-Col. P.C. Fenwick, NZMC in command with several RAMC officers temporarily attached courtesy of the DGMS.

New Zealand hospitals, with the exception of No 3 New Zealand General Hospital did not receive Imperial or any other troops but their own, and the fact that special types of cases always went to special hospitals led to a waste of beds so that at times when the division was not fighting the hospital beds were not fully employed.

In the Salisbury Plain group of units No 3 New Zealand General Hospital, at Codford, was so remote from the ordinary routes of evacuation from France and had so few beds- which hardly sufficed for our own and the British sick in the immediate district- that it had no admissions by convoy. Much representation to Southern Command had so far failed in increasing the hutted accommodation so as to make the complement of beds up to 500. Attached to the hospital was the Venereal Disease Section, a very important department which, as it was a Detention Hospital, enclosed in barbed wire and supplied with a guard, had been first attached to the Command Depot for rations and discipline. Admissions varied between 30 and 50 a week, the proportion of infection being 77 per cent. gonorrhoea, and 22 per cent syphilis. Major Falconer Brown, NZMC still in charge, was visited early in the Summer by Colonel Harrison, RAMC of Rochester Row, and by this officers recommendations, certain necessary improvements were effectuated; the section was attached to No 3 General Hospital, the staff and accommodation were increased, and the Syphilis Case Sheet, AIF 1238 was introduced to general use in the NZEF Colonel Harrison had expressed his entire satisfaction with the methods of treatment in use,- based on the Rochester Row technique- and with the prophylactic measures which had been adopted in England. For the first six months of the year 1138 cases of venereal disease had been admitted, of which only 223 came from France- 50 per cent of the infection, acquired in England originated in London. Prophylactics were on sale at all New Zealand canteens at a nominal cost, and ablution rooms were provided in each unit; men were warned, as far as possible, of the dangers of infection and the methods of prevention; but practically all cases admitted with the disease had had failed to use

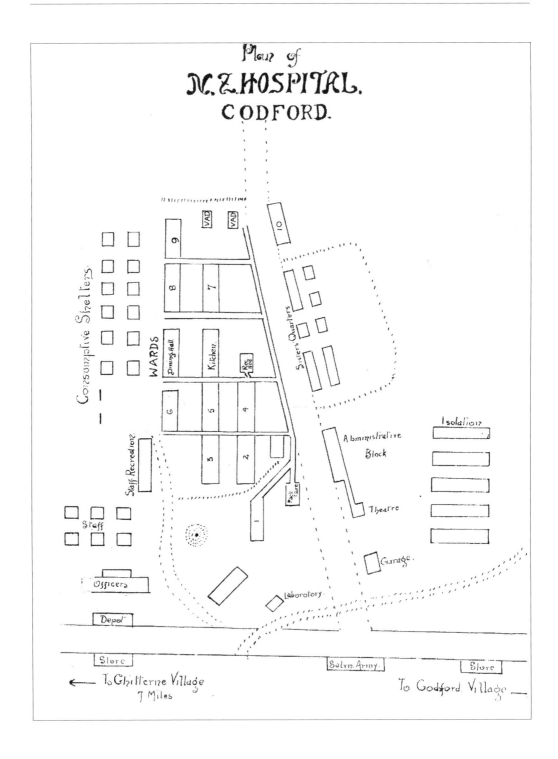

Plan of
N.Z.HOSPITAL.
CODFORD.

either preventatives or the ablution rooms. At the end of the year there were 400 patients in the venereal section with 200 convalescents attached. This was not a very high percentage, but sufficient to warrant strong efforts directed to reduction. The estimated cost to the State by this wastage was stated to be £70,000 per year.

At the Command Depot, numbering some 2,000 men on the strength, Major Bernau, NZMC had replaced Lieut.-Col. Peerless, NZMC as SMO. The additional medical officers were now attached and under Major Bernau's direction classification was brought to a closer discrimination. By means of a card system, each man's status and an epitome of his history was recorded, which simplified the sorting process considerably. The opening of the Discharge Depot had relieved this unit of 'C'class men, which was very desirable. Physical training was now energised and having in view a possible shortage in manpower, a vigorous campaign of combing out was initiated.

The chief medical considerations in the camps and depots during the year had been the virulent epidemics of septic pneumonia and purulent bronchitis. In the first term of the year the 31st and 32nd Reinforcements had suffered from an epidemic of measles, rubella or morbilli – contemporary reports say both – which was complicated by fatal broncho-pneumonia. 75 cases of pulmonary infection resulted in 35 deaths, mostly at Brimsdown Bottom Isolation Hospital, Tidworth, during February, March and April. The disease arose on board ship and is reminiscent of the similar outbreak amongst our soldiers returning to New Zealand by the 'Britannic' in July, 1902 at the end of the South African War. It was stated that the more serious form of the disease- whatever it was- was contracted at Newport-News, Virginia, where the ship had called to coal. Some of our men had visited a US camp where the disease had been prevalent and where purulent bronchitis as a complication had been severe. The ventilation on the transports, especially at night, was defective, owing to the necessity for keeping the ports closed in the submarine zone, and for this reason the epidemic assumed graver proportions.

In view of the seriousness of the outbreak and the necessity for determining the specific cause of the complications, Lieut.-Col. Marshall Macdonald, NZMC, the Consulting Physician, and Major Richie, NZMC, Bacteriologist at No 3 NZGH, were detailed to assist the small RAMC staff at Brimsdown Bottom Hospital. Pathological investigations of fatal cases revealed conditions of acute bronchitis with copious purulent secretion, areas of consolidation and broncho-pneumonia, and emphysema with signs of generalised infection. The Bacteriologist noted the presence of streptococcus longus, associated with B. influenzae, pneumococci and staphylococci. A streptococcus was occasionally isolated from blood cultures. The invariable presence of B influenzae as determined by culture of the sputta by Dr Eyre of St Thomas's Hospital was a remarkable finding, as it put this type of pulmonary infection in the same category as the influenzal pneumonias seen later on during the year. The similarity of the necroscopic and laboratory findings with those reported in New Zealand during the winter epidemics is also worthy of note. Similar cases had been observed in France in the winters of 1914, and 1916; few if any in 1915. Purulent bronchitis was a frequent complication of wounds more especially of the chest, and usually the bacillus of Pfeiffer was the organism most constantly found, although there were no epidemics of influenza at this time.[1] The presence of streptococcus as in Trentham in 1916, was a characteristic of the Sling epidemic of early 1918, but as another investigator, Capt. Lowe, NZMC, Bacteriologist No 2 NZGH, had by blood agglutinations shown a definite lack of immunity to the pneumococcus in New Zealanders, all were agreed to adopt an immunising vaccine prepared by Dr Eyre in collaboration with Captain Lowe and containing mixed organisms.[2] The vaccine was known as MCV [Mixed Catarrhal Vaccine] and had at first the following content:

Pneumococcus	50 to 100 Million per half c.c.
Streptococcus	10 to 50 Million per half c.c.
R. Influenzae	10 to 30 Million half c.c.
Staphylococcus aureus	200 to 500 Million half c.c.
Micrococcus Catarrhalis	25 to 75 Million half c.c.
B. Pneumonia	50 to 100 Million half c.c.
B. Septus	50 to 100 Million per half c.c.

The vaccine was made compulsory for all reinforcements; it gave rise to little obvious reaction administered in two doses at a week's interval, and yielded some evidence of immunising power during the influenza epidemics in England.

The lengthy report on the Sling epidemic furnished by the Army Sanitary Committee on February 28th, 1918, after pointing out the known fact that measles in armies was noted for the increasing severity of the cases during the progress of the epidemic and that the case mortality in such epidemics in the American Civil War had, at times, reached 20 per cent, while in the siege of Paris as many as 40 per cent. of the sick had died, insisted that a specially high case of measles was unnecessary to explain the high case mortality in this outbreak. Its seriousness was explained by the simultaneous presence of other catarrhal infections, a condition aggravated in the crowded and ill-ventilated ships and leading to massive mixed infections. Measles, cerebro-spinal fever, influenza, and acute tonsillitis had affected the troops on board the Willochra after sailing from New Zealand, but the full virulence of the enhanced infection did not mature until shortly before landing.

Another and more serious outbreak was that which occurred on board the troopship Tahiti, in August, 1918. The transport carrying the 40th Reinforcements including 21 officers, 10 NZANS and 1080 men called at Sierra Leone towards the end of August, where she had a rendezvous to form part of a convoy. Contact was made with HMS *Mantua*, a cruiser infected with by a serious and fatal form of influenza. Within a few days of the sailing of the convoy, influenza broke out in the Tahiti, and practically the whole ship's complement was affected. A very fatal broncho-pneumonia which complicated the more serious cases, caused 68 deaths at sea before landing at Plymouth, and of the surviving sick, 116 in number, who were transferred to No 3 NZGH, three died of purulent bronchitis, and one sister, NZANS of cerebro-meningitis. It is hardly possible to realise the difficulties of dealing with such a pandemic on board a crowded transport in a submarine zone, where ventilation was limited by reason of the closing of the portholes at night, and where practically everyone suffered from the disease, including the three medical officers, the nursing sisters and the NZMC orderlies. Much could be said of the zeal and fortitude of the OC troops, Lieut.-Col. R. Allen, DSO, and the devotion of the NZANS and the medical officers who were unremitting in their attentions to the sick. The deaths which occurred daily and in daily increasing numbers until no less than 20 bodies were committed to the sea on the 4th October, had a depressing effect on all, and led to a despondency and apathy in the sick, which in many cases seemed to determine a fatal issue. The cause of the outbreak was closely investigated in Codford, Captain Lowe, NZMC coming from Walton and working in close collaboration with Captain Eagleton, RAMC, pathologist at Sutton Veny, who had previous experience of the Sling epidemic.

Interest in the epidemic, however, was soon diverted by the most serious of all outbreaks, the influenza epidemic of October and November in France and England. Several thousands of cases in the NZEF were reported during this epidemic which affected the division in France and the camps in England; the total loss from pulmonary complications probably exceeded 150 and in most instances the fatality rate in the pneumonic type was extraordinary high. The New Zealand Stationary Hospital reported a complication incidence of 12 per cent in all cases of influenza admitted in October and November, and a mortality of over 50 per cent for the pneumonias. On 5th October , the disease was made notifiable in the British armies in France, which had an incidence of 112,274 cases with 5,483 deaths during the winter crisis."

It was ironic that after the carnage of four years conflict, in the final months of the Great War, virulent disease ravaged the battlefields and the home front with relentless savagery.

The machinery for demobilisation was well in hand by the end of the hostilities, the category men were concentrated at Codford.

'The New Zealand standing medical board in France was now no longer required, the president, Major Bowerbank, NZMC, with his staff, was recalled and established at Codford for the purpose of finally boarding the 'B' group to be concentrated there. All case sheets and documents were forwarded to the depot – the medical history sheets had previously been filed at the office of the ADMS in London – and a board of from 10 to 14 medical officers was set up in specifically devised quarters with a large NZMC staff, the whole so organised and administered that at least 400 men could be adequately boarded in one day. The assistance of the specialists at No 3 NZGH was made available in doubtful cases and the service of the VD section furnished criteria for estimating the present condition of those who had records for venereal infection. The Board dealt with only 'B' and 'C' class men not requiring any treatment, and in the great majority of cases suffering from minor disabilities which did not at the time suggest serious pensionable disability; but it was precisely this class of men who later furnished the most intricate problems set before the Pension's Boards in New Zealand, hence the necessity for considerable care in the preliminary boarding.'

Notes
1 Official History of the War, Diseases of the War, Vol. 1, page 213
2 Eyre and Lowe Prophylactic Vaccines against Catarrhal infections. Lancet 1918. Vol. II, page 484.

Sources
Hornchurch During the Great War an illustrated account of local activities and experiences by Charles Thomas Perfect, published 1920
New Zealand Medical Services in the Great War 1914-18

4

Letters from a 'Six Bob A Day Tourist'
L/Cpl Henry John Hatherley
46th Battalion Australian Imperial Force

Henry John Hatherley was born on 29th August 1988 in a suburb of Hawthorn, Melbourne; he had one sister, Ida and was known to his family and close cousins as 'Son' and to the rest of the world as Harry or Jack. Both his parents were born in Australia, while one of his grandfathers was born in Devon.

After leaving school he was apprenticed as a tailor in his home city; after completing his apprenticeship he took a position as a tailor in Colac, a country town about 80 miles from Melbourne. Harry loved to ride and to sail on the local lake.

When he joined up he was a lot older than most of his comrades, twenty-seven years and seven months of age while most of the others were between eighteen and twenty. As he was an only son the law was that he could not enlist without his parents written consent; his father consented but it took two years before his mother agreed; Harry enlisted in March 1916.

Harry met Jack Laing and Jack Box while they were at training camp in Australia; before they went overseas they were told to pick their mates, Harry told his son John "We were the three Jacks, Jack Hatherley, Jack Laing and Jack Box."

The following letters to his parents and sister offer valuable first hand accounts from the perspective of an Australian soldier, impressions of England, of life in the Codford Command Depot, the wastefulness of war and life in the trenches of the Western Front. Perhaps because Harry was older, he was able to observe and comment on the world around him with a degree of detachment.

Sunday 29th September 1916
A line to let you know how things are going. By what I can see the English Army is no better than ours. The Australian Army is under what they call Southern Command, which includes Canada and New Zealand, South Africa and India. The British troops are called the Imperial Army. All Australian Officers are over us except the very high Commands whom are all English Officers.

When we first landed in England we were not recognised until 48 hours after. All troops coming from Australia have to bring their own food all the way from Australia for the first 48 hours. Have to carry it along our selves.

Harry's mother Louisa; Harry on his 21st birthday, 29th August, 1909

Broadmeadows Training Camp in an outer suburb of Melbourne. Harry third from left second line from top; Jack Laing fourth from left.

Royal Mail ship ? left Melbourne 16th August, 1916, for England

When we arrived in this camp we remained two days doing nothing, just eating tinned meat and biscuits, which we brought with us and tons of food in the Camp. After the two days are up, we are handed over to the Australian Imperial Force and then they feed us. Red tape to start with.

All Australian troops arrive here with leather equipment on costing two pound ten each, the sort I was telling you about. When we arrived here it was taken from us and thrown in a heap to rot and we were then given webb equipment [1]. Not allowed to wear the leather at the front. This leather equipment is costing the Australian Govt millions of pounds and is given to you a week before you leave Australia and taken off you a week after you arrive here and thrown in the dust heap.

We all arrived here with two splendid pairs of boots, you saw them. When you get here they are taken off you and thrown in a heap with thousands of others to rot, I suppose, and we are then given a pair of English black boots. Not allowed to wear tan boots in France. Millions more wasted. This is only one or two of the many ways they are wasting our money. [2]

Our fellows are getting killed in thousands, every week in the Somme battle. I have spoken to several officers I know who have come back wounded from the Somme and they told me [two of them Officers] things are in an awful mess over there. Some Officers have got no idea where they are or what they have to do half the time and its nothing for them to get a dozen different orders in as many minutes.

They say the Germans ought to be able to break through anywhere along the Somme line. The conclusion they come to is that the Germans are in a sight bigger mess that we are.

While in London and different parts of England I took particular notice and can say that every man of the fighting age in England is in the Army or the navy. Zeppelin raids in London have done no damage to speak of. London of a night is in pitch darkness and you can't see a yard in front of you, but it makes no difference, the streets are still as busy. London in many ways is disappointing although a very big city [make a dozen or more of Melbourne] is not as large as I expected. We hear of it being dirty but the streets are just as clean as Melbourne streets and all the main streets are wide and some exceptionally wide. Nearly all the London streets are wooden blocked the same as ours.

I went out to the East end to see things and you bet we looked for the worst parts, but came away disappointed. Everything very clean, the streets and lanes kept in good order. All the houses are built in one long terrace running for the full length of the streets. Some parts are bad but could be worse. Canals run in and out among the houses with barges and boats on them and the water in them is awful, they are about thirty feet wide.

St Paul's from the outside view is nothing to look at, very dirty, and if you did not know which Church it was, you would pass it without giving it a second look. Pigeon's fly all over the building and the mess they make over the buildings and the entrance is a disgrace. I don't believe it has been cleaned up for years. The pigeons are very tame. The inside of St Paul's is beautiful, the ceiling is a work of art, monuments are erected all over the floor of statesman and soldiers. Under the floor is where they are buried.

Here Wellington, Nelson and Roberts are buried. The first two have splendid tombs. The Houses of Parliament and Westminster Abbey are next door to one another. The first is a fine building but not up to my expectation. We could not get inside. The Abbey is nothing to look at from the outside. All these buildings are built of the same stone, a sort of white sandstone turned black with age and where the water runs down it washes white again, so you can imagine these buildings look very dirty.

The Abbey is by far the most interesting to see in London, both from an historic point of view and for beauty of the building and the tombs inside. It is far above what I expected to see. To stand in the centre of the Church and look along the Nave is passed me to describe the beauty of it. It is recognised to be the finest piece of Gothic architecture in the world. This building or parts of it were built before William the Conqueror came to England.

Here you can see nearly all the tombs of the Kings and Queens, including Elizabeth, Mary Queen of Scots, Henry VIII and all his wives. Edward the Confessor, two Princes of the Tower and the rest of them, Queen Victoria and Edward VII were buried at Windsor. Many of these tombs are covered over with sandbags in case of Zepps. The Abbey is getting rather crowded with tombs. What strikes you as funny is that the great Kings of England have very small and simple tombs, while others we hardly hear about have very large and more elaborate tombs.

When we first entered the service was on; we heard the organ and the boys singing.

Harry on the rantan (the town) in London in 1917. He is wearing a new uniform.

These choir boys belong to Westminster College, which is attached to the Abbey, they live there. We went and saw the College and the boys; they are the best looking and cleverest lot of boys I have ever seen, although they only range from ten to sixteen years of age. All wear the silk top hat, either Eton or Beaufort suit, and look very nice. Most of them were playing games, wearing navy blue knickers, short black socks, white shoes, tan belts and white silk shirts open at the neck. Others walking about had a mortarboard hat and varsity cloak.

Church service was also on when I entered St Paul's, and although it is the leading church of a city with a population of seven and a half million people I counted only twenty two people in the Church and half of them were Australian Soldiers and the other half like our selves, sight seeing, so if you subtract that lot, there was no one at the service.

The choirboys were singing, and after the service the big organ played or rather roared. The building is built in such a way that in parts it echoes if you speak in almost a whisper, so you can imagine the organ sounded like one continuous roar. Under the floor is the basement or crypt, just like the Winter Tea Gardens, with a stone floor. Under the floor of this they bury all the great men of England. All have just a slab of stone level with the floor on which is inscribed the name etc. The only two who are buried above the floor are Wellington and Nelson, both have fine tombs.

I am sending a book on the Tower of London which explains it better than I can, I am also sending post cards on it. The Tower Bridge is next door to the Tower of London; I have always had an idea the bridge was named after the design of it, but it is named because it is next door to the Tower. I was disappointed in it. The towers are not very high and the bridge is about half the width of Prince's bridge; the Thames is about three times the width of the Yarra.

There are some fine buildings being built in London, one of them twice the size of our Parliament House, but no body working on them; it looks as if all building was stopped when the War started and never been touched since. The only building they are working is the Commonwealth Building in the Strand, nearly finished. A fine building and called Australia Building it is situated in the busiest and finest site in London.

While in London I wanted to change some pound notes and asked several people where the Commonwealth Bank was, but none had ever heard of it, let alone knew where it was. We knew it was situated somewhere near the Bank of England and after hunting about for an hour or two and asking everybody, I saw a little messenger boy and asked him. He said he had never heard of it but he had often noticed a lot of Australian soldiers standing outside a doorway down the next street, perhaps that was it. We went down the next street, saw them standing outside a doorway with a little signboard over it, Commonwealth Bank printed on it.

Well Dad I will write you a letter next time on the rag time Australian Army, I can hardly see now it is getting dark. Give my best to Mother and Ida.

3rd October 1916

England is beautiful and so quaint and pretty, it is one great garden with little villages dotted all over it, even the big towns are not like ours just big villages and just as quaint. We landed at Plymouth, which is of course in Devonshire. England is just as I expected, in every way, but more beautiful, it is just as you read about it, the little village with the little church and the grave yard around with some of the tomb stones falling over and the little cottages with the thatched roof and little square windows, low little doors and brick floors and everything so beautiful and clean. It reminds me of that poem 'The cottage was a thatched one'. That poem describes it exactly.

The roads or lanes as they are called are past describing; they are all like fairyland. The little streams of water running through the country and villages with little rustic bridges, as you see it now so it was hundreds of years ago. The little inns with sign posts outside as it was in the coaching days of old. For 180 miles we travelled through country like this, passing hundreds of those little villages, all alike, you could not tell one from the other. The country is not flat anywhere, just a mass of rolling hills, with little dells like fairyland in between. When I walk through one of these villages of an evening I pinch myself to see if I am awake or dreaming. You may laugh but you would do the same. I realize I am in England. If I saw Pickwick walk out of one of these cottages I would not be surprised."

9th October 1916

I am getting London leave this Thursday for four days; we all get this leave before we get to France. Along this road are 72,000 Australians encamped, also the New Zealanders. I met one of my pals from Colac who enlisted with the first lot; he has been fighting ever since the war started and got wounded a couple of months ago.

Yesterday, Sunday, I went for a walk to Stockton village and went inside the church. Under the church is one great vault where they bury the big heads; all around the inside of the church are big tombstones of the heads of Stockton House dating back to 1590, the lettering is on bronze plates, it takes you all your time to understand it, its all in Old English [thee and thou style]. It gives you the family tree of Stockton House; they are married to the Duke of Dartmouth's daughter s and lord knows who. On the tombs it tells what things they had done for their country; one of them had fought with the Dutch against the Spaniards in 1500 odd years. Stockton House includes some thousands of acres all around the House.

Stockton

You enter the main entrance gate with the thatched lodge house and enter the big park lands full of oaks and elms and walnut trees, great big trees with the grass all under them so green, just like one big lawn. These parks are thrown open to the public on Sundays. The main drive runs for about half a mile when you come to the village. I could not describe this village; it is so pretty, all thatched roofs. The people who live here all work on the Estate, it has a school and the church I was telling you about; the minister lives here, also the Estate agent. The churchyard has all the graves around it, some dated in the 14th century; the churchyard and all the little gardens around the cottages all beautifully kept. At the top end of the village is another big entrance gate to the private grounds. These great homes of England are just as you read about.

The village people are very humble to you; I bought a glass of milk off one, went to the door, an old lady came out, as soon as she saw me she grabbed hold of her skirt each side and gave me a little curtsey and addressed me as Sir; she was very excited.

15th October 1916

From Plymouth to Codford is about 180 miles and we were travelling by train. We had a bun and a cup of tea at Exeter. At about 5 that evening we arrived at Codford, Codford is between Salisbury and Westbury. At Westbury you can see the big white horse you read about. From the station we had to march two and a half miles to our camp, passing through Codford village about a mile from the station. Every half-mile along the road is a camp of about a thousand men, just put down amongst the trees.

Codford 27th October 1916

Our huts are very nice and warm, each one has a heater and plenty of coal for it, we have it burning all night and make toast with it. Gas with mantles on each hut too. Each man has four big blankets and a waterproof sheet. Four tables and seats in each hut to have our meals on and thirty men to each hut- plenty of room. Of a morning we have cold ham and fried hot tomatoes as a rule, sometimes tin pork. For dinner roast meat or boiled, sometimes beef, sometimes mutton, very good meat; another time baked in a meat pie, one for each hut on a big dish, or, a meat pudding beautifully cooked; about once a week stew. Two sorts of vegetable, potatoes and haricot beans, cabbage, onions or turnips.

We get allowed half a small loaf each man first thing in the morning and it's gone by lunchtime. A quarter tin of jam and half a pound of margarine for eight men, gone by lunchtime also. For dinner at night we are supposed to keep the bread, jam and margarine, but you see it is all gone by lunchtime. The tea we have to drink has milk and sugar and is very good and hot. All this you may say is very good but we don't get enough by a long way and we have to work very hard and to come home to no dinner at night is no joke. It is a disgrace to the Australian Govt. I always go down to the village and buy bacon and eggs and such things, but most of the fellows have no money and have to go without. I am having tea and cake in the village at the Church of England hall, it is half past seven.

At 6am and run out for roll call; at 6.10am fall in again; 7.45 with full pack go on a route march for about eight miles; get back at 10am; go to drill grounds on top of a steep high hill, have to crawl it is so steep, full pack and rifle all the time. Get to the top and fall on the ground and lay there until you get your breath; then drill until 12.30, an hour at each thing; with a smoko for ten minutes every hour. The same thing in the afternoon without the march, fall in at 1.45pm until 5pm. We are trained the same as a runner or a boxer; I can tell you it nearly killed me for the first couple of weeks. I was soft but I am getting as hard as nails now and in the pink of condition. On a Saturday we march to another Camp and about ten thousand of us start on a long route march about fifteen to twenty miles with a good band in front and a bugle and kettle drum band too.

We start off down the road with the band playing a treat all along the country lanes through village after village, the lanes winding in and out among the hills, over little bridges and streams. The elms and the oaks arching right over the roads and the hedges on each side full of berries, every time we stop we get some. The lanes are just wide enough for two carts to pass so when we march we take the whole road up.

The band plays for about a mile then has a rest, then the bugle band starts. This is the time we would not change places with the King of England. About forty bugles and drummers start to play as soon as the band stops. The drums give one loud roll for about a minute, then stop dead with a bang on the big drum and a loud sharp note on all the bugle, then another long roll with another sharp stop. You can hear it through the hills for miles. Everyone throws out his chest and then all the bugles start to play all the calls.

The villages all come out to look at us pass and when you look back you can see the long line of soldiers for miles winding in and out among the trees, all Australians. This is where all mothers should come and see their sons marching, it would be the proudest moment of their lives and not one regret. All though I am an Australian, there is no finer race of men than the Australian. He may not have the looks but in build he makes two of the English soldier and three of the French. I have seen them all. He is not as manly in his ways as the English, but just like an overgrown kid. Whenever you see an Australian he is eating or chasing one another, just like school kids. I take particular notice of these things and you can't help noticing it.

The English race is different to us in appearance, if you mixed a thousand English and Australians together all dressed alike, you could sort them out in five minutes. There is such a vast difference in their appearance, ways and speech.

We are not called Australians here, but Anzacs. I was walking in Hyde Park the other day and a woman with a little girl was walking along, the little girl said "Look at the Australian" and the woman said "no, not Australian- Anzacs, say Anzacs" and the kid said "Anzac."

Codford, England 28th October 1916

In my last letter I gave you our life day by day in our Camp. At five o'clock in the evening I generally have a hot shower and then we go down to the village for the evening about a mile away. There are two picture shows and all sorts of shops to buy what you want, just tin sheds put up since the Camps started. Things are very dear, apples about the size of a plum three pence each, good grapes for sixpence and nine pence per pound up to three shillings. The black grapes they grow in England two shillings and three shillings a pound are the best and largest grapes I have ever seen, they are the size of a big plum and very black.

To walk about the country in these parts is just the same as walking in Fitzroy gardens only much prettier. The elms are bigger and taller and the lanes are just the same width as the paths in these gardens. Very few oaks nearly all elms.

There is a pretty village not far from here named WYLYE. I thought it would be a nice name for our house and looks pretty on the finger posts about here WY-LYE. We all had to vote on conscription the other day and you can take it from me it will be turned down by the Army over here. They all say we came here of our own free will and will force no man to come against his will. It is for the people in Australia to say not us.

We are not in the Signal school here, but could get in when we like. Jack Laing won't go in he thinks we will be separated if we do. I will try and talk him into it. I went over to Stockton Church again to copy some of the names on the tombs but it is hard to follow. Jack bought a Kodak in London so I will send you some photos.

England   Sunday 29th October 1916

A line to let you know I received all your letters up to September 10th. If you intend sending a parcel always put a bit of velvet soap in and some woollen thing as I will be going to France any time now and the Winter is setting in. It does nothing but rain in England but have not felt the cold yet.

I don't think I will have a chance to go to Wales; they will not give me any leave. Evelyne Williams writes me every week, she offered to make me a pair of mittens and has asked me to come there for ten days. I would like to but don't think there is much hope.

I was standing, this morning, Sunday, looking across the hills when all at once all the village church bells started ringing. Then where I was standing in our camp I could see five villages with the little church towers standing above the trees and each has a bell, it sounded so pretty, not a sound anywhere but the bells. It is autumn now and all the trees are turning yellow.

I am in the YMCA hut writing and church service is just starting now, they are singing the first hymn, it is 7 in the evening. I will join them in a minute.

England   Friday 3rd November 1916

By the time you get this letter I am almost certain to be in the trenches. We are supposed to have fourteen weeks in England, but you are lucky if you get eight or ten weeks. As you know by now they are knocking them over pretty fast, but if I go under I will go game.

Jack Laing is in the pink of health and getting fat as a pig. Jack Box is in the hospital, he looks very bad, can't eat or keep anything down. We visit him every day; he is not strong enough for this life.

The weather is bad here, rain, rain, rain all the time. We have easy times here now; we only have a march once a week, too wet at times. Every time it rains we get into our huts and as it is always raining we don't do much.

The nearer we get to war the less sincere it seems to get, nobody troubles about it. In this big Camp here are English, New Zealanders and Australians and of a night they are all mixed up together, but they don't have anything to do with one another. You never see an Australian or a New Zealander speaking with an English soldier. We would not be more distant from one another if we could not speak their language. I have not had a conversation with one yet, why I don't know. If you were to ask all the other Australian fellows they could not tell you why, in fact I don't suppose they have noticed it. We mix more with the New Zealanders.

The English soldier is very clean about his dress and general appearance, always carries a little cane, but our fellows never trouble about dress. Their boots are never clean, tunic on any way and if a button falls off it stays off. Some have caps on, others hats on, put on any way, no badges on some and all badges on the other. Hats hit up the side on one and the next down all round. All the Tommies hair is cut very short, ours is never cut unless you go to a barber and pay for it and you can guess a lot don't worry about it.

The Tommie is very quiet and you never hear him swear, but the Australian is awful. The Tommies get one and four pence per day and they know how to live on it. They will go into a shop and ask the price of this and that and finish up getting a quarter of a pound of something, seldom spend more than two pence at a time and easily makes his pay last the week. We get paid two pound at a time and it lasts the majority of three or four days. He will go into a shop, buy the best of everything and spend less than a bobs worth.

A Commissioned Officer in the English Army before the war broke out got four shillings a day, now they get ten shillings. A Staff Sergeant Major gets three shillings and sixpence and Private one and four pence. Now you understand why we are called the six bob a day tourists.

England   Sunday 5th November 1916

A week ago everything was green and in a few days the elms turned a rich golden brown not like the colour they turn in Australia and to see them all over the hills is a sight worth seeing.

When making socks make them long and wide at the top; when sending a parcel always put in a tin of medium Havelock tobacco.

It has rained all week without a stop and will continue for another six weeks by the look of it. I am in the best of health, never felt better.

England   Tuesday 7th November 1916

Another mail came in tonight, I got one from you and Ida, Ida's had the gum leaves in, also one from Nell Alsop and Nancy Tait. Some received papers today so I might get some tomorrow. Don't worry about me Mother, I am enjoying myself and we have everything we want. Our huts are as warm as our own homes and we have the best food and plenty of it now. Today we had for breakfast bacon and fried tomatoes with bread and margarine and toast; dinner roast beef and potatoes and green peas, stew and rice custard; bread, margarine, treacle and tea with every meal. What more could you want? And well cooked too.

Aunt Harriet's watch is going good, I wear it on my wrist all the time. I think I will send my silver one to the William's to mind for me.

Did Ida get the Zeppelin brooch I sent her? I bought it in the street near St Paul's in London, it was Flag Day in London at the time.

Today is Cup day, 7.45 in the evening so it will be about half past six Wednesday morning now.

England   10th November 1916

Just a few lines on the Australian rag time Army. The nearer you get to the front the worse it gets, and by what I can see of the English Army it is no better. The first thing we had to do when we got here was to tie our puttees at the top instead of at the bottom. For a week we were taught nothing but saluting and had lectures on it, who to salute and not to salute. Although only a few weeks off the trenches we spend hours learning how to present arms and over two hours every day loading and unloading with no cartridges, old rifles made before the South African War, over eighteen years old and entirely different in every way to the ones we will use at the front, got no others.

In our camp of two thousand men we have exactly sixteen bayonets and as there are exactly sixteen of a guard on our Camp who must have a bayonet, when one is sometimes missing the whole camp is turned upside down looking for it. At the guardroom is the klink, where as a rule there are sixty men in it. They have a good time in there smoking and playing cards, but get no pay while they are in there. The guard have to watch them and if they want to buy anything or have a shower the guard have to go with them with fixed bayonets, wait until they are finished and bring them back again.

The other night two prisoners wanted to buy something at the canteen so two of the guards with fixed bayonets took them down. After a couple of hours had gone and no sign of either guards or prisoners, an Officer went and had a look for them. He found the four of them dead drunk in the canteen. He tried to get them to come away but it ended in one of the biggest riots you ever saw; beer bottles, glasses and everything flying in all directions. All the guard had to be called to bring the four back.

The other day I had to go on guard at a Court Martial; everything carried out in great style. A guard with fixed bayonets in the room and Officers of all ranks there, and the head Officer in a chair. They put through three or four prisoners with great dignity, when a big, hard faced fellow was brought in. The Officer started to address him but he would keep chipping in; at last the Officer told him to be silent; that did it. He shook his fist at the Officer and yelled out "I'm going to have my say, you are a bloody bastard, f——— you f—— you all." Well Ida if you had been in the room, you could have knocked them all over with a feather.

Another fellow who came over with us has been in the klink ever since he came here. The other day they let him out as his time was up, and the next morning he came on parade with us; after drilling for about an hour he started to walk off. The Officer asked him where he was going. He said he had had enough of drilling and was going back to the klink. Anyway he went in again and they can't get him out! Another fellow at a Court Martial upset the table with ink, papers and everything else on.....!

The English Officers treat their men like dirt, you would not believe it unless you saw it; they try the same game with us but they soon take a tumble. They are awful dandies! In London I saw crowds of them on the Strand with eyeglasses in their eye and a long bit of tape hanging from it, big caps twice the size of their heads, a very full overcoat reaching not very far beneath their waist, very full riding pants, tight at the knee, and high flash tan boots to the knees. Always carry a flash stick and stand about the corner of the streets smoking a cigarette, all have gloves on too. These are the men who are leading the British Army today.

We have often heard the expression "wake up England" but you want to come to England to understand what it means. The whole place is asleep and they say it is just beginning to wake up. God knows what it was like before.....!

England 24ᵗʰ November 1916

Just a line to let you know I am in the best of health, my cold is better and I have just had a tooth out!

I hear the coal miners are going from bad to worse over there and they are not much better here in Wales. We had our first fall of snow the other day, snowed for two days, had quite enough, don't want anymore for my part.

Today I bought a pair of Australian tan boots, the same I showed you, for two bob off another fellow, brand new, never been worn. You can buy them here off the fellows going to France for three pence to sixpence up to three shillings a pair, brand new. Fellows from hospital who have been wounded are drafted to our Battalion and get a new rig out including two pairs of tan boots, and of course the first thing they do is sell on pair. We use our tan boots here until we go to France; then they give us the English black boots, a fine boot too.

Talk about a rag tag Army, it gets worse, I have not done any drill for twelve days, sit in the hut making toast, sometimes go to the village for a walk and have afternoon tea there. Have not had a rifle in my hand for three weeks and expect to go to France any time now.

Another draft of men from our Company were picked out yesterday to go to France next week and they are teaching them to present arms and to salute and to do right and left turn by numbers. This is a fact; I have not seen the rifle we use at the front since I left Australia; the ones we use here were made over twenty years ago, altogether different to what we will use at the front; got no others!

Of a morning when the bugle sounds to get up, nobody thinks of getting out of bed, not until the 'cook house' sounds an hour later does anyone start to get up, and they would not get up then only someone has to get the breakfast or go without.

You hear a lot about the discipline of the English Army and that you can't drive it into an Australian. I have seen both sides of it here and I say that it is impossible to drive discipline into an Australian; if they drilled them for the next twenty years they would be the same, they are different altogether to the Englishmen. He will do whatever he is told to do the moment he comes into camp and everything he does, he does in the correct way. Walking through the Camps here you will see a Tommie on sentry, he will turn in the correct way, march up and down, hold his rifle correctly, never smile or talk to anyone. Walk a bit further on and you will see an Australian on sentry, he will be sitting on his rifle or leaning on it, perhaps talking to someone or yelling out to every one who passes. They are everlastingly putting them in the klink for it but it makes no difference! If you came along at night he would most likely be asleep. All they say is "it's a lot of damn rot this guard work here, they won't catch us sleeping when we get across the other side"- meaning France.

A Tommie has his hair cut very short, buttons polish up a treat and not a thing out of place on his dress, but our fellows dress does not trouble them. If it came to a fight between the two I know which side I would get on, our fellows would eat them!

One thing about things here, we get well fed. Of a morning we get porridge, bacon and fried tomatoes or tripe or fried smoked fish and coffee. Dinner, roast beef or boiled mutton with potatoes, carrots, turnips and cabbage, very seldom stew; tea, golden syrup or jam and margarine. The jam they make here is a long way ahead of Australian jam, it is beautiful, blackberry, strawberry, never see plum or melon or any common jams like that. I can't tell the difference between butter and the margarine we get. Although in the way of food things are pretty dear in England, there seems to be plenty of everything and the people seem to have plenty of money to buy it.

Speaking to several men back from the front, they say you never see a German, and in a charge you never use a bayonet. The Germans won't wait for it and if they can't get away they surrender. One fellow in my Battalion, back from the Somme, was in two charges before he was wounded and told me, as soon as you get up to the German trenches, they throw up their hands and go down on their knees to you calling out "mercy comrade". He said it is an awful sight to see them.

What struck him more than anything else he had seen, that the Germans were about done, was that a charge he was in his battalion, the 14th captures 300 odd Germans in one trench and the prisoners in that mob consisted of men from battalions ranging from 72nd to the 178th . So you can imagine how they have to put dozens of Battalions together to form one.

England 27th November 1916

It is a long time since I got any letters from Hawthorn, of course I expect a lot went down with that Australian Mail boat a few weeks ago and that accounts for it. Today I received a letter from the shop at Colac, dated 15th October, so perhaps will get some more tomorrow.

The cold over here is awful, everything is frozen; the ground is frozen as hard as a rock, even the mud you can't break with a pick! All the water is frozen, even in the taps, and if you hang a shirt out to dry and go and get it first thing in the morning, it is frozen hard as a board and you can't even bend it.

Our huts could not be better, they look after us well in that way; every hut has a stove in to warm the room and electric light on. We also have straw mattresses for our bed; Jack Laing and I sleep together, we have eight thick

Harry, 2283 Pte 46th Bn 1st AIF

blankets on us and are as warm as toast all night.

What I want you to send is a pair of woollen gloves like I had at home, I bought them very thick; we must have them and very thick socks, have to wear two pairs at a time it is so cold; a good woollen vest would be good too.

The cold here is passed describing. They say the men in the trenches after being in just a few hours fall down with the cold and can't get up, have to be carried out!

At present I am in the best of health and hope all at home are the same.

Codford 1st December 1916

A short note to let you know I am leaving for France tomorrow morning, Saturday 2nd December 1916. Only told this morning! All we are allowed to take with us is one change of underclothing, one towel, one pair of boots [the ones we have on only] and shaving outfit, also waterproof sheet. Carry it all on our back. We will be in France about a month before we go into the trenches.

If you don't receive a letter for a while don't be surprised, sometimes they won't let you write for a time. Today I received fourteen letters including two pounds from you. No parcels yet. I am sending my silver watch to Evelyne Williams to mind for me.

Ten to one I will not get the parcels now that I am leaving here, will let you know if I do. I am leaving England in the pink of condition and best of health. I must thank you very much for the money.

Well I must close now as I have no more time to write, getting everything ready to move off.

Codford 2nd December 1916

Leaving for France at 5 o'clock this afternoon. Just had a Church service and took communion. Went down to the village for lunch and had fried eggs and sausages; also went to the Post office to change the money order, but they won't change it, must go to Salisbury Post Office and of course can't get there so will have a hard job to change it, I think!

I have sent my watch to Eve Williams in Wales to mind for me. Aunt Harriet's watch is still going strong. Jack Laing is going with me but Jack Box was not picked to go so will have to say goodbye to him for a while.

When sending parcels always put in a tin or two of Havelock tobacco, medium, something to eat and something to wear, such as socks and handkerchiefs and under clothing. No good depending on the Army for them because they have to be in rags before they will give you new ones.

Somewhere in France
A.N.A. Day 26th January 1917

A line to let you know I have received 30 letters and 4 parcels in the last week including a parcel from your shop. You must thank the girls from me. I got it the day I came out of the trenches.

The cake was beautiful and in splendid condition, nothing could have been nicer.

Harry in camp in Codford, 10th January 1917, one week before he went to France

The bootlaces were very acceptable as I have none and was about to use string. I got the parcels today, one from your shop, one from Colac, which had a tin of cream in it, [always put a tin of cream and pineapple in it.] The other two I have not opened yet.

Among the letters were eight from you Ida, two from Mother and six from Nell, one from Aunt Harriet with a pound in it, [money order], postcard from little Nell. Post card from Aunt Thomas and Aunt Salina, two from Wales saying they had got my watch alright and the rest from Colac.

Today I received Mother's money order from London saying I could change it at any French post office, so you see I still have two-pound orders with me. If you send any more money, just send an ordinary pound note in a letter, I can change them easily but money orders are very hard to change. I had a long run in the trenches, under shellfire all the time, several falling only a few feet from me. but have had the luck to escape so far. All the time I was in the trenches there was six inches of snow on the ground and all the water holes had a foot of ice on them. The water in our bottles was frozen all the time and although there was snow and ice everywhere we could not get a drop to drink. If we went to a shell hole for a bit of ice we could not break it with a pick even, so hard. Our boots are frozen hard as rock and if we take them off we can't get them on again, our feet are always frozen, its agony, that is the worst trouble, our feet. To give you an idea of the cold, boiling water freezes as hard as rock in twenty minute. This weather has been on for the last month and is still on.

When walking on the roads or open ground we are always falling down, the ground is so hard and slippery that we can't keep on our feet. The tips of my fingers are frost bitten and my feet are sore otherwise I am in good health.

Send me socks and gloves and balaclavas, and when sending tinned stuff, send tinned rabbit or sausages, something we can heat up on the fire. I have just opened another parcel from Wales full of little home made Welsh cakes and cigarettes. They are very good to me and ask me to send for anything I want, just as if I was asking you, they said, I wish you would thank them for me.

You say the dog is bad but you do not say if he got better. Let me know. I will close now and write later.

France 6th March 1917

We have just been out of the trenches today and were paraded out for hot showers and the only clean clothes they gave us was socks and singlet. Our feet are always cold to such an extent that they pain, the only time they get warm is when we go for a long march. Our battalion has a fine band, one of the best, I have heard it play of an evening in the street. The old church in the village although it has no clock, strikes the hours out, and of a still night when we are in bed, we can hear it tolling out the hours.

Just next to this village is a flying station and the machines are buzzing overhead like bees all day long. I went over to it and they are beautiful machines and are coming and going all day long. The men are dressed in soft leather clothing, lined with fur, from their feet to their heads, can't see a bit of them not even their face.

At the front our guns fire night and day without a stop, you would not believe unless you saw it yourself. Just imagine guns of all sizes along our front firing all day and night, each gun firing thousands of shells each day and we have thousands and thousands of guns. The push has not started yet, God help the Germans when it does. Ida asked me if we would win this war, I don't think at all I know we will and no one knows it better than the German soldier himself. I have seen it myself. He is no match for the Australian, and surrenders as soon as we get near him. The last time I was at the front his dead were laying everywhere. He doesn't attempt to bury them and we are driving him back every day. We never give him a nights rest. He is fed up with the war and it is only his artillery that saves him. We will win never worry about that.

I was in a raid on German trenches the other day and of course there was the usual rush for souvenirs. We got a box of cigarettes off a dead Fritz.

France 10th March 1917

This is Sunday today and the first nice day we have had, the sun is shining brightly and very little wind. As I said before the whole division is out of the line resting and this morning we had a Divisional church parade. That means nearly all the men of our division, including four brass bands, also General Birdswood and Staff.

All the different battalions of the division are billeted in different villages, just around this particular part, about two to each village, and they all march to one centre for the parade.

The parade was held on the side of the hill just outside our village and we were all lined up in the shape of a square with the bands on one side and the parson in the middle with the bible resting on three drums, one on top of the other. The bands played the hymns and we sang "Lead kindly light" and "All people that on earth do dwell."

After the service General Birdwood presented medals to the men who had won them during the last months. Afterwards he made a speech on the wonderful work we had done this winter in the trenches.

While in the trenches this winter we had opposed to us the 1st and 4th division of the Prussian Guard, General Birdwood told us. The 4th Guards morale was very low and all the prisoners said they were fed up with the war and had no chance of winning, but the 1st Guards were certain of winning as they were told that the English would have to surrender in a few months because of the submarines. That is the only thing the German soldier has any faith in, and if they fail I don't think that the German heads will get them to swallow any more tales.

No one at home realises what the Australian s have been through and have done this winter. I have seen and been in it, so can say that there are few better soldiers than them. I have seen them in trenches day after day, night after night, with everything frozen, snow falling and mud nearly up to their waists. No place to lay down even, no sleep for days at a time, and high explosive shells of every kind raining down upon them. We had to carry the tucker up to them. The saps were too bad to walk in so we had to walk over no mans land with shell holes and mud up to our knees and shells falling all around us. This is in broad daylight too, impossible to run in the mud.

When we get into the front line we jump into it and sink in the mud up to our waist. All along the trench men are standing with bayonets fixed all the time. Just where I jumped in four men were lying in the mud wounded and another dead, a shell had just landed in. So we handed the tucker over and got orders to carry the wounded back with us. We put them on stretchers and started off. The one I had to help had had his leg and hand smashed. He asked for a cigarette and then laid back smoking it and said "anyway I'll get a trip to Blighty out of this" meaning England.

All the other fellows in the trench standing at their posts, when we got into the trench, just turn their heads and with a grin ask whether its turkey or roast beef for tonight. Every one of them is the same, nothing makes them downhearted. I'm not praising up our men, I am just telling you what I see and hear myself.

While my battalion was in the front line, all the mud was frozen hard as iron and dead Germans everywhere, in front and behind us and all our fellows thought about were souvenirs and in broad daylight would crawl over the top of the trenches and go through their pockets to see what they could get.

France 18th April 1917

I suppose you have been wondering when I was going to write to you, for I think it must be some time since I wrote, but when I write to Mother I mean it for all of you at home.

For the last few weeks I have had no chance to write at all. But remember I always do when I get the chance. Today I received a dozen letters including two from Mother, two from yourself with photos of the house in, one from Nell Alsop, Aunt Harriet, Aunt Salina. Mill Kemp and Dads second letter, also several for poor Jack Laing. All letters dated up to the 25th February. I don't think you will get any letters last mail only cards, Rene ought to get one though.

We are back in a village miles behind the line, once again. This is the first fine day we have had. I am sitting up with my back against a barn in the back yard of a house. A French woman is digging the garden about twenty yards away, about the same distance off a crowd of our fellows are playing two up, a little further on some more are playing football. The band is playing in the street and the bugle is sounding 'Retreat.' The retreat is always sounded when the sun is setting. Overhead about a dozen flying machines are sailing about making a loud buzzing noise.

The last stunt we had we lost little Jack Laing. I miss him very much, we were always together. He will be reported missing I suppose, but I know for certain he was wounded in the foot and that would mean a prisoner too. We went over the top together and he was as game as any man there. I would like to give full particulars, but of course we are not allowed to. Perhaps later on I may be able to give you more news about him. The charge we were in is considered one of the most gallant charges the Australians have ever made, as we had no cover whatsoever and had to charge over a thousand yards, through barbed wire, rifle and machine gun fire at point blank range and shell fire of every description. We took the trench and held for about six hours, ran out of bombs and had to retire over the same ground under the same fire.

We were the first to attack the famous Hindenberg line, and I can always say I was one of the first to enter this line. I went over in the first wave and never got touched. Enclosed you will find a bit of paper I took off a German N. C. Officers field bandage which I used to dress his wound while in the trench.

He was shot clean through the chest and was out in a shell hole a few yards from the trench. I called to him to come in. He got up and walked into the trench. I undressed him to the waist and dressed his wound for him. He could not speak English and although the bullet must have missed his heart by a fraction of an inch he was still sitting up in the trench six hours later when I had to leave it and get out. The bit of paper was the only thing I bought out of the famous Hindenberg line, so it is worth keeping [give it to Mother] I also dressed many of our own fellows wounded while in that trench.

It has just come out in the battalion news that Jack is wounded and missing, and as I said before he is almost certain to be a prisoner. I wish the photos of the house were not so dull, they would have been good otherwise. I could not help smiling when I saw the name of the house, but for all that it is a pretty little name and village too, and will always remind me of my all to short stay in England.

Yesterday I walked into a house, just walked into the kitchen and asked the woman to boil me some eggs. I sat in front of the fire and the little baby came and sat on my knee. I ate some eggs with salt and pepper only, no bread. They can hardly get enough bread for themselves, it is very scarce in France. Afterwards the mother started to give her little girl [about six years old] lessons. There are no schools in these villages near the line and no men to do the work for them.

I know about a dozen words in French and it is marvellous what a long conversation you can have with such a limited number of words. I am almost sure that I get all letters and parcels sent to me. You say there are a couple more parcels for me, but I have not received them yet, but no doubt I will get them later on.

Yesterday I bought half a block of beautiful currant cake at the canteen [English cake] for five and a half francs. Well I must close now as it is getting late. I am in the best of health and spirits and hope you are all the same. Give my best love to Mother and also a good kiss from me and remember me to dad and tell him I was very pleased with his two letters.

Jack Laing. Regimental number 2284, 46th Bn 1st AIF

Instructions found on the top of a German shell dressing Harry applied this dressing to a German during an Allied assault on the Hindenburg line. Apparently you never use your own dressing on someone else – it is strictly own use.

Gebrauchsanweisung.

Roten Verbandstoff und **Wunde**
nie mit **Fingern berühren.**

Mit beiden Händen anfassen, wo rechts
und links „**Hier**" steht –, die Hände
hochhalten – stark auseinander ziehen.
RotenVerbandstoff auf die Wunde legen.
Binde umwickeln und knoten.

France 19th April 1917

A line to let you know I got your letter from Port all right, also the photo taken at Letas and the postcard of the Port. I must have just come out of the big battle at Messines in which I was in all through and most of the time in the very front line. It was a fine battle and a great victory.

Being an open battle and in hilly country I had a fine view of it, being able to see for miles on all sides, and it was a sight worth seeing. I was in that fight for six days and hardly six hours sleep all the time and the last eighteen hours I was in a shell hole 150 yards in front of the front line and all the time we were being bombarded with his big shells.

Perhaps you don't know what it means. It means that shells were falling at the rate of ten or twelve a minute and landing anything from ten to fifty yards off our hole, and every now and then one would cover us with dirt and dust and at the same time expecting the Germans to counterattack at any moment, that bombardment on us did not stop for one minute in all of that eighteen hours. This will give you a faint idea of the number of shells used in a battle.

There were eight of us in that hole [one killed since], what they call a strong point to give our front line, warning if he is attacking. Perhaps you will think we sat there shivering with fright, but I will tell you how we passed the time away.

First thing we do is take turns to keep a look out to see if the Germans are coming over an hour on at a time, two of our fellows could sing and they sang duets by the hour. I went into that battle with two magazines in my bag and a book up my coat [A trick of hearts] and read the lot right through in that shell hole. After a while I crawled over to another shell hole to [you know] a matter of five or six yards and found one of our fellows lying dead in it so had a look to see what he had in his bag and found a tin of golden syrup and sardines and as we were short of tucker we were highly delighted.

This will sound a bit tall to you, Ida, but I think you know me better than to think I would lie to you under the circumstances. That was one little part of the battle I was in, but not the worst by far and the way the boys in my brigade, after being driven back half a mile were called upon to line up in three long lines, lines in full view of the enemy and under awful shell fire told to advance right down the hill, with no cover for over a mile. We lined up just as we were on parade, not a man out of place and then went forward in perfect line, just walked for over a mile, took the trench and held onto it for days until we were relieved.

After we came out of the line, our Army Corp Commander, lined us up and gave us a great speech. He said the work our brigade had done was beyond praise. He had especially selected our brigade to do that difficult advance down that slope as he had heard of our brilliant charge at Bullecourt and knew he could depend on us to do it. All the brigade got drunk that night.

In the trench we took over two miles in from our old front line. I got a letter off a dead German, he had several on him, but I took this one as it was small, enclosed you will find it. Tell Aunt Harriet I got the parcel with the ten-shilling note in it, thank her for it. I also got her money order changed last night so I am well off at the moment.

France 29th April 1917

I believe the mail left here yesterday, and I want this letter to go by it, but we, like you, never know when a mail is leaving. I received both of your letters, also a parcel from Aunt Harriet with a woollen vest etc. in it, yesterday. Today is Sunday, a beautiful day, rather warm, in fact I am sitting in the shade as the sun is rather hot.

All the country around is ploughed up. France is all cultivated, no parts like in Australia, and no fences at all. I believe you could walk from one end of France to the other without getting over a fence.

The Somme which is the name of a country in France is very hilly, not unlike Burwood for hills, but more so. About every mile or even less is a village. Between these villages is cultivated land, not a tree, not a house, shed or even a fence is to be seen, just narrow white winding roads running from one village to another, so you can understand that each place has about half a dozen local roads leading out on all sides to the next villages, making France one network of roads. All the main roads are very straight with big trees planted on each side, mostly elms. All along the Western front, troops not in the firing line, are billeted in these villages, so far back from the front line as twenty or even more miles. A battalion coming out of the line for a rest, gradually marches from one village to another, putting in a few days at some or perhaps a week or two in another, until they get right back to the furthest village; then they start working back to the front line in the same way.

Now the Somme where the great battle was fought last year, and the Germans driven back so many miles, all the villages were destroyed, [I fought all along this front all winter] not even a wall of any kind is left standing, that meant no billets for the troops behind the line, and as the men could not live in tents during the winter, the British had to build thousands upon thousands of wooden huts, with heaters in them, to take the place of the villages; also make new roads, put railways down and lay water on to all these great camps, this meant pumping stations all over the place. All these huts are made in parts and can be taken to pieces and carried forward as we advance, so you can understand what a great move it was on the part of the Germans when they retired destroying all of the villages at the same time.

I might state that on all this great battlefield of the Somme, consisting of hundreds of square miles there is not one full square yard of ground that has not been hit by a shell. I have been all over it, and at Pozieres, [where there is not even a brick or a piece of wood to be seen,] they are erecting a big wooden cross in memory of the thousands of Australians who have fallen there. The cross stands about fourteen feet high and painted white with black lettering. I saw two or three little cemeteries there with a few men buried in them, you can guess the rest. All over the Somme there are cemeteries with little white crosses over each grave, with the name of each soldier on it!

But on all the great battlefields I have seen only four German cemeteries with about one hundred buried in them, all told. What he does with his dead I don't know. All the crosses on his graves are painted green and are very nice too.

We have just come out of the line for a much needed rest, when Fritz started his big retreat from Bapaume, and our battalion along with many others were called on to make the road from Pozieres to Bapaume, and the first days work on that road, I saw the greatest sight I have ever seen. All that winter we had fought in the trenches in snow, ice, mud and water, hardships that no one could imagine, but those who were there, were seeing the fruits of our hard fighting.

All along those miles of road, thousands upon thousands of men were working to repair that road, carrying old bricks in sand bags from all the destroyed villages within reach, and throwing them into shell holes on the road, anything we could get hold of, so as the transport and heavy guns could follow the advancing army. Day after day, night after night, until the railway to Baupame was repaired. The traffic went along the road, not a yard of space in between, and all the time it rained, then snowed, then continued to snow until everything was covered in it, but still the traffic went on. Motor wagon after wagon, then limber after limber, then thousands of Australian Infantry, with all their transport and travelling kitchens; next battery after battery of field artillery, then dozens of ammunition limbers, with six horses on to each; followed perhaps by an English regiment with band playing in front, next the grandest sight of all, the Indian Lancers, thousands of them with beautiful horses. We would all yell out to them to stick it into Fritz, and they would laugh and show their white teeth. More horse transport and dozens of motor wagons, then great heavy guns with anything from a dozen to twenty horses pulling them. More Australians then Light Horse followed by more English infantry. The English crack cavalry regiments with half a dozen kettle drums in front with the bag pipes playing for all they were worth, followed by the Scots, all in their kilts, swaying together as they marched along and the snow falling until every man, horse etc. was covered in it.

Next day the traffic started to go both ways, coming and going until the road was one moving mass. Day and night, night and day, this went on, and still the snow fell. Now and again the great guns would get bogged, and the traffic would get held up for a while, then the language would start, but in all the great army, no one was down hearted, everyone had a smile on him. We were following in the wake of the German army! It was a great day. The greatest day the British army had ever had in all its history, and the grandest sight the British soldier had ever seen. Dad, you cannot understand the proud feeling of us all as we stood on the great battlefield of Pozieres [on the very spot where thousands of Australians had fallen in that great charge of last August,] and watched the great army on the march. I have seen Bapaume and all the villages the Germans destroyed on their retreat and he did the job properly, not a house or shed left standing, even beautiful churches, so that we could not billet in them. He had perhaps some reason for doing this, but the beautiful iron railing fences around these churches, which were no earthly use to us in any way, not even for cover, he has broken down and smashed up, and left there just for spite and no other reason.

About three miles the other side of Bapaume I came across one of his little cemeteries, about sixty graves all done up very nice, and at the top of it he had put a big crucifix, life size, which he had taken from the village nearby; and not two hundred yards from this cemetery he had destroyed a beautiful church. The cemetery was made and the church destroyed all in the space of the last two months, and as I looked at that crucifix, and then at the church, I don't think a man could look upon a greater mockery of the Christian religion.

As I have told you in previous letters, I have been in a great charge on the Hindenberg line. As usual it was snowing, when we marched up in the dark to the front line to do the charge, then we fixed bayonets and lay in the trenches, waiting for dawn. You have heard the feelings of soldiers waiting like this to charge, but it is not true, we waited in that trench for over three hours before we charged; and the saying that a man goes through awful torture waiting, is all rot. I am telling you how I felt, and I know all the others were the same. In the first place I had no fear at all, not even the slightest fear, and for over an hour I slept in the trench; a few yards away from me two fellows were having an argument and it nearly finished up in a fight until the Officer stopped it.

When the word to charge came we all jumped up and started to run [overcoats and all on; it was daylight]. After the first couple of hundred yards we were all blown out, so walked the rest of the way, could not have run if you paid us, we were loaded up so much, and the ground was all shell holes. We did not know where Fritz's trench was or how far away, just kept going, then all at once Fritz opened up with his artillery, then machine guns and rifles from in front and only a hundred yards off on our left. I looked around me and fellows were falling all around and the bullets were bizz bizzing, just past me in all directions, and great shells bursting all around, but still we kept walking, until we could see the flash of his machine guns, then we ran at them, through the barb wire, and at that moment Fritz gets over the back of his trench and off, he would not wait for the bayonet. I got into his trench which was about ten foot deep and about three feet wide at the bottom with big dug outs about twenty feet deep. Jack Laing came up to me and we had a look around. We had charged over a thousand yards of flat open country, not a bit of open cover, and up hill at that, and against everything the German could throw at us. We were shelled all the time we were in that trench, and I dressed many of our wounded, they are heroes, no matter how awful the wounds, they never groan, and to the very last smile and may pass away with a lighted cigarette between their fingers.

These are not lies Dad, I am telling what I saw. These are the men Australia has sent to fight for her, she might well be proud of them. For nearly six hours we held the trench, but ran out of bombs and men were sent up to us with more, but they never reached us. In the middle of all this Jack and I found a lot of mail parcels with boiled eggs, cakes, tinned fruits and boxes of cigars, and I can tell you we had a feed. A mail must have arrived for Fritz, just before we came over as the parcels were not even opened. Germany short of food, don't you believe it! Being cut off from our front line and no communication, we put all our wounded in the dug outs and were told every man for himself. It meant staying in the trench and surrendering or make a bolt for it back again in broad daylight with the Germans picking us off with rifles and machine guns. Not one man in my battalion surrendered. Over the top again, our fellows fell like sheep all around me, my overcoat got caught on the barbwire, and I dived into a shell hole, three others jumped in after me, one with his finger shot off. Then our artillery put a barrage right on top of us, and we lay in the shell hole for about half an

The High Strret, Codford

Green Lane junction with High Street

High Street by Cherry Orchard

Talbots Stores at bottom of Chitterne Road Junction with High Street

hour, not sixty yards off Fritz's trench. When our barrage lifted we decided to chance it and off we went.

When I got to our line I picked up my blankets, which we had left before the charge, and walked two miles behind our line to my dug out, made a fire and boiled some tea, and ate some biscuits; then got into bed and slept until six next morning; then what was left of us came back here for a spell. This is just a rough outline of what I went through that morning.

France 5th July 1917

Well Ida, as you see the war goes on and by what I can see, it will continue to do so for a long while yet, to give you my candid opinion, I can't see any end to it yet, but you can take it from me it will not end this side of twelve months and to my idea it will be well over two years from now at the least.

I have a new uniform on now so feel quite a toff, clean my boots every day and polish up my badges, and never felt better in my life, never looked better and was never so fat before. I never get a days sickness, never a headache and only one cold since I landed in France and no man has ever had a harder or rougher life than I have had this last six months.

On the Somme in winter I have been wet through for weeks and months at a time, very little to eat, slept in the mud and water, out all night crawl back at dawn into a little dug out of mud and water, too tired even to take my pack, just fall down asleep with mud up to our waist and never a wash for weeks and crawling with lice as well as under shell fire all the time.

At Bullecourt a few nights before the charge we had to work up in the front line all night, every night and come back at dawn to our dug outs a couple of miles behind the line and many a time at day break we had to come back with snow on the ground a foot deep and falling, just too tired to even walk, just struggle for a hundred yards and fall onto the snow and lay there and sleep, with big shells falling all around, until someone wakes you up and you struggle on for a couple of hundred yards and then fall again covered in snow and sleep.

In the German trench at Bullecourt I was covered in blood, my overcoat was soaked and my hands covered with it. German and Australian blood, through dressing their wounds, my face was black from the powder of the big shells and mud over everything. That's how I looked after I came back from that trench.

After a man comes out of the line for a rest, has a good wash and a good feed and a good sleep, he is as good as new again. I had a letter from Jack Laing's aunt in Essex and she has heard nothing of him yet and at Headquarters, London either. I don't like it myself, I think they should have heard by now but its often six months before they hear, so I have not given up hope yet. We are about to get paid at this minute, forty francs a fortnight, so will have to close. Enclose you will find a railway ticket I bought to go to Amiens with, also a pass in French and English, a cigarette I got off a dead German, a receipt from the photos and a tram ticket. Give them to mother.

Harry on leave in Amiens, 25th June, 1917

TO THE MEMORY
OF

JOHN ORD LAING
PRIVATE 46TH BATTALION
KILLED IN ACTION AT BULLECOURT, FRANCE,
APRIL 11TH, 1917,
AGED 23 YEARS.

In Memory of John Ord Laing

St John Ambulance Brigade Hospital
A.P.O. S11
B.E.F
France

My Dear Mother,

You will see by the above address that I am in hospital. I was wounded by shell, on 19th October, in four places. One bit hit my left leg, well above the knee, going right through and causing a compound fracture of the bone, another bit hit me on the same leg, making a groove on the front of the shin bone, another went through my left arm, above the elbow, but did no damage to the arm, only a flesh wound, the other bit hit me in the hip [right] but only made a little wound.

I will be kept down at the base, in this hospital, for three months [until my leg sets] and then sent to England for goodness knows how long. In the first three days I was operated on twice and put under X rays once, but through it all I have been in splendid health and can eat like a horse. We are fed on the best of everything and plenty of it. I will give you my meals for every day: breakfast 7am porridge or fried bacon or boiled egg, as much bread and butter as we want, cup of tea; 11am beef tea; dinner 12 noon roast beef or fowl or fish, potatoes, carrots, turnips, rice custard or sago custard or stewed fruit and custard; Tea 4pm bread and butter, bread and jam, perhaps a boiled egg, cup of tea; supper 7pm cup of cocoa, bread and butter. I also get a glass of stout at dinner.

One thing about this wound, I will miss winter in the trenches and I can tell you I was dreading it. A funny thing about it is I will spend this Christmas within a mile of where I spent last Christmas day. I was wounded about a mile and a half outside Ypres by a high explosive shell, which fell two yards off me, so you see I was lucky.

I am lying on my back and cannot move and will have to lay like this for four months but don't worry about me; I am happy and contented here in a nice warm room and clean bed. I often lay in bed and listen to the rain outside and I know where I would rather be. By the time I get an answer to this I will be in England.

Don't forget to send that money to Evelyne fifteen pounds, cable it. Well Mother I must close now, hoping you are all well at home and give my love to Ida and Dad and remember me to all the relations.

With fondest love and kisses

from your only son,
Son.

St John Ambulance Brigade Hospital
France 7/11/17

To E Williams

Dear Madam, L/Cpl Hatherley is suffering form a severe gun shot wound of the left leg, which is fractured in the upper part of the thigh. He is progressing quite satisfactory at present but is not likely to be sent to England for some weeks as the Surgeons generally keep patients with fractured thighs for some time on account of the journey and the fear of the leg being in any way injured while travelling.

L/Cpl Hatherley is in good spirits. I told him I had written but did not say you were anxious about him.

Yours Truly,
C.E. Lodal
[Matron]

St John Ambulance Brigade Hospital
France 3rd January 1918

My Dear Mother,

As you see we have had Xmas and New Year over and the way they looked after and treated us is beyond praise. On Xmas day I ate until I was almost sick, we had a bottle of beer or stout each as well as champagne. When we awoke in the morning every bed had a big stocking hanging at the foot of it full of lollies, nuts and goodness knows what. I also got a box from the Australian Red Cross. For breakfast we had ham and eggs, dinner roast beef and four sorts of vegetables, also Yorkshire pudding, much as we want, plum pudding and brandy sauce, nuts, bon bons and lollies and a bottle of beer or stout, tea, sardines, bread and butter, cake, jelly, hot mince pies, also an apple. Supper a cup of cocoa, toast, biscuits and cheese, in the afternoon a glass of champagne and about 8.30 in the evening another glass; we also got two fine cigars each.

While dinner was on a splendid band played outside. During the afternoon they brought a big bran tub around and we had a dip in it and got little note-books, mirrors and different things. Xmas eve a lot of nuns sang Xmas carols outside each ward. During the week they gave us concerts in the ward.

Well now as to myself. It is just eleven weeks, seventy-seven days tomorrow since I was wounded, all that time on my back and my leg in a splint and I am in the pink of health and fat in the face and body, well they laugh at me, eat like a horse and sleep like a top, in fact that is all I do. About three days ago I was sent to x-rays again and I had a look at the photos. The bone is pretty badly broken, [I would like to show you the photo] and by what I can see will be pretty short, about two inches by the look of the photo, of course they can't tell until they take the splint off and measure it, but you can take it from me it will be about that short. Anyway the bone is set pretty strong again, well, to give you an idea last night the Doctor said I could go to the concert in the Concert hall and this is never done unless the bone is properly strong again, he said he would take the splint off in a weeks time. The concert was given by the VAD's (I might tell you about the VAD's later on, you have heard of them I suppose). I was put on a stretcher and taken to the hall and placed right in front. All the stretcher cases are put in front [one stretcher case from each ward] in two rows behind them. The Sisters, nurses and Doctors are at the back. All the walking cases are organised in front of the corner. The concert was a sort of pantomime, dancing, singing, beautiful dresses, lights on scenery and everything just like an Xmas pantomime. The VAD's are all young women who come out to help in the hospitals, they are all from good families in England and a fine looking lot and of course this sort of things is right into their hands as most of them can sing and dance beautifully. I had a good time and got back to bed about 11 that night.

The wound in my leg is getting on but will take a long time to heal yet. When they get the splint off the leg will begin to get more life in it and I suppose will heal a bit more quickly; they took the tubes out a few days ago.

I got your Xmas cards and all the girls including Bibs Harrison's, Ida's and several others. They got the fifteen pounds in Wales. With fondest love to you all.

France 8th January 1918

It is just six o'clock in the evening and a snow storm is raging outside, been on all day. They had me already to go to Blighty at eight o'clock this morning but owing to the snowstorm it was put off. I have my Blighty ticket tied on to me and printed right across it in red letters is "helpless." I am what they call a special case and will be sent to a special hospital, most likely London.

My leg is still in a splint but getting on well, the skin is healing fast and the tubes are taken out of the femur, very little pus coming from it. The Doctor has not measured my leg yet, but he said it would be about one and a quarter inches short, but take it from me it will be a good two inches. The other wounds are almost better.

It will not be long before I can walk, perhaps they will send me home before then, but I hope not, I would like to be able to walk before they send me home. In another ward in this hospital is a young Australian, only a lad, he has a broken spine and paralysed from the waist down. He has been in here a long time now and the Doctor said he may live for a month perhaps two, or he might last two years and he knows this. He laughs and jokes with them all in the ward, never downhearted and has a smile for everybody. Is he not a hero? Heroism at its greatest. No great headings in the papers about him, no VC's or Military Medals, no one to see him but the Doctors and Nurses, and no chance of seeing his home, not even Blighty. That's an Australian for you. He is the talk of the hospital.

Well Mother this is my last letter from France to you, the next will be from England. I am in the pink of condition. I will knock off writing to you now as it is too cold to hold the pencil any longer.

Bethnal Green Military Hospital
London
Monday 14th January 1918

As you see from the above address I am in Blighty once again. I left Etaples last Wednesday morning about three o'clock and arrived in London a little after nine in the evening. I left the hospital a little after midnight in an awful snowstorm. Taken off the bed on a stretcher, carried outside to a waiting motor ambulance, driven about one and a half miles to the Red Cross train, beautifully fitted out, put into a nice bed, like on a ship, started off about three o'clock. About six o'clock, a hot cup of tea and bread and butter was brought to me.

Arriving at Calais at daybreak 7.30, put on a stretcher again and carried on to the boat., still snowing, taken down below to the big saloon room, beautifully fitted up, Officers ward, with cots, put into one, cup of hot coffee and biscuits brought to me, felt quite pleased with myself, but was beginning to feel done up and cold.

One of the men played the piano to us, at midday a lovely plate of stew was brought to us, the best I have tasted since I left home. Off at last, very rough, but did not feel sick. Arrived at Dover after one hour and twenty minutes run across. Had a cup of coffee and biscuits again, put on to a stretcher, carried to an ambulance train, put into bed, felt done. Started off, about half way another cup of tea and a big meat sandwich. Arrived at Charing Cross, put on to a stretcher, carried to motor ambulance, young girl in navy blue uniform got me a cup of coffee and cigarettes, then got inside with us and off we went, they left the back up so we could see.

Along the Strand into Whitechapel Road, right into the heart of the East End, Jews quarters, into a great big building, put into bed, cold and absolutely done, temperature 102 degrees, washed my face and hands, gave me a cup of hot milk and then I fell asleep.

I don't like this place, no comforts, not the same attention. I have not been comfortable since I arrived here although the leg is going good. Had the splints taken off and another sort, not as big put on. The leg is quite fat again and the skin nearly healed. It is almost certain I will be sent home before I can walk. Still waiting for an Australian mail. Well no more news just now.

No 3 Australian Auxiliary Hospital
Dartford
March 19th 1918

Dear Evelyne,
I would have written to you before but I have been too ill. The Matron came in to me and showed me your letter and asked me to write to you. My leg went all

septic as soon as I landed here and they had to operate on it but it did no good and in a week or two they had to operate again. My leg is all cut open, great gashes all over it and I think I have a stiff knee now.

For three weeks I was in agony and all the time they kept injecting morphia into me and at times I got too weak and they would not give it to me and I would cry with pain for hours and beg them to give me the morphia. Evelyne I never knew anyone could suffer like I have the last few weeks. I am getting on so well the last few days and can eat a treat. They feed me on the best of everything, even the best of grapes.

The Sisters are so good to me, they can't do enough for me. I hardly have any pain in the daytime now but it comes on in the night, nearly every night they have to give me morphia. You said something about your brother coming down to see me, I would very much like to see him again, but tell him not to come down for a week or two yet as it is a long way down here as I might be bad just as he comes or perhaps sleeping under morphia. If I keep picking up like I have this last few days I ought to be pretty good in a fortnights time.

I have not written home yet, I do not feel like it, I wish you would for me Evelyne tell them everything. I promised to keep nothing back from them. I thank you for the papers you sent me.

Yours ever sincerely,
Harry

No 3 Australian Auxiliary Hospital
Dartford
4.4.18

Dear Miss Williams,
Am writing to let you know that L/Cpl Hatherley left this morning en route for Australia.

The moving up to where he left caused him no pain whatsoever, and you may rest assured everything was made just as comfortable as possible for his comfort. | He went away in extremely good spirits and really he looked awfully well and comfortable.

The watch arrived the day before yesterday and I promised Hatherley I would write to you.

Trusting you are not worrying yourself about the lad.

I am, Yours faithfully,
Rubi I Rippon [Sister in Charge]

Harry spent fifteen months on his back after being wounded at Passchendale whilst returning to the front line with two other soldiers; he was hospitalised first in France,

H.M. Hospital Ship "DUNLUCE CASTLE" *(Publication Officially sanctioned by the Lords Commissioners of the Admiralty)*

HM Hospital Ship Dunluce Castle
that took Harry half way home

Caulfield Repatriation Hospital,
Melbourne

Out of hospital and walking

Harry and May, Melbourne, 23rd June, 1962

then in England and finally in Australia for a long period with a permanent legacy from active service, a stiff left leg. Harry returned to tailoring in the country and it was there he met his wife May Victoria Richards eleven years his junior; they had a daughter and two sons, Nancy Mary, John Evan and William Henry. In 1961 Harry revisited the battlefields and England with May; he died of a heart attack in the Repatriation Hospital in Melbourne on 17th December 1962.

Notes

1 The reason webbing replaced leather was that leather reacted badly to trench warfare conditions.

2 British Army Officers wore brown boots, the lower ranks wore black.

Source

John Hatherley: The family were very close knit; Aunt Harriet was the sister of Harry's mother who was married to a Mr Williams who came from Wales. His two sisters Evelyne and Lucy Williams treated Harry as if he were another brother, he was a favourite of all his female cousins, hence the large number of letters and parcels he received. Evelyne and Lucy came from Ystalyferain Wales and owned considerable property there.

Ida ran a dress making business and he received parcels from her and from the girls who worked for her as well as the girls he worked with at Colac.

No doubt the silver pocket watch was of value, after he sent it to Wales the watch Aunt Harriet gave him broke, so he ended up with no watch at all.

Harry's best mate Jack [John Ord] Laing was born in St Kilda, Victoria; he trained as a commercial artist and as an art student exhibited in oils. The two men had trained together, shared their blankets for warmth in Codford and wartime adventures in France; Jack disappeared in action and was never heard of again, he was one of the countless soldiers 'Known Unto God.' He is listed as Killed in Action on 11th April 1917 at Bullecourt aged 23 and is remembered on a panel 142 in the cemetery at Villers-Bretonneaux.

Jack Box became sick in England and never recovered, so he didn't go to France with his two mates. John Hatherley doesn't know what became of him, it is likely he was repatriated to Australia. If he died it was not at Codford, he is not in the War Grave Cemetery neither is he listed in the military records available to me as dying in WWI.

According to Casualties WWI web site Australia's enlisted personnel including the Australian Flying Corps numbered 416,809; 331,781 of these men and women served overseas. Total casualties; captured, missing, wounded or killed 215,585; killed 53,993, wounded 137,013 plus 16,496 gassed.

ANA Day on 26th January is an Australian national holiday. It commemorates the day Captain Cook raised the British flag at Botony Bay, claiming Australia as a British Possession.

5

'Bright Day's Done'
The ANZAC War Grave Cemetery

A small plot of land in a tranquil corner of the village close to St Mary's Church was established as a Military Burial Ground by deed of gift after the Great War. Planted with Irish Yews and Beech trees the ANZAC Cemetery is tended by locals under the auspices of the Commonwealth War Grave Commission. It is the largest New Zealand War Grave Cemetery and the second largest ANZAC War Grave Cemetery in the United Kingdom. The plot contains 66 New Zealanders and 31 Australians from WWI and a lone Welsh Guardsman from WWII. Wiltshire burial grounds are the last resting place of 636 soldiers and airmen of the Australian Imperial Force and 173 members of the New Zealand Expeditionary Force.

New Zealand and Austrailia Cemetery, World War I

Inside the hedge from Benis Path is a single grave, directly behind it two more; there are three rows of graves with an aisle in the centre; four individual graves and finally a long row along the western boundary. These are the ANZAC graves; the WWII headstone is beneath a tree to the east of the Cross of Sacrifice.

1] Fletcher, Pte. Harry David 7455. 13th Bn. Australian Infantry. 29th July 1917. Enlisted Sydney New South Wales.

2] Harris, Pte. Albert Arthur, 640. 4th Coy Australian Machine Gun Corps. Died of wounds 27th July 1917 aged 23. Son of Arthur and Eliza Harris of Ranelagh, Tasmania. [a]

3] Patience, Pte. Frank Nicholas, 7795. 16th Bn. Australian Infantry. Died of pneumonia 27th October 1917 aged 19. Son of Joseph and Elizabeth Patience of Georgina, Western Australia; born in Greenough.

4] Couchman, Pte. Arthur John 2881. 51st Bn. Australian Infantry. 15th February 1917. Died of bronco-pneumonia aged 30. Widowed mother Mrs S. M. Couchman of North Fremantle, Western Australia; enlisted Fremantle 10th July 1916; born Dartford, Kent, England; worked as a labourer.

5] Williams, Pte. James Thomas 6859. 16th Bn. Australian Infantry. Died of influenza and cardiac failure 18th February 1917 aged 29. Son of Mr. J.M. & Mrs. M.E. Williams of Kalcuddering, Kounongorring, Western Australia; was a farmer before enlisting in Toodyay, WA.

6] McIlroy, Pte. Gabriel 6607. 15th Bn. Australian Infantry. Died of bronchitis 19th February 1917 aged 39. Son of Patrick & Ann Christina McIlroy; a gold miner born at Charters Towers, Queensland.

7] Flanagan, Pte. John Richard 6762. 16th Bn. Australian Infantry. Died of pneumonia 19th February 1917 aged 43. Son of Luke & Annie Flanagan; a civil servant born at Tatura, Victoria.

8] Morton/ Lessells Pte. [served as John Morton –true family name John Macindish Adamson Lessells] 6809. 15th Bn. Australian Infantry. 19th February 1917. Enlisted Brisbane, Queensland.

9] Bickley, Pte. Thomas George 6852. 16th Bn. Australian Infantry. Died of bronchitis 23rd February 1917 aged 37. Son of Absolon & Mary Bickley; husband of Rose Bickley of Wagin, Western Australia; born at Fremantle; worked as a labourer.

10] McGrath, Pte. James Charles Patrick 7026. 15th Bn. Australian Infantry. Died of pneumonia 2nd March 1917 aged 21. Son of Patrick & Margaret McGrath of St Lawrence, Rockhampton, Queensland; enlisted St Lawrence; schooled at home; worked as a station hand. Inscription: For King and Country He Gave His Best, Thy Will Be Done.

11] Gorman, Pte. Thomas Michael 6019. 15th Bn. Australian Infantry. Died of sickness

14th March 1917 aged 25. Son of Patrick John & Mary Gorman; born at Brisbane, Queensland; enlisted Petrie Terrace, Queensland.

12] Connelly, Pte. Percy Francis 3144. 49th Bn. Australian Infantry. 19th March 1917. Enlisted Banalow, New South Wales; died of pneumonia. This headstone has an inscription which read: In Loving Memory Erected by His Comrades 8th Reifor. 49th Bn. 13 Training AIF. Rest In Peace.

13] Holder, Pte Harry, 7251. 16th Bn. Australian Infantry. Died of cerebro spinal meningitis 28th April 1917 aged 32. Son of Harry & Grace Leggo Holder of 109 St Leonard's Avenue, West Leederfield, Western Australian; born in Cornwall, England, emigrated to Australia apparently with his family when he was 27; worked as a farmer. Inscription: 'Duty to this plane completed, Admittance to a higher plane won'. In all six brothers enlisted, Harry's younger brother John Leggo Holder was 14 when the family arrived in Australia. John was a clerk when he enlisted in Subiaco, WA as Pte 2431a in 51st Bn. Australian Infantry. He was killed in action in France when he was nineteen and a half and is remembered on memorial panel 568 HAC Cemetery Ecoust-St Mein. The records show that Harry Holder Snr. states a third son was totally incapacitated in the conflict. A search of the Australian Roll of Honour does not indicate any details that any of the other brothers were killed.

14] Salisbury, Spr. Charles 16486. NZ Engineers. Died of sickness 28th May 1917 aged 32. Husband of Norah A. Salisbury of 18 Newton Rd, Auckland.

15] Wishart, Pte. Andrew Anderson 8/4057 . 1st Bn. Otago Regt. NZEF 10th July 1917 aged 21. Son of George Blyth & Agnes H.M. Wishart of Makarewa, Invercargill.

16] Protheroe, Dvr. William 6/3133. NZ Army Service Corps. Died of sickness 15th July 1917 aged 38. Son of Alexander Protheroe of Elgin, Ashburton, Christchurch.

17] Holland, Pte. Francis Arthur 28885. Auckland Regt. NZEF 6th September 1917 aged 30. Son of Matthew & Elizabeth Holland of High St., Maryborough, Victoria, Australia.

18] Keys, Rfn. Frederick Charles 32346. 3rd NZ [Rifle] Brigade. Died of sickness 15th April 1917 aged 35. Son of Benjamin Hunt & Annie Jane Keys of 94 Marine Parade, Napier.

19] Dumbleton, Cpl. Ronald 8/2901. Otago Regt. NZEF died of sickness 5th April 1917 aged 26. Son of William & Lucy A. Dumbleton of Pukcuri, Junction, Oamaru.

20] Browning, Pte. Frederick Henry 34797. Otago Regt. NZEF. Died of sickness 31st March 1917 aged 33. Son of John & the late Mrs Browning.

21] Watson, Pte. Walter Robert 31568. Canterbury Regt. NZEF died of pneumonia 20th March 1917 aged 27. Son of Edward Wilfred & Eliza Watson; husband of Beatrice E. Watson of Fox Hill, Nelson.

22] McDonald, Pte. Gordon 28186. Wellington Regt., NZEF Died of meningitis 5th

March 1917 aged 25. Son of John & Ellen McDonald of Te-Ore, Pongaroa, Wellington.

23] Allen, Pte. William 31453. Canterbury Regt. NZEF died of sickness 23rd February 1917 aged 29. Son of Joseph Allen of Bexley, Canterbury.

24] Tombs, Pte. Charles 31552. Canterbury Regt. NZEF 17th February 1917 aged 43. Son of Job & Elizabeth Tombs; born at Sefton, Canterbury.

25] Delaney, Pte. J. 32149. NZ [Rifle] Brigade. 17th February 1917.

26] Button, Corp. Albert James 1870. 51st Bn. Australian Infantry. Accidentally killed 23rd November 1916 aged 23 or 24. Born Melbourne; enlisted Fremantle W.A.; worked as a hotel clerk. [b]

27] Smith, Pte. Michael, 2782. 45th Bn. Australian Infantry. 5th December 1916 aged 38.

28] Osborne, Pte. T.E., 45th Bn Australian Infantry. 10th December 1916 aged 33.

Both private's Smith and Osborne have crosses as headstones and an inscription: Erected by his comrades A Company 12th Training.

29] Ryan, Pte. Richard Charles Gladstone, 2465. 50th Bn. Australian Infantry. Died of bronco-pneumonia 16th December 1916 aged 21. Son of Richard & Margaret Ina Ryan of Streaky Bay, South Australia; born & enlisted at Talia; worked in farming. Inscription: Dearly Beloved Second Son of Margaret & the late Richard Ryan.

30] Beattie, Pte. Edwin, 2389. 47th Bn Australian Infantry. Died of pneumonia 1st January 1917 aged 22. Son of John & Mary Elizabeth Beattie of Fern Hill, Coomera, Queensland.

31] Kinane, Pte. Lawrence, 2538. 49th Bn Australian Infantry. Died of broncho-pneumonia 6th January 1917 aged 19 or 20. Son of Daniel & Catherine Kinane; born in County Cork, Ireland; came to Australia aged 18[?] worked as a farmer; enlisted Warwick, Queensland..

32] McGregor, Pte. David Edward, 6621. 15th Bn. Australian Infantry. Died of broncho-pneumonia 23rd January 1917 aged 36. Son of Mrs Isabella McGregor; born at Bega, New South Wales; worked as manager of a cheese factory. He had two brothers in the AIF Lieut. McGregor of 121 Light Horse ' Mentioned in Despatches' & Sgt. Major Wallace McGregor of 25th Battalion 'Military Medal.' Neither man appears on the Australian Roll of Honour so it would appear they survived the war.

33] Brookes, Pte. Harold Vincent, 2628. 47th Bn. Australian Infantry. Died of sickness 5th February 1917 aged 19. Son of William & Mary Brookes; born at Ipswich, Queensland.

34] Parkinson, Pte. Alfred Henry, 7109. 16th Bn. Australian Infantry. Died in Sutton Veny Hospital of broncho-pneumonia 26th March 1917 aged 37. Son of William Jones & Isabella Louisa Parkinson; born in South Australia; worked as a miner as did his brother Pte Charles Frederick Parkinson, 3914, of 11th Battalion. He was killed in action somewhere in France between 22-25th July 1916 aged 30. He is remembered on panel 63 at Villers–Bretonneaux. Inscription reads: In the path of duty was the way to glory.

35] McMullen, Rfn. William, 23416. 1st Bn. NZ [Rifle] Brigade. Died of sickness 13th February 1917 aged 21. Son of James & Rose McMullen of 20 Arabi St., Mount Albert, Auckland.

36] Jefferies, Pte. Job 6/2173. Canterbury Regt. NZEF 12th February 1917 aged 27. Son of William & Ada Jefferies of Kangahu, Karamea.

37] Kelland, Pte. John Bodley, 31294. Wellington Regt. NZEF. Died of sickness 11th February 1917 aged 21. Son of George & Mary Kelland of Manaia, Waimate West.

38] Boland, Pte. Edward James, 26982. Canterbury Regt. NZEF 4th February 1917 aged 31. Son of Francis & Annie Boland of Darfield; husband of Nellie Bolland of Darfield, Christchurch.

39] Winterburn, Rfn. Betram, 28568. N.Z. [Rifle] Brigade. Died of sickness 4th February 1917 aged 40. Son of Arthur A. Winterburn of Tory St., Nelson.

40] Telford, Rfn. Thomas, 13132. 3rd Bn. 3rd NZ Rifle Brigade. Died 2nd February 1917 aged 44. Son of James & Mary Telford of Baccus Marsh, Victoria, Australia.

41] McFarlane, Pte. James Malcolm, 25284. Wellington Regt. NZEF died of pneumonia 26th January 1917 aged 23. Son of Peter & Helen McFarlane of 'Hopetoun', Woodgrove, North Canterbury.

42] Shaw, Pte. Alexander Davison, 27966. NZ [Rifle] Brigade. 15th January 1917 aged 36. Son of Elizabeth Shaw of 170 Coventry Street, South Melbourne & the late Thomas Shaw; born at Sandford, Victoria.

43] McCloud, Pte. James, 8/2084. Otago regt. NZEF. Died of sickness 28th December 1916 aged 23. Son of Samuel McCloud of Papatahi, Featherstone, Wellington.

44] Garlick, Rfn. William, 17708. NZ [Rifle] Brigade. 13th December 1916 aged 29. Son of Charles & Maria Dorothy Garlick of Taneatua, Bay of Plenty.

45] Glastonbury, Rfn. Albert George, 25860. NZ [Rifle] Brigade. 5th December 1916 aged 34. Son of Mrs. M.A. Glastonbury of Ohingaiti.

46] Darch, Pte. A.J., 87276. 'F' Coy. Royal Army Medical Corps. 25th November 1916.

47] Foster, Rfn. Edward, 20134. NZ [Rifle] Brigade. Died of sickness 14th November 1916 aged 34.

48] Pollock, Pte. Alexander, 3587. 57th Bn. Australian Infantry. Died 21st February 1919. Enlisted Derby, Victoria.

49] Ziesler, Cpl. or Sgt. Charles, 3961. 51st Bn. Australian Infantry. Died of in No 3 New Zealand General Hospital of sickness 26th June 1918 aged 46. Son of William &

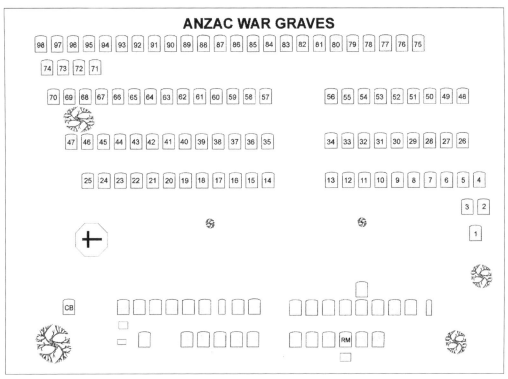

Map of the ANZAC Cemetery

Clerk of the Works Hut World War I known locally as the Scout Hut

St Mary's Church and St Mary's Cottage from Cemetery

The Cross of Sacrifice

Majors Avdrew Wears and Jackie Kopievsky, Australian Liaison Officers,
Anzac Service, 25th April, 2007

War graves and roses

Lucy Ziesler; husband of M.M. Ziesler of 68 Outram Street, Perth; born in England. Inscription: In loving memory of my dear husband and our dear father.

50] Clarke, Pte. Sydney James, 3762. 49th Bn. Australian Infantry. Died of brocho-pneumonia 21st June 1918 aged 28. Foster son of Mrs. E. Noud of Goondiwindi, Queensland; born & enlisted at St George, Queensland.

51] Cattermole, Pte Frank James, 3861. 48th Bn. Australian Infantry. Died of sickness in London 14th June 1918 aged 19. Son of William James & Amelia Jane Cattermole of Bordertown, South Australia; born in Victoria. Inscription reads " Dear Boy you have gone but we can never forget your smiling face."

52] Chilton, Pte. Thomas William, 1588, [also listed as John William Auton]. 53rd Bn. Australian Infantry. Died of sickness 30th March 1918 aged 29. Son of Mrs Sarah Ellen Chilton; born at Ripon, Yorkshire, England. Inscription "He died that we might live- ever remembered by his loving uncle, aunt and cousins." He seems to have been a farmer who arrived in Australia when he was 22 and enlisted in Coolamon NSW. He had been wounded at Suvla Bay in 1914 and in France in 1917.

53] Jennings, Pte. Clarence Albert, 3861. 32nd Bn. Australian Infantry. Died of measles & purulent brochitis 22nd March 1918 aged 21. Son of Robert Edward & Mary Ann Carrison Jennings of Port MacDonnell, South Australia. Inscription "He has done his duty."

54] Stratford, Pte. Henry Thomas, 5117. 31st Bn. Australian Infantry. Died 4th March 1918. Enlisted in Brisbane; worked as a labourer.

55] Cameron, Pte. Oscar, 3367. 59th Bn, Australian Infantry. Died of chronic nephritis 24th January 1918 aged 37. Son of Christopher & Agnes Cameron of Shelburne, Nova Scotia, Canada.

56] Cathcart, Pte. William Rea, 7716. 16th Bn. Australian Infantry. Died of diabetes 25th November 1917 aged 30. Son of Thomas Cathcart of Windsor Terrace, Ballymena, Co. Antrim, Ireland. Went to Australia at the age of 24; worked as a book-keeper; enlisted in Perth WA. Inscription "Gone but not forgotten."

57] Bourke, Pte. Walter Edward, 51681. Auckland Regt., NZEF 25th October 1917 aged 36. Son of Eliza & the late Patrick Bourke of 35 Esplanade, Mount Eden, Auckland. Born at Dargaville.

58] Kcarse, Pte. Thomas Walker, 6/2382. Canterbury Regt. NZEF 25th October 1917 aged 23. Husband of Mrs. C. L. Asselin [formerly Kearse] of 25 Holmwood Street, Newtown, Sydney, New South Wales.

59] Holmes, Pte. Arthur, 23/2204. NZ Maori [Pioneer] Battalion. Died of sickness 22nd March 1917 aged 33.

60] Whitelaw, Pte. Alexander George, 37903. Canterbury Regt., NZEF. Died of pneumonia 10th January 1918 aged 36. Son of Peter & Agnes Whitelaw of Makarewa, Invercargil;. born in Scotland.

61] Thomas, Rfn. Samuel, 26207. 1st Bn. 3rd NZ [Rifle] Brigade. Died 14th January 1918 aged 21.

62] Alley, Pte. Francis Lignori, 10287. Otago Regt. NZEF died of sickness 1st January 1917 aged 22. Son of John & Elizabeth Alley of Salisbury Road, Gisborne.

63] Moody, Pte. Francis Robert, 62358. Canterbury Regt., NZEF died of phthisis 22nd February 1918 aged 31. Son of Francis Rolfe & Mary Moody of Kihi Kihi, Waikato.

64] Charleston, Rfn. John, 33301. NZ [Rifle] Brigade. Died of meningitis 15th March 1918 aged 39. Son of John Charles & Clare Charleston of Cardiff, Wales; husband of F. Charleston of 109 Aro Street, Wellington.

65] Morris, Pte. Frank Kemp, 64558. Otago Regt., NZEF died of bronchitis 20th April 1918 aged 32.

66] Perwick, Pte. Thomas Patrick, 39307. Otago Regt., NZEF 4th May 1918 aged 28. Son of Alfred & Catherine Perwick of St Patrick's, Balfour, Southland.

67] Harvey, Pte. John Charles, 40212. 2nd Coy. 2nd Bn. Canterbury Regt. NZEF Died of nephritis 7th May 1918 aged 25. Son of George & Eleonora Margaret Dorothy Harvey of Sandy Bay, Riwaka, Nelson.

68] O'Neill, Pte, Patrick Thomas, 30449. NZ Machine Gun Battalion. Died of sickness 23rd May 1918. Son of Mrs Jane and the late Mr O'Neill of 151 Taranaki St., Wellington.

69] Tucker, Pte. Harry Edward, 10899. Wellington Regt., NZEF. Died of sickness 15th June 1918 aged 26. Son of John Tucker of Weardale Orchard, Havelock North.

70] Dunne, Serjt. William Patrick, 13890. Otago Regt., NZEF died of sickness 19th June 1918 aged 31. Son of Patrick & C. Dunne of Totaratahi, Oamaru.

71] Moore, Pte. John, 79989. Canterbury Regt., NZEF died of pneumonia 13th April 1919 aged 37. Son of Thomas & Helen Moore of Sumner, Christchurch; husband of Mary Moore of 13 High Street, Kaiapoi, Canterbury.

72] Hape, Pte. Hona, 16/536. NZ Maori [Pioneer] Battalion. Died of sickness 11th April 1919 aged 26. Son of Hope & Hera Inumia Tangiora of Opoutama, Napier.

73] Gilmour, Cpl. William, 10/3886. NZ Medical Corps. Died of influenza 7th April 1919 aged 52. Youngest son of the late John & Isabella Gilmour of New Plymouth.

74] Kearse, Rfn. Bertie Ernest, 25/1771. 1st Bn. 3rd NZ [Rifle] Brigade. Died of sickness 16th July 1918 aged 40. Son of Thomas F. Kearse of 15 Owen Street, Wellington; husband of the late Ada Kearse. Born at Wanganui.

75] Hayes, Pte. Daniel, 63153. Otago Regt. NZEF. Died of pneumonia 31st March 1919 aged 24. Son of Ann & the late John Hayes of Outram, Dunedin.

76] Aicken, Rfn. William Michael, 72925. NZ [Rifle] Brigade. Died of pneumonia 28th March 1919 aged 27. Son of William & Jessie Aicken of Aickens, Westland.

77] Freitas, Pte. David, 47553. Canterbury Regt. NZEF. Died of sickness 21st March 1919 aged 35. Son of Mr F. & Mrs M.A. Freitas of Three Mile, Hokitika.

78] Sexton, Rfn. Michael, 65462. NZ [Rifle] Brigade. 18th February 1919 aged 30. Son of William & Bridget Sexton of Westport.

79] Hayes, Q.M.S. [W.O.II] Charles William, 5/242B. NZ Army Service Corps. Died of pneumonia 16th February1919 aged 34. Son of Porter Theodore & Elizabeth Hayes of Auckland; husband of Emily Hayes of 25b Hanson Street, Newtown, Wellington.

80] Maley, Lce. Cpl. Archibald James, 8/3001. 1st Bn. Otago Regt., NZEF 15TH February 1919 aged 24; born at Mataura.

81] Wakelin, Capt. William Richard, 6/2891. Canterbury Regt., NZEF 5th February 1919 . Eldest son of Mrs G.A. & the late G.K. Wakelin of Blenheim.

82] Griffin, Pte. Alexander John, 81179. Otago Regt. NZEF. Died of sickness 22nd January 1919 aged 29. Husband of Mrs E.M. Griffin of Bonny Glen, Marton, Wanganui.

83] Jordan, Major Benjamin Stevens, 6/1109. Canterbury Regt. NZEF. Died of accidental injuries in a plane crash 24th May 1918 aged 34. Son of Mr S & the late Ellen Jordan of Rangiora; husband of Elsie C. Jordan of 136 Bishop Street, St Albans, Christchurch. [c]

84] King, Pte. Walter Edward, 16761. Auckland Regt. NZEF 14th December 1918 aged 27. Son of John Henry & Johannah Augusta King of North Loburn, Canterbury.

85] McDonnell, Pte. James William, 17806. 1st Bn. Canterbury Regt., NZEF died of pneumonia 18th November 1918 aged 27. Son of Eliza Amy & the late William McDonnell of 97 Barbour Street, Linwood, Christchurch.

86] O'Connor, Pte. Graham Wakefield, 60184. Auckland Regt., NZEF died of pneumonia, 9th November 1918 aged 24. Only son of Charles & Ellen Nina O'Conner of 28 Omahu Road, Remuera, Auckland; born at Christchurch.

87] Mincher, Pte. Oswold Alan, 26885. 2nd Bn. Auckland Regt. NZEF died on pneumonia 15th November 1918 aged 30. Son of James & Elizabeth Mincher of Northcote, Auckland.

88] Guthrie, Rfn. William George, 57070. 3rd Bn 3rd NZ [Rifle] Brigade. Died of pneumonia 29th October 1918 aged 40. Son of William & Jane Guthrie of Havelock North, Napier.

89] Byrne, Lce. Cpl. Vincent John, 4/535. NZ Engineers. 19th October 1918 aged 27. Son of Thomas Vincent & Frances A.M. Byrne of Kumara, Westland.

90] Saville, Pte. John George, 73523. New Zealand Reinforcement. Died of bronchitis 15th September 1918 aged 30. Son of Frank & Sarah Saville; husband of H.J. Saville of 13 Craighead Street, Timaru. Born in Durham, England.

91] Elton, Pte. Charles Edward Stuart, 38792. Wellington Regt. NZEF died of sickness

15th September 1918 aged 25. Son of Arthur & Elizabeth Elton of 207 Coutts Street, Kilbirnie South, Wellington.

92] McEnteer, Pte. Claude, 76955. "E" Coy. 40th New Zealand Reinforcements. Died of bronchitis 13th September 1918 aged 20. Son of James & Elizabeth McEnteer of Grey Street, Waihi; born at Thames.

93] Pilkington, Pte. Zell Eric Ivon, 75251. Machine Gun Sect., 40th New Zealand Reinforcements. Died of pneumonia 12th September 1918 aged 20. Son of Mr. W.A. & Mrs E.D.B. Pilkington of 1 Grey Street, Devonport, Auckland.

94] Magee, Pte. Joseph, 52446. Auckland Regt., NZEF. Died of sickness 2nd September 1918 aged 40. Son of late James & Mary Ann Magee of Ireland.

95] Stevenson, Pte. Bertram Onslow, 11587. NZ Medical Corps. Died of meningitis 24th July 1918 aged 36.

96] Wade, Pte. John, 61006. Canterbury Regt. NZEF. Died of phthisis 23rd August 1918 aged 34. Son of John E and C Wade of Winchester Road, Temuka, Canterbury.

97] Westerby, Pte. William James, 75618. N.Z. Medical Corps. Died of sickness 30th August 1918 aged 30. Husband of Lillie M. Munn [formerly Westerby] of Greytown, Wellington.

98] Nicolson, Pte. Archibald John, 29844. Otago Regt. NZEF. Died of pneumonia 14th July 1918 aged 23. Son of Donald & Isabella McDonald Nicolson of Deveraux Road, Winton, Southland.

The single grave from WWII is sited close to the hedge bordering Church Lane beneath a large Beech tree. Lance Sergeant Christopher Thomas Brown was in the 2nd Battalion Welsh Guards stationed at Codford with 6th Guards Armoured Tank Brigade. Born on 29th August 1909, the son of William and Elizabeth Brown; Christopher Brown enlisted in Middlesborough eight days before his eighteenth birthday on 21st August 1928. From 1929-1930 he served in Egypt, transferring to the reserves two years later. He was recalled to regular service in 1939, promoted to Lance Corporal on 17th June 1940 and to Lance Sergeant three months later.

Christopher Brown was found dead of gunshot wounds in the head in the room adjoining the Sergeants Mess on 8th April 1942. He was found laying with his head on a kit bag and a rifle on the floor by his side, medical evidence at the inquest stated that the skin around the wound was discoloured by explosive and the shot had penetrated the brain. He was thirty-three years old and left a widow and two sons.

One other grave RM is marked on the map – buried in the local grave section.

Brigadier General Russell Maynard MBE was drowned in Italy on 15th July 1988 after rescuing a group of teenagers at Fregene near Rome. For this heroic action he was posthumously awarded the Medaglia Civile Di Valori by the Italian Government. The citation says, "Alerted by cries of help, he did not hesitate to dive into the sea to go to

Russell Maynard's grave

the rescue of six young people who were about to drown. General Maynard generously succeeded in saving to lives of all the young people but, overcome by fatigue, was himself swept away by the waves and drowned. He sacrificed his own life for the most noble ideals of altruism and human solidarity." Russell Maynard had lived St Mary's Old Rectory since 1981with his wife Marguerite and his children Matthew and Rebecca.

This beautiful and peaceful cemetery is today a place of pilgrimage, it also a place to reflect on the tragedy of so many young men who arrived in the vigour of youth and never returned to their loved ones. In 1917 40 of them died, in 1918 a further 34; as far as we can tell 73 of the men were in their 20's and 30's, 8 were in their 40's, 4 were 19 and 1 aged 52. Pneumonia and sickness accounted for the majority of the deaths, 56 that we know of. Few of the men seem to have been married.

It is impossible to look at the gravestones with their simple inscriptions without a feeling of deep sadness. Shakespeare's quotation from 'Antony and Cleopatra' perfectly evokes the pathos of the Great War - "the bright day is done, and we are for the dark." For these men and millions like them, the bright day burned all too quickly and darkness descended upon a generation.

a] Private Albert Arthur Harris known to his parents as 'Sonnie' was the eldest son of Arthur and Eliza Harris; he came from Ranelagh in the Huon Valley and was an orchardist with a passion for horses. His sweetheart Amy became pregnant with their son Reginald before he left to fight; Sonnie was never to see his child, he died of peritonitis as a result of bullet wounds received in Malta in 1917. Machine gun crews were the target of every enemy weapon on the battlefield; the officers and men of the British Machine Gun Corps were nicknamed 'The Suicide Club' with a casualty rate in excess of 33%. Reg knew very little about his father, he was orphaned at 16 when his mother died; Amy had never married.

In November 2003 Sonnie's great granddaughter Georgena Kemp decided that her 'Pop' was going to become a real person in her life, her research has ensured that we have a glimpse of the young man who volunteered to fight.

b] Corporal Button was killed in a training accident at No. 2 Camp Codford, when a

Sonnie Harris

Sonnie Harris's grave

live grenade thrown by Private Taylor of 51st Bn. landed in a bay full of men waiting their turn to practice. The other men escaped almost unscathed; Corporal Button froze, he was seriously injured and died before reaching hospital. At the Inquest it was recorded that "A bullet had passed completely through his brain, death being due to a fracture of the skull. Deceased had a few wounds on his legs but they were quite slight."

c] At the time of his death on Friday 24th May 1918, Major Jordan was second in command of the New Zealand Command Depot at Codford. He was a passenger on an Airco DH6C6518 piloted by 2nd Lieutenant Joseph J. Daley from New York based at No 8 Training Depot Station at Netheravon. The crash occurred when the outer port wings collapsed as the aircraft began to pull out of a loop and dive manoeuvre to 1000 feet. The Training Depot had been formed 1st April that year and was responsible for basic and advanced training; the crash was its first fatality.

William Shakespeare - "Antony and Cleopatra" Act V, Scene II . Iras to Cleopatra - "Finish, good lady; the bright day is done, And we are for the dark."

Note
Sutton Veny has the largest War Grave Cemetery in the UK- the village was the Australian Command Depot in WWI.

Sources
The War Dead of the Commonwealth: Wiltshire Section published The Commonwealth War Graves Commission, London, 1961.
Information on Private Harris, Georgena Kemp
On Corporal Button: *The Warminster Journal* & Terry Crawford, author of *Wiltshire and the Great War*.
On Major Jordan *For Your Tomorrows* by E. Martin, Rod Priddle & Christopher Green. Fuller accounts of Corporal Button and Major Jordan are to be found in *Warriors For The Working Day: Codford During Two World Wars* by Romy Wyeth published by Hobnob Press in 2002.

6

Country Delights
Doreen Shelinga

Doreen is a member of the Cole family. She lived in Codford from 1920 until 1950 when she left for Australia. She wrote this essay in 1948 recording her childhood memories:

'When we were children my brothers and sister and I used to spend much of our time playing in the Chitterne Brook near our home. When dry in the late summer this stream revealed a collection of rusty tins, broken crockery and old boots, which provided much valuable play material, and we passed many happy hours there engaged in extensive building projects. With the coming of the autumn rains and February thaw however, this winterbourne came into full spate, and our imaginary cities were inundated with water. So our attention turned to other things, for in the early spring the trout came up this small tributary from the river Wylye, only to get left in the deeper pools near the hatches when the drier weather came again. These wary fish would remain stationary with their heads tucked under the boards at the sides, but with their tails and bodies in full view. What a delight it was to us to visit the brook, armed with rabbit wires attached to the end of long sticks, and by careful manoeuvring slide the nooses over their tails and catch them behind the gills. Quickly pulling the unfortunate creatures out of the water we would wrap them in large leaves, put them into a rush basket and run home with them, where they were deposited in a large sink kept for this purpose. After a few preliminary gasps the trout would revive and we would then enjoy their company for as long as they cared to continue ours. A country child can always get "something for nothing", and perhaps it was these early successes with fish which led us when older to go further afield in search of new acquisitions. We gathered in their seasons- cowslips, primroses, bluebells, rhododendrons, mushrooms, blackberries and nuts. The joy of all these ventures was derived I think, not so much from achieving the objects in view, although there was satisfaction in this to be sure, but also from the long walks usually necessary to reach their situations. In the spring time there was little to compare with the sight and the smell of a field filled with cowslips, the vision of primroses and bluebells under the fresh green foliage of an April wood, or the first view of a rising bank of rhododendrons; and in the early autumn the return home with a well filled basket of blackberries or mushrooms is a pleasure indeed. At one time we always got up at about four or five o'clock in the morning to look for mushrooms. We had been told that you must always pick them before the sun is on them, but we soon realised that this was just another way of saying "the early bid catches the worm," for later we gathered fine mushrooms at all hours of the day. There was certainly something about the atmosphere of an early walk on the Downs on a misty September morning, which was missing on an afternoon or an evening jaunt. Sometimes we took our tea with us on these gathering expeditions, and had a picnic in the open or under the trees. The food always tasted better after the appetite had been sharpened by a long tramp, when the stomach had been satisfied we played games of cricket, rounders or hide and seek. I associate picnics too with another feature of country life- the Hunts "point to point" race meetings. Meals on the grass always preceded the business of looking at the runners, studying form in the ring, buying tickets at the tote, watching races and cheering the winners. I liked the atmosphere of friendly rivalry which pervaded these meetings, and maybe the odd hope of "getting something for nothing" also served in drawing us to Kingston Deverill, Larkhill, Thingley and Chewton Mendip during the spring months of March, April and May. June and July brought the haymaking season to the farm again, and attention had to be given to the more serious matter of providing next winter's feed for the cattle. The scent of newly mown grass never fails to stir the emotions of one born and bred in the country. On many occasions I have gone out of doors, to stand and watch fascinatedly, the way in which the cat was jumping to catch the large moths which hover over the flowering grasses at this time. Sometimes, after a busy hot evening spent sweeping hay from the fields and making with it a rick, we would take our swimming costumes and go down to Sherrington Mill Pool for a bathe. I have enjoyed swimming more a ten o'clock in the evening, than at any other time, and a good supper following at eleven thirty does not lose it's savour either. Harvest followed haymaking, and "when all was safely gathered in," the church festival never failed to attract a much larger congregation than usual. Whether it was the sight of the sheaves of corn, vegetables, fruit and flowers arranged in a setting of Gothic architecture, their rich mingled smells or the genuine thankfulness which caused the increase, I do not know. I rather fancy that the pleasure derived from the lusty singing of the old familiar hymns had a lot to do with it. Winter too had some delightful aspects. Although I have never been colder in my life than I was during the severe winter of 1947, there were days when I had to acknowledge the sheer beauty of crystalline trees and bushes, sparkling like a transformation scene in a pantomime, and I felt that Christmas and it's attendant celebrations always more than compensated for the greyness of November and December. At one time we used to go out carol singing, to the accompaniment of an American organ carried in a horse drawn milk float hung around with lanterns. At some of the houses we visited, our treatment was extremely generous, and we got far more out of the expeditions than a full collecting box. Many other organised entertainments of the countryside took place in the winter. Just before Christmas the village Cricket Club held its annual Whist Drive. On many occasions fifty card tables had been filled with keen players eager for the prizes of poultry, joints of meat, wine, fruit, chocolates and cigarettes. It was a special feature of these competitions that the booby prize winners should always kiss publically under the mistletoe, and this always aroused merriment. However any special occasion is a good excuse for a celebration in the country. There was always a dance on New Years Eve, a large bonfire with fireworks on November 5th, a flower show and fete on the first Monday in August, whilst at events like the Jubilee of King George V and the coronation of George VI there were excellent programmes. On May 6th 1935, the Jubilee of King George V, all differences of "church" and "chapel" were forgotten, and after a united service of thanksgiving in the morning, almost the whole population sat down to an excellent lunch, set out in a very large granary which had been cleared out for this purpose by a local farmer. In the afternoon a fancy dress procession with decorated wagons and lorries, paraded the main village street, headed by a hurriedly organised band. The standard displayed by the competitors was very high and I still have photographs of the scene, which prove to me that my appreciation was not heightened by my youthfulness and the novelty of the occasion. Sports occupied the afternoon, and I remember how keenly the veterans race [for men over fifty] was contested and with how much amusement it was regarded by the younger members of the gathering, especially as two less agreeable old characters fell over each other and had a rather heated argument as to who had caused the mishap. Later their differences were resolved when everyone sat down to an excellent high tea which had been prepared by some of the industrious ladies of the committee. As soon as it was dark a firework display took place, then all who were not too tired repaired to the village hall to dance until one o'clock the next morning. Village life owed much of its humour to individuals, who, because they differ a little from the average are well known to everyone. Such a person was Tommy, the young man who brought the newspapers round. You could always tell where he was by his merry whistle, and to encounter his cheery smile in the morning was a tonic for the day. Then there was Alice, always referred to as "the postgirl" although she had begun her daily rounds during the 1914-18 war. Her uniform had never changed in style from then until the recent war [WWII], then she appeared in a modern trousered outfit, which she declared was "very comfortable and more convenient for riding a bike." Another old woman who always caused a smile was Eva. She told fortunes with cards, and earned much money at fetes with this kind of entertainment. You never had to ask where she was situated, for her frequent high-pitched cackle always denoted the spot. If you had gone into the local public house, you would have been almost sure to meet the old seedsman who warmed his beer in a little saucepan which the publican kept under the counter for him, and we had many a laugh at our old doctor who treated his patients with methods of "trial and error." I recall too, an old busybody on the Parish Council, who was always against any innovations in the village, as he didn't want the rates to go up. When the subject of street lighting was being discussed at one meeting, he stood up and argued that he couldn't see "why it was necessary for the young 'uns didn't want lights at night time, and the old 'uns 'and't got no business to be out after dark!" Dull, living in the country? I don't think so!

7

The Village
Harry Cole

Among the twenty or so villages which lay in this lovely valley of the river Wylye
from Wilton to Warminster, Codford would not perhaps be counted among the
most beautiful. It has none of the old world charm of neighbouring Stockton, or the
unspoiled rural setting of Sherrington, which make them so much desirable to people
seeking rural retreats. Parts of it may lay claim to beauty, especially around the fine
stone bridge over the river just outside the park, and the area around the nearby ford
from which the place probably takes its name – Co-ed-ford, the wooded ford – where
there are some fine trees, as indeed there are in other parts of the village although in
1914 there were many more. In Domesday Book the name is written Coteford.

Stockton Lodge, circa World War I

William Cobbett in his "rural rides" written in the early nineteenth century has little to say of the place, except to wonder why two such large churches should have been built within a few hundred yards of each other, the chancel of either he says being large enough to contain the whole population. This would hardly seem feasible unless the population at the time was very small.

Codford has no fine old manor house, such as Stockton House or Boyton. In fact the Lord of the Manor of Codford was the Yeatman-Biggs family of Stockton, nor has it any predominating residence, new or old to give it distinction. Even the new housing areas developed since the last war [WWII] cannot be said to have contributed anything of aesthetic value to the place. There are some nice Georgian and early Victorian houses, mostly hidden from view by walls and hedges, and the smaller houses, chiefly in the main street. A pair of old cottages opposite St Peters Church is not without interest. On the wall facing the road is the date 1722 and the letters I.C. The story goes that Isaac Crouch who owned the property and lived in the adjoining house, had two daughters, who quarrelled continuously about a lover. Unable to stand the repeated bickering over the swain who did not settle the matter by marrying one of them, he had two cottages built and put one daughter in each.

The village would appear to have grown haphazardly, having two parishes may have had something to do with this, and straggles alongside the main road which narrows badly at the lower end, where the Chitterne Brook runs under the road to join the Wylye. St Peter's Church in a fine position at the top of the hill is situated quite close to the highway whilst St Mary's Church is tucked away at the lower end of the village under the curve of the Downs and adjoins East Farm House. The house is on the site of an ancient hermitage, and the stone fireplace from it now forms the porch of Mr Frank Sykes house at Stockton.

1914-1918

To the end of 1914 Codford was just a typical Wiltshire village with two parishes, two churches and a chapel, with at the time considerable congregations attending them all. A school in each parish where the children went until they were old enough to leave. There was only one public house, the George Inn, now called a Hotel. At one time the Brewery was behind the Inn, and stood on the ground which has become the garden. The water was drawn from a well now behind a pair of cottages. There was also an off licence which sold beer only for six days of the week. In past times there had been two other Inns, "the Fleur-de Lys," which was situated at the French Horn and seems to have some connection with the wool trade which flourished in the district and the "Kings Arms" reputedly situated by the ford. No trace, however, except an old pewter mug bearing the name Chris Cook, The Kings Arms, Codford St Mary remains of either.

The carriers cart went once weekly to Salisbury, and twice to Warminster. In 1914, a carrier started a Motor Carrier Van service from Chitterne to Salisbury which picked up in Codford. The van had solid tyres, and transported live and dead stock as well as passengers. There was at that time, only two cars in the village. The Doctor drove on his rounds in a pony and trap. There were bicycles of course, and the railway with the station over a mile from the village. The post went to the station on a handcart late in the evening, pulled and pushed by two men, or three if the post was heavy.

The shops consisted of two grocers, a draper, butchers, saddler, cycle shop and blacksmith. No telephone or electric light- coal was 24/- per ton, rent and rates were low. Income Tax if you paid any was 1s/2d in the pound, and food was cheap. Housewives for the most part were careful, thrifty and hardworking- they had no modern amenities such as piped water or washing machines. They did have a store of practical knowledge and made the little money they had go around, by a host of well proved methods of making ends meet. A pig in a sty, jam making, home remedies in cases of illness, wine making [lovely stuff some of it] and mead, potent and palatable.

Cider was made locally, although rather rough.

Much of the children's clothes were made at home, and new clothes were mostly made to last. Skirts were long, and the rest of the ladies garments were substantial and voluminous. The young girls made the best of themselves, but cosmetics and make-up were not used. For a girl to use lipstick or nail varnish would have branded her as someone better not to know. Girls up to 14 or 15 wore their hair long and their greatest pride were the long curls done up each night in curling paper.

Men, were for the most part soberly and solidly clad. Moustaches, and whiskers of all shapes, colours and sizes were wore by the older men, but they were well on the way out. This solid and staid habit of dress was reflected in their deportment. People of forty or so were elderly, and at sixty seemed quite old. Perhaps it was the life of manual work which began earlier which aged people quickly.

On the whole life proceeded at a leisurely pace; they fed the chickens, milked the cows, ploughed the fields and scattered, then they had a pint or two at the George on Saturday [2/- a pint] and went home to bed. On Sundays they went to church or chapel, paid proper respect to the Squire and Parson, looked the whole world in the face, and owed not any man.

Entertainment usually took the form of concerts in the schoolroom by the Glee Singers. Mrs Ashton, the wife of the Rector of St Mary's Church, was very musical, and did much to encourage music in the village. She composed many anthems and hymn tunes anonymously and a Church Choir Book for village use.

An annual Flower Show was held, an important event always well supported, usually on the last Saturday in July. There were children's parties at Christmas time, not forgetting the Bell Ringers Supper on New Years Eve and the annual fairs at Warminster, Wilton and Salisbury.

Politically the village was about equally divided between Conservative and Liberal, with considerable interest and excitement being shown at election times. The emergence of the Labour Party as a major political group had not yet affected the rural areas.

It was to Codford that the First World War brought all the traffic of a military camp, and the main road, which at that time was totally unsuited for any volume of heavy traffic, rapidly became a sea of mud.

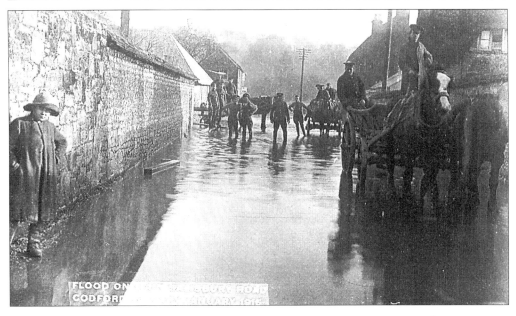

Floods, Codford St Mary, January, 1915

Codford Flood, January 1st

Flooding, January 1st, 1916

Interior of Y.M.C.A. Hut,
Camp 15, Codford, Wilts.

YMCA Camp 15

The abnormal rainfall of 1914 and early 1915 had caused considerable flooding in the village and the area from the Park Lodge to the west of Chitterne Road was under water. The ford had disappeared and the footbridge was impassable. The land round the station, into which from late 1914 large numbers of men, and vast quantities of materials for camps were poured, was churned by horses, carts, and traction engines into a quagmire which had to be seen to be believed. The flooding which had occurred over the whole area of Salisbury Plain had brought a condition on the roads with which the local authority had neither the equipment, or the resources to cope, and the place inevitably earned the unenviable notoriety as Codford on the Mud.

Over the Plain, the consequences of the flooding were much more serious. Large numbers of troops from overseas [mostly Canadians] trained under appalling conditions, and many died from Cerebro- Spinal Meningitis, brought on by the it was said, by the wet and the cold. Whatever the cause, many who left their homes in distant parts of the Empire to fight for the Motherland, left their bodies in her care in England without having seen the battlefields of Flanders, or heard, to quote Wilfred Owen, "what passing bell for those who die as cattle, only the monstrous anger of the guns."

Mud was everywhere. Newly enlisted men were under canvas here and there in the area, and the need for better quarters than tented camps was vital and urgent. Water supplies were negligible and contaminated by floodwater. The contractors had recruited hundreds of men from all parts of the country to help in the building of proper accommodation. Special trains brought workmen out each day from Salisbury to work on the camps, and all sorts of temporary huts and buildings were being erected anywhere and everywhere to provide for the invading army of soldiers and civilians.

It seemed like chaos, and it was- fifteen camps to be built as well as a hospital and its accompanying buildings. RE; ASC and the necessary services such as stabling, water supply, electricity, drainage etc, all had to be erected and installed without any of the present day equipment for trenching and building. It was done by hand, pick and shovel, and muscle power.

A branch railway line was run from the siding at the station to near East Farm and northwards. Horses, carts and steam wagons did the hauling, ropes and tackle did the lifting, and some shape of things to come emerged. The village was submerged in the feverish activity of preparation for waging war on a scale hitherto unknown. Gunfire surrounded it, indeed was in it.

In the main street every vacant plot including front gardens, where there were any, sprouted temporary shops, cafes, barbers, tobacconists, photographers, grocers, butchers, boot and shoe shops, chemists and tailors. The Wool Stores, a legacy to the village of an industry long transferred to Yorkshire, became a cinema, complete with orchestra pit. The reading room where chess was once regularly played, became a café.

At the rear of St Mary's Church a huge Army Institute was put up, and various religious organisations all had provision for the spiritual welfare and social needs of the men who were there, and still coming. In fact, Codford had all the accessories and equipment of a fair sized town, and that it was with inhabitants of every type.

CONGREGATIONAL INSTITUTE FOR SOLDIERS, CODFORD.

Congregational Institute

View of troops on parade in Camp No. 6 from Little Wood.

The first occupants were English troops, newly enlisted, full of enthusiasm and patriotic fervour- men from all walks of life, with but one object; to get to France as quickly as possible. As more of the camps became available, men from overseas began to fill them. They came from distant parts of the Empire – Australians, great big men, rough and ready; undisciplined by our standards but great fighters and eager to be in the war. They had little respect for law and order, and they left the George a shambles after one hectic evening, but as fighters [and the First World War was a fighting mans war] they were superb. Of a similar type, but quieter in manner and tidier in appearance, more amenable to discipline, were the New Zealanders. They were fine men too, tall, but lighter in build than the Australians. A few South Africans were also stationed here.

These were the inhabitants of the camps from 1915 to the end of the war. Their number at its peak was ten to eleven thousand but decreased as time went on.

In the middle of this frenzied activity and conglomeration of people was the village, who lived in it you did not know, what they did or where they worked was also unknown, that it had any life of it's own nobody could say, its entity had disappeared . Certainly some farming was going on, but in a limited way by a few older men. Many of the younger men had gone away so farming activity was curtailed. In addition, all the best horses, and large quantities of hay and corn had been requisitioned for the use of army transport. Never had the village seen such mule teams as came to Codford – some of them 16-17 strong. Dairying was restricted to a few small cow keepers.

Thomas King Harding, the owner of the Ashton Gifford Estate, rode forlornly round his devastated acres vainly endeavouring to save what he could. Troubled in spirit, he fought unavailingly against the advancing tide of military occupation. He died in 1916, and Ashton Gifford House was then occupied by military personnel.

Looking back to the military occupation, one now realises that a fundamental change was taking place, not only in Codford but in the country as a whole. There were changes among the occupants of the village about the same time as the outbreak of the war. Both Manor Farm and East Farm changed hands within a short time of each other, also two smaller farms. Canon Maclean, who had been rector of St Peters Church, retired in 1915 and was succeeded by the Reverend Edward Denny. Dr Ward, who had served the village for many years retired and Dr Lewis took his place. A new schoolmistress was appointed to St Mary's school. All these people had meant a lot to the life of the village. It was as if a shutter had been pulled down on the old order, to be raised five years later on a new. Whether a better one was a question to which no answer was possible, but changes were going on. Although the upheaval in the pattern of daily life was accepted, including the disappearance of Sunday as a day of rest, the seed of a new set of values had been sown. True, the harvest was not yet, new horizons were to come into view.

The war was over. "The Captains and the Kings departed." Yes, the King had been to Codford. His visit was not officially notified but his coming had been rumoured , and about half a dozen were gathered on the triangle of ground near the village when a car with several officers in it came by and one called out "Your King is coming, give him a cheer," and there was King George V. The car stopped and he got out with accompanying officers. He chatted with them and acknowledged our greeting, then went on to Sutton Veny for an inspection of the troops.

Armistice Day, November 11th 1918, now kept as a day of Remembrance, was as far as Codford was concerned, an occasion of frenzied excitement. Waves of happy Australians, accompanied by any female they could persuade to join them, swept up and down the main street, linked together across the road. They shouted, sang and surged along, sweeping everything before them – safety lay only in flight.

Celebrations for the victory of the Allies were widespread. Gradually the men returned to their homes in Australia, New Zealand and South Africa. Several girls went with them to face life in a new country under conditions very different from those of their homeland, and a few of the men who had come from the Dominions found sweethearts here and stayed. The Australian Badge of the Rising Sun was cut into the chalk slope of Codford Down – a silent reminder of those strenuous years, as are also the graves of about 100 men by St Mary's Church. The epidemic of Spanish Flu, which followed immediately after the end of the war, was responsible for some of those deaths.

The Rising Sun: Australian Badge on Misery Hill

1918-1919

The village now had to get back to peacetime conditions. It had to emerge and re-establish itself. The war, which had brought sorrow and bereavement to almost every family in the land, had touched Codford too, and of the men who had left in such high spirits to engage in the war to end all wars, eighteen failed to return.

In other ways the village people had not suffered. Rationing which had been imposed hardly seemed to matter. There seemed to be always enough food and fuel, and there was money about, more than had ever been thought possible.

Farm workers wages had risen considerably and were supplemented by their wives working in the many places requiring help. If people had any room to spare they took in boarders of whom there were many requiring accommodation. Work on the camps was well paid, and many girls who would formerly have nothing but domestic service to look forward to, found better pay and more interesting work in the shops.

The population of the village was substantially increased. There were still many whose business with the army kept them on duty, gradually the men who survived the war came home and if possible took up their lives again. There was a state of prosperity, which previously had not been known. A bus service began to run to Salisbury and Warminster and goods hitherto out of reach, became obtainable. The carrier still went with his horse and van but his days were numbered.

The young people began to look for interests outside working hours. The Choral Society began again in 1919 under Mrs Aston, and attended the festivals at Devizes. A football and social club was started and the football team achieved some success in the local competitions. Whist drives and dances began in the dining hall of one of the camps, and even a fancy dress New Year's Ball. There were no bands available so a piano and a violin played for the now called "old time" dances. A cricket club was formed and ground laid out in Stockton Park and the Comrades of the Great War started a club in the Wools Stores.

1920-1930

People were becoming more socially minded and there sprang from this, perhaps, the most ambitious idea- the setting up in 1920 of a Red Triangle Club. The YMCA had erected several large temporary buildings for the use of the troops, and one of these was taken over as premises in which to start and run the social club. A caretaker was installed and a useful nucleus of members enrolled. Among the activities of the Club was a debating group and this proved quite exciting on occasions. One debate which had for its subject "Bolshevism, is it a workable system ?" brought down upon the members the spectacle of a specially organised panel of speakers from the Conservative Association. Never was there such a lively meeting, and very early on all the accepted rules of debate were forgotten. Nor were the arts neglected, for the Club held a well-supported Arts and Crafts Exhibition for a year or two covering most of the hobbies and spare time occupations of people at that time.

The Codford Concert Party came into being in 1920- Harry Pellissier and all that- and this may be said to be the first attempt of an organised entertainment group in the village. The party met with considerable success and travelled around neighbouring villages and towns with their programmes. The girls were attractive in their costumes, and the men included some good singers with two first-rate pianists as accompanists. They were full of enthusiasm, even if talent was limited, the one act plays and sketches were the early productions in this village which has now achieved considerable prestige and standing in the field of dramatic presentation.

The boom time which followed the war of 1914-1918 and which reached its peak in 1920 was brought about by the shortage of all sorts of consumer goods and food. The U-boat warfare had been more serious than anyone knew, and from many points of view this ignorance of the true position was a good thing. Had the people known we were within measurable distance of starvation there might have been many serious consequences- but peace had come- we thought for good- we had money in our pockets- we would have a good time.

Prosperity reached the farming community as well, and the price of livestock soared. History was made in the village in 1920 when a saddleback sow was sold for three hundred and forty guineas- the fact was widely published abroad and in this country- the price would be equivalent to two thousand pounds today [1964]. Incidentally, the local barber trimmed the pig up before she went on her triumphant tour. Probably the first and last time he had barbered a pig! Hay and corn had reached record high prices and many farmers bought their farms, only to find that after a few years the high prices disappeared, and they were ruined by the disastrous depression of the late twenties.

It was in the Red Triangle Club of 1922 that the village first heard the marvel of radio. Major Allott had built a receiver and a large gathering came to hear this new wonder of science. It was not entirely successful, being subject to the teething troubles of all new inventions, but it worked sufficiently well for people to realise that they were hearing something , which they had never thought possible.

The Annual Flower Show began again and was looked forward to each year with eager anticipation by local gardeners, several of whom were employed as such in the district.

The Boy Scouts had a troop under a scout mistress; they were a lively lot of youngsters and had many happy gatherings.

In the village initial enthusiasm began to wane and by 1924 or 5 some of the more ambitious projects were wearing a little thin. The Red Triangle Club had to close down because the building could not be maintained. The rather flimsy construction of wooden sections, began straining at the seams. Membership declined and it had to close, with the result that many activities had, for a time, had to be curtailed. The Ex-Service Men's Club suffered a similar fate and the Football Club suspended operations at about the same time. However, much had been learnt, and the committees were by no means discouraged, even though some of the Concert Party members had decided to get married!

A number of people who had been living in the village ended their work with the military authorities and left for other districts, and so Codford began to revert to its entirely agricultural character. On the credit side at this time of waning interest, was the formation of a branch of the Woman's Institute in 1924. The Codford Branch had some talented ladies as president, the first of whom was Mrs Arthur Jeffries. They have proved themselves as an active and progressive body, ready participants in many village events.

The repeal of the corn production act was felt. Farmers were losing money and corn prices collapsed as did the value of livestock. Tractors had not come into general use, and farmers could not afford to buy them. In order to make ends meet land, which had been cultivated, was put to grass. Wages fell and unemployment began to raise its ugly head.

In the country as a whole the depression settled on industry. The government had no remedial means of work for the unemployed and there was little opportunity for alternative work in the countryside for many who lived there or who had returned from the war. Quite a number of younger men left the village for towns and districts where there were prospects of employment and the money which had been so easily come by in the days of the war went just as quickly.

The unrest, which permeated the whole country, began to find expression in the countryside and the rise to power of the Labour movement began to spread. The elections in the twenties saw the emergence of the Labour Party as a major political force in the constituency, and at more than one public meeting, women were reduced to tears by the eloquence of their speakers.

Motor cars were now seen more frequently and a garage and petrol station opened, petrol in two gallon cans at two shillings and fourpence a can; happy days! A go ahead young man acquired a second hand "Overland" and started a hire service. One evening he had a call from a lady to go to Warminster Hospital and pick up an elderly man. When he got there it turned out to be a corpse. Rigor Mortis had set in and the difficulty was to get the body into the car. He solved this by putting a board across the tops of the front and the back seats and so came home to Codford with the cold feet of the corpse tickling his left ear.

The doctor had a car which he drove for many years, and in which he had several narrow escapes. It bore many honourable scars when he finally parted with it. Motorcycles were more commonly seen and popular with the younger men. The bus service developed and started trips to the seaside, journeys, if not hazardous were not without incident. One lady making what was probably her first journey of this kind to Weymouth sent a telegram to her relations at home telling them of her safe arrival.

Some revision came about in the social activities of that time. The Social Club carried on in a limited way in a smaller venue. For others there were the occasional whist drives and dances which were well supported, especially the Christmas whist drive, when live poultry were given as prizes. A home for these activities was found in a surplus army building which had been purchased by the County Council for a school extension. The school extension was the first idea for a central school for the neighbourhood. The Church authorities proposed to build it. A very large effort combining several parishes was initiated and a fete to eclipse all previous fetes arranged. However fate intervened and the day was completely ruined by rain. Notwithstanding, a sum of £448 was raised for the school, but the school was never started and the money was devoted to a college for training teachers in Salisbury.

The building did provide a stage where concerts and plays were performed by local groups and school children, and it became known as the "Little Theatre." It was in this place that the Citizen House Players from Bath performed a passion play. Another evening's entertainment included tableaux, and the Pears Soap advertisement "Bubbles," was a striking performance by a local child. Freddie Bartholomew of Warminster, afterwards a Hollywood star, also appeared there. An acetylene gas plant supplied the lighting and this was very temperamental if not unreliable with consequences that are better imagined. The dancers liked the occasional black-out.

Occasions for general rejoicing were always welcome and one such opportunity did occur in 1925, the Gold Wedding celebrations of the Rev. Canon and Mrs Denny at St Peters Rectory. They, together with their family, entertained all the parishioners to high teas on the lawn. A Loving Cup, subscribed for by all the parish was presented to them. Canon Denny came to Codford early in 1915 from a London parish and had a great deal of work to do during the war with a floating population. He was a fine parish priest.

The General Strike of 1926 which although it caused considerable interest and concern in the village did not affect life there to anything like the extent it did in the towns. The local grist mills were working. Flour was obtainable locally. Meat, milk, butter, were all available from farms in the neighbourhood and we got by without any great hardship.

An event which did cause considerable interest and feeling in the village happened in 1926. This was the union of the benefices of Codford St Peter and Codford St Mary. The idea had been mooted that one church would lose its Rector and become redundant. Quite what was to happen was not understood locally and speculation and gossip over afternoon teas were rife. Canon Denny, Rector of St Peter's was an Irishman and much respected by the parishioners, was opposed to the scheme as were many others. He was outspoken in his objections and said it would cause dissention. It was, he said, "setting Imperium in Imperio." We were not quite sure what "Imperium in Impero" meant but it had a fine resounding ring about it and made a fine rallying cry for opponents to the scheme. An enquiry was held in the Little Theatre and the union was approved in 1928. Canon Denny died in 1928, and Canon Meyrick who had succeeded the Rev. E.H.Ashton at St Mary's in 1924, came to St Peters Rectory in 1930 and nothing further was heard of "Imperium or Imperio!"

A great snowstorm occurred in December 1929. For days preceding Christmas Day of that year, a bitter wind blew from an easterly direction, so fierce and strong that it was difficult to stand against it. On Boxing Day the snow began to fall and by the next day the roads were impassable. Visitors stayed with their friends for most of the Twelve Days of Christmas, whether they were welcome or not. The food situation was not too healthy as for some time it was only possible to get about with difficulty. More snow fell in a shorter time on that occasion, than in 1962-63, but fortunately it did not lie so long, and as mechanical aids for road clearance were not then available, the roads would not have been opened so soon.

1930-1939

The first Sunday in 1930 was the evening of the great wind. It came from the southwest and gradually reached its climax in the early evening. Roads were littered with falling trees and hundreds were brought down in the neighbourhood causing damage to property and some injury to persons. Many vehicles as well were marooned on the roads. It was as though the decade was being given a parting kick for having failed to live up to its early promise, for 1920 was a year of prosperity, high wages and prices; 1929, a year of acute economic depression, unemployment and low wages, truly a wind of change.

Radio was now well established and personalities in this new medium of communication began to be known. Music and singing of the sort that up to then had only been heard on gramophone records flowed into the humblest home. The Savoy Orpheans Dance B was a regular feature. Talks and discussions widened our outlook; the radio was our guide, philosopher and teacher. We even began to listen to weather forecasts and fat stock prices. The daily paper contained yesterdays news, we wanted, and were getting today's! The radio filled our evenings with music and drama at little expense.

The economic depression was not acute, money was short, there was not much left for holidays at home or abroad. Leisure time activities had to be found locally, and the social groups carried on bravely. The Tennis Club was set going and established itself well, the dance on New Year's Eve, which they started, is still a very popular annual feature. In 1931 the Codford amateurs gave their first performance in the Wool Stores. Two one act plays with some solo items between comprised the programme, and the Society, which it was said was "launched out of boredom and supported by somebody's overdraft" was afloat. That it was to become front-page news never entered anyone's mind. Emboldened by their initial success they followed with a three-act play and this was equally well received. The Society was not regularly constituted; people were invited to take part on the strength of their possible ability and for the first few years' changes in cast and producer were frequent.

Another merger took place in Codford in 1934. As the Union of the Benefices had taken place in 1928, so the civil parishes of St Peter and St Mary became united under an order of the Ministry of Health. The local office of the Tax Collector and Overseer disappeared and Parish Council was brought into being. The election for this took place on March 25th 1934, seventeen candidates being nominated for nine seats and elected by a show of hands. Mr H.E. Wightwick was subsequently elected Chairman of the first Council.

Another result of the union was that the parishes now only had one representative on the Rural District Council instead of two, so one would have to go. It looked at one time as if a delicate situation might arise, as by an unwritten law one member was usually drawn from Conservative and one from Liberal, or Church and Chapel. The dilemma was quite amicably settled however, as a neighbouring parish was without a member, so our surplus member popped in there and everyone was happy.

The year 1935 was a red-letter day for the village, as for every place in the country. King George V, who had come to the throne in 1910, celebrated his Jubilee. Nobody could have foreseen or anticipated the enthusiasm and good will engendered by this event. For more than a decade the country had been suffering from depression and it seemed that people felt they had to celebrate – and celebrate they did. Ever before or since in the fifty years of this history has the village been so united in a common purpose. Everybody entered into the arrangements with spontaneous good will, and the day of the celebrations, May 6th was perfect.

A Service of Thanksgiving, a half-mile long procession of decorated vehicles and a fancy dress parade with every conceivable costume took place. The local butcher was "Glaxo builds bonnie babies." There were Henry VIII and Anne Boleyn, Deweys "Jubileers" and Robin Hood. A cine camera picture of the procession was taken and shown later. A dinner for all the village was held in the large Institute at St Mary's. There were toasts, sports with an amusing veterans race, dancing and fireworks and a huge fire balloon, [which drifted seven miles before it descended,] sent up. Altogether a memorable day in the life of the village! To mark the occasion a tree was planted in Cherry Orchard in 1936, the year in which King George V, the object of so much spontaneous affection, died. That year was memorable too in that a new king acceded to the throne and abdicated all in the same year.

An ominous shadow of things to come loomed when a parish meeting was held in March 1937 to consider arrangement for provision of gas masks, and the appointment of an Air Raid Warden.

The meeting discussed as well the celebrations for the coronation of King George VI, and a committee was appointed to carry out the arrangements. The coronation date was May 12th, and the preliminary plans were on much the same lines as in 1935, with a few exceptions. For some indefinable reason there was not the same feeling as on the previous occasion. Not that there was any lack of loyalty or enthusiasm, but the Jubilee celebrations and the events of 1936 had somehow overshadowed the preparations. It seemed that the burst of excitement and fervour exhibited on that occasion could not be regenerated, and so it proved. Joyful it was, the procession excellent with some outstanding and ambitious costumes, decorations no less varied, dancing as enjoyable and high spirited, but it was perhaps a little too close in time to the Jubilee. We had done it before- and we had no fireworks.

An interesting sidelight on the Coronation ceremony occurred in the summer. The owner of Ashton Gifford House, who was a peeress and had attended the Coronation thought the school children would be interested to see her robes. She was a small, regal figure, in stature not unlike Queen Victoria, and on the appointed day the school children were taken to the house to see probably the only real life Peeress they had ever seen fully robed.

An outbreak of foot and mouth disease occurred in the autumn of 1937. Practically every farm in the locality was affected. The burning of the carcases was going on during dark and foggy days and the unpleasant smell seemed to hang around the area for weeks.

Among the other Parish Council affairs of 1937 was a letter from the Wilts Planning Committee on the preservation of trees, and it was decided by the Parish Council that the Jubilee tree in Cherry Orchard be scheduled for preservation. However, the tree was uprooted in 1954 by the order of the Planning Committee of the Rural District Council to make room for houses. It was replanted in Broadleaze, where of course it died- so much for the planners!

To mark the Coronation of King George VI a small recreation ground for children was purchased in Chitterne Road in 1938, and by a curious freak of fortune, this too was taken by the County Council in 1950 for a Police Station, so Codford has no permanent record of either King George VI's Coronation or the Jubilee of King George V.

The village activities in their several ways were continuing with varying degrees of success; St Mary's Church Choir won a trophy at the Devizes Music Festival and this was proudly displayed in a local shop window. The Codford Amateurs were producing their plays and gaining wider recognition by their successes in the County Festivals. In the autumn of 1937, they entered a competition run by a national daily to perform a three-act play specially written by J.B. Priestley. The country was divided into six areas with a different adjudicator for each area. The winners of each were to go to London and perform the play on one evening at the Fortune Theatre, Drury Lane.

A Captain Roscoe had been secured as producer and rehearsals began. On the evening of the performance the Wool Stores was packed and the adjudicator listened with varied emotions. That was the end of our adventures we thought. We should have known better than to think we could act, and resigned ourselves to accept what we thought was inevitable. To our complete surprise, and everyone else's, we woke up one morning to learn from the newspaper that we had been placed first in our area. The excitement was terrific. We had achieved the front page of a National Daily and were being looked at by the London critics.

On January 19th 1938 we went to London for our performance in the Fortune Theatre. Our name was in lights on the front of the house, "the Codford Amateurs". What a day that was, and how far we had come in seven years. The house was full and included many friends who had made the journey to see the play, and a happy memory is of one well-known local figure striding up and down outside the Theatre complete with opera hat and cape. No, we didn't win the final. That would have been too much, but we were placed fourth with commendable remarks from the Adjudicators Miss Diane Wynyard, Claude Gurney and Lionel Hale.

Up til 1938 nothing much had been done in the village to alter its appearance or character. The temporary shops and other legacies of the war had been cleared away, and little or no fresh building had taken place, although several businesses, which had come temporarily to the village in the first war, did stay on and found permanent premises.

The Parish Council had previously discussed housing, street lighting and water supply, and in connection with water a well attended public meeting in 1938 was warned by one worthy gentleman of the danger of providing people with water out of pipes. "What," he exclaimed, drawing himself up with indignation, "they will be demanding baths next!" Added to this awful thought was the threat, "Your rates will go up by nine shillings in the pound." That clinched it- no water!

But houses were being built by the local authority and the first eight were erected and occupied in 1938, and oddly enough they had baths which were regarded as a joke, as there was no provision for hot water except a small copper, and no water supply except on hand pump outside between eight houses. They were not central in the village, but they were there. The village had started to grow and they had baths.

The rumbling of army tanks at night was now being heard and the Parish Council were concerned about the noise so they decided to see what could be done about it. There was even talk of a by-pass road. Nothing came of the complaint and in view of the international situation at the time, nothing could, for the ominous approach of another war was felt more heavily as 1939 went on. Then came that fateful day in September- we were at war again!

1939-1945

It was with a feeling of dull resentment that the village accepted that another war had started. The sense of security, engendered by the National Governments of the thirties, was now shown to be false, and there was a feeling that somebody, somewhere, had let us down.

But the grim situation was with us, for stabbing the darkness of the night sky were the probing pencils of light from the searchlights. An eerie feeling of danger always seemed to be with them and their restless search of the heavens. Then suddenly they would be gone, making the darkness seem more intense.

The presence in the village of military personnel presaged the fact that troops were to be stationed here again, and it was not long before there were a Company of the Forty-third Wessex Division R.E. in our midst. They were men from the Trowbridge and Chippenham area, and they settled in our midst like old friends-which they soon were. Camps began to be built again, not as one might have supposed where they stood before – that would never do! No, fresh sites had to be found – in some cases adjacent to former sites and, in others, entirely new. The main difference from the First World War, was that there was not that same upheaval in the daily life of the village. The construction work went on at a faster pace. Transport was not a problem, the roads were better, mechanical aids were available, and the contractors brought the men to the sites and then took them away again. There were no temporary huts or odd buildings set up. The huts for the troops had not so much had to be built but assembled, and almost without notice the camps were there – not so many or so wide spread as before, so they caused less interference with the business of the farming fraternity, for which they were duly thankful.

With the outbreak of war practically all social and other activities came to a stop, except for the Woman's Institute, which carried on, war or no war! They actually celebrated their 21st anniversary in 1945 in the Congregational Church Room.

In other ways the village soon became aware of the situation- rationing, the call up of all the eligible young men, and a severe shortage of petrol. The black-out regulations were a source of worry to Police, Wardens and villagers alike, and getting around at night with so little illumination was a nightmare, especially when livestock had to be dealt with. We were also getting to know "Lord Haw Haw"- "this is Jarmany calling"- and his nightly radio broadcast of British disasters. He might have had more effect had it not been for Sir Winston Churchill who unfailingly cut him down to size! Even so, the situation was grim.

The return of men from Dunkirk reminded us that the war was actually getting closer, and every able bodied man and woman was enrolled for some job in case the need arose. As well, we had the Wardens Home Guard, and the Woman's Voluntary Service. We had no arms of course, but heavy old farm carts and implements were looked out to provide road blocks. It was believed that the invasion would be some time in September 1940. So the river was dredged, to make it impassable for tanks and pill boxes set up at strategic points. We waited, and nothing happened. Autumn drew on to winter, the bombing of the big cities continued- we were not, it seemed, to be called up for any defence. We were relieved but not relaxed, as the bombers passed high overhead and were caught in the silver sword points of the searchlights, for we knew of death and destruction being carried to towns and cities in our own land.

Evacuees arrived unexpectedly after several false reports of their coming had been circulated, and the business of finding people willing to billet them was a headache. The truth of the saying "An Englishman's home is his castle" was brought home to us. Arrangements for the evacuees were very poorly organised. Plans there might have been, but not anything like the preparations necessary for such an emergency, added to which, much of the available accommodation had been taken up by relatives and friends of men stationed in the village. Where room was available, there was often nothing in the way of equipment, so this had to be borrowed. For some reason everyone seemed to want girls- not boys! The number we had to deal with was not large, and eventually all were accommodated somewhere. To have said that they were happy would have been untrue- everything was against them, all so different. The darkness frightened them, their husbands and fathers were in London, and many soon returned to their homes. A few remained and were quite happily absorbed into the village and its life. In addition a preparatory school for boys, complete with staff, came from Bognor to Ashton Gifford House in 1940. They too, did not leave and became the well known preparatory school "Greenways."

This was a different war from the first one, not so much man to man, but machine against machine. Our Air Raid Wardens did their nightly patrols, our other services were well manned but not required, for with so many military personnel in the village

Pillbox, Station Road

Greenways School

there was little need for them, although there were a few incidents from enemy action in the parish, no damage to life or property occurred. Bombs were dropped close enough to shake the houses but nothing worse.

It was the Sixth Armoured Guards Brigade who now occupied the camps. They were a fine body of men, and probably the most popular troops to have been in the village in either war. It was in the Officers Mess at the Institute Camp, that Rex Whistler the artist painted murals and pictures on the walls. Those were later removed and preserved. He was killed in action. Also in the Welsh Guards were two fine singers, David Lloyd the Welsh tenor and Tudor Evans. Both were heard frequently after the war on BBC programmes.

The present Queen carried out her first public engagement when she inspected the Grenadier Guards in Stockton Park prior to their departure for France and D. Day in 1943 and were succeeded by the Eleventh Armoured Division, but their stay was comparatively short.

After they had gone the Americans arrived, and what a contrast this was. Their enormous transport vehicles with teams of drivers, and the mechanization of everything to do with the war was, for us, an education in modern methods of warfare. Somehow, they never looked like soldiers, and certainly many of them, it seemed, had never wanted to be. Those that came here were mostly from the country places, quiet towns, homesteads and farms. Softly spoken, happy, kindly natured men, who missed their homes and loved to sit in the houses of the village people, smoke their endless American cigarettes and cigars, and just talk about their Pops and Moms. Delightful companions they were just as we had met them in books, and brought home to us the fact that all Americans do not come from New York, or are Chicago gangsters. They made many friends, and we were impressed by the fact that they were proud of their British ancestry – if they had any. What a party they gave our school children at Christmas, for they at any rate, had no rationing problems!

A large American Club was set up for their use in the Wool Stores, and it was during their stay that a visiting ENSA Company, including Gracie Fields, gave a performance in the large repair depot in the paddock of Manor House. They left in 1944 and were replaced by another batch. As different as "chalk from cheese." Most of them appeared to have come from large cities. Their numbers were not great, as the war was at last drawing to a close, so they were not with us for long.

Another group of men stationed here for some time was the Pioneer Corps. They were the "jacks of all trades" for the camps, and included a wide variety of men; conscientious objectors, men with impaired eyesight and other physical handicaps. One of the most noteworthy was Sidney Wooderson, the runner, who at the time held the record for the mile. He ran at a local sports gathering during the war held in the field behind the New Road Service Station and did the mile on that occasion in four minutes ten seconds.

There were also German prisoners of war. These were used quite widely on the farms, and many were likeable men and good workers, but rather apt to pick things up which did not belong to them. Under the circumstances this could be understood as

Grenadier Guards in New Road

Honour Guard American Veterans 50th Anniversary D-Day Landings, 1994

it's no fun being a prisoner of war in an enemy country.

The Woman's Land Army brought girls from the towns and cities into the village for a new experience of country life. They worked well, and soon adapted themselves to the rural lack of home conveniences to which they had been accustomed. A few married and settled down to life here.

As had happened in the previous war, some of our girls left their homes for the United States to marry there, but no Americans stayed here, as had been the case with the Australians, New Zealanders, Scots, Irish, Welsh, Belgians and later the Poles. Their descendents added to our population, and provided variety in our village.

Now the war was finally over [brought about by the use of the atomic bomb] we rejoiced and started to look at local life again. We realised the full horror of the new forms of warfare and wondered if we had reached the point of no return.

1945-1950

Now began what might be described as the modernisation of the village- the full flood of the welfare state. The sensational result of the 1945 election, when the Labour Party was swept into power with a large majority, was evidence of a change in outlook of the nation, and followed a pattern of political thinking which had emerged after the First World War. This time there must be no mistakes. The eight men from the village who would not return must not have given their lives in vain. A brave new world would be born out of the holocaust of evil which had afflicted the world for nearly six years. The lights came on again!

For the present we were concerned with getting back to normal, and a spontaneous, largely attended gathering celebrated the end of the war in the Y.M.C.A. Club. It had a happy family atmosphere and was very different from the hectic excitement which had signalised the end of the First War. Rationing, of course, was still in force, and like most other people all sorts of "dodges" were employed to obtain coupons for things which had been in short supply for years. The farmers were the best off for food, and they could do a deal for sweets and clothing if they could get the contacts. They did not indulge in the spiv's way of buying coupons- theirs was a much more subtle business.

One foggy evening in 1945, a war scarred veteran returned to Codford from service in Burma. As he came down the main street he met his Uncle whom he had not seen for two or three years- uncle was carrying a sack. "Hello J.B." said Uncle, and went on his way without further comment. Curious, his nephew followed, and Uncle made his way to a cottage where he counted out some Swedes and received coupons in exchange. This business was repeated at another point of barter, and Uncle was then free to welcome his nephew home!- business before pleasure!

Pig keeping had a boom, two pigs a year could be killed for home consumption. Nobody ever stipulated how big they should be, so some hefty pigs provided bacon and lard in abundance. Pig Clubs were run, sties sprang up like mushrooms, and many a deal was done on a "rasher for raiment" basis.

Clothing was perhaps the worst thing to get, and some of the men folk looked shabby- not that it mattered.

To celebrate the peace and to mark the event in some permanent way, it was decided to raise funds for a sixth bell in St Peter's Church. A fete was held in 1946 at the Manor House, and the Bishop of the Diocese was present [he was no mean skittler either!] The sum raised was £285, of which no less than nearly £100 came from the jumble stall. It was the biggest scramble for bargains ever seen, and indicated the clothing shortage. Where it all came from was a mystery- equally mysterious was where some of it went! But the bell was added to the five already there and all of them retiring in 1947.

The Parish Council were again exercising their minds on parish matters, and at one meeting a question was asked about fish and chip papers making the village untidy. Nothing much in that perhaps- village tidiness had been mentioned before, but we <u>had</u> got a fish and chip shop- that was certainly a sign of the times.

Housing was also a matter for concern , and it was finally decided to ask for thirty houses under the Housing Acts. The dearth of houses led to one of the unoccupied camps being taken over by squatters who just moved in and took possession, and nothing could be done but allow the people to stay there, which they did until they could be re-housed. In the meantime the huts were taken over by the Rural District Council.

Another disturbing feature at this time, were reports of hooliganism. For some reason the village was without a resident Policeman and it was thought that this had something to do with the trouble. The Chief Constable said it was impossible to appoint a resident Constable in Codford until a house could be made available for him, so we just had to wait patiently until this was the case.

Our social events began again, although most of the younger people in the village, especially the girls, had not lacked invitations to dances in the war. The Poles, who had arrived in the village from Italy and other theatres of war on the Continent, had some excellent musicians, and what was quite the best band ever heard locally, and were soon giving regular performances in the Wools Stores.

The Football Club restarted in 1947 with a junior team, and this was afterwards developed into a Youth Club. The need for permanent quarters for this and a village centre, revived interest in such a project. There was at the time a YMCA Club in the village for the servicemen. It had been built by the War Charities Commission on land belonging to Mr Charles Edwards, who had strongly objected to it being built, but without avail. He was a quite remarkable man, a fairly tall, strong figure with a foreward thrust of the head, a long white beard and a patriarchal appearance. He looked like an old time revivalist in his black "wide-a-wake" hat, and was opposed to anything of a frivolous nature, being very earnestly religious, and having a great reverence for his godly forebears.

His voice was surprisingly thin and reedy and the house he lived in was extraordinary, with "DAT DEUS INCREMENTUM" on the lintel and two monkey puzzle trees in the front garden. He was in business with his younger brother John, a much more earthy and practical man, and whilst Charles travelled widely in connection with the business, John looked after the office in London. They were wealthy, and after the death of Charles, John expressed a wish to give the village a piece of land in memory of his parents. It was on this piece of land the YMCA stood, but for some reason best known to himself, John did not make a specific bequest of the land, known as "Broadleaze" in his will. After his death which occurred in October 1946, the Trustees and Residuary Legatees were approached, and they agreed to carry out the wishes of John Edwards in respect of the land. Contact was then made with the YMCA who agreed to sell the building which they would otherwise have to demolish.

This fortunate chain of circumstances was responsible for the founding of the Codford Club in 1947, and a committee was set up to run it, not without misgivings on the part of some people! Happily, these were unfounded and the venture has proved itself to be an important acquisition to our village life, as well as a valuable property. A grant was obtained from the Ministry of Education to adapt the premises, and local events were organised to raise money for the same purpose. Among these, was a Bank Holiday Fete and Flower Show, this was continued for some ten years or more; the Woman's Institute gallantly undertaking the Flower Show section of this annual event. [The Woman's Institute do other things beside making jam!]

The Codford Amateur Dramatic Society which had been in abeyance for the period of the war, began again with renewed enthusiasm. They had been able to do little during the war, although at the request of the County Drama Advisor they had a small mobile demonstration team who toured several villages and towns to show how village theatricals could be improved in wartime. A new County Drama Advisor had been appointed, and in 1948 a new group was formed, called the Woolstore Country Theatre Club. They were not competitive in any was to the Codford Amateurs. Its purpose was to provide a wider field of activity and interest in dramatic work than had been possible with the Amateurs. It attracted wide support, and held weekly meetings in the Woolstores. The secretary was Mrs Sneyd, whose experience and ability in drama had been of so much value to the Amateurs. The idea of a Theatre Club had attracted attention in other places in the country, but Codford was probably the first to be started in a rural area.

Street lighting had been repeatedly discussed by the Parish Council, and various ideas to get it installed were proposed, all without result, and early in 1949 it was reported that there was no change of a permit for a lighting scheme from the Ministry of Transport unless the plan conformed to their requirements. That was the end of lights!

1949 also marked the end of the Codford Nursing Association, a body which had been of great value to the village since 1905. Its functions were being taken over by the Ministry of Health, so it activities ended and the funds were made into a trust to provide nursing comforts for any person requiring such help – another link with the old life of Codford had been severed.

The first post war council houses were now ready for occupation, and out of a host of applicants the Council made their recommendations. The houses had water laid on which was connected to the supply installed by the Military Authorities. This led to a demand by other residents for a water supply, and this demand was implemented when it was discovered that one place other than a council house had been connected to the supply. It happened to be the Off Licence premises, and one was prompted to ask if the proprietor knew the story of his well and was nervous over what might come up in the next bucketful. Some year earlier, in the days of a previous licensee, friends used to foregather in the back kitchen for a quiet little booze. Late one evening, Charlie joined a few pals there after he had been down to the eel stage and come away with some good eels which he left in a bag on the well cover before joining his friends inside.

Later, steamed up with good warmed cider and ginger, he picked up his bag and wended his way homewards, but on arriving there he made the unhappy discovery that there was a hole at the bottom of the bag, and some of the eels were gone. The one thing not done in cases of this sort was to make enquiries [you were sure to hear if any eels had been seen in the street!] , but no such news was forthcoming. "Gone down a drain," thought Charlie. Months later, when the bucket was drawn up from the well, there was a fine fat eel in it. Here was a mystery. How had the eels got into a sixty foot well? Charlie might have enlightened them, for whilst he was inside enjoying convivial company, the eels had squeezed through a hole in the bag, and slithered under the ill fitting well cover down into the water – a very fishy business altogether!

1950-1960

The Rural District Council eventually took over the water supply from the War Department, and by 1951, piped water was available for anyone who wanted it, but not without some grumbling about the cost of having it installed.

The Reverend C.H. Meyrick who had come to Codford in 1924 and been the Rector of the combined churches since 1928 passed away suddenly at the end of 1951. He had taken an active part in the life of the village, played cricket with the local team, acted with the Codford Amateurs, sung with the Choral Society, in addition to his work as the Parish Priest. He will be remembered for his many activities.

Proposals by the Rural District Council to build a further forty-eight houses in the village met with opposition from the Parish Council. It was too many, they said, and those not wanted by Codford people would be occupied by outsiders! Furthermore, it would completely alter the character of the village and necessitate additional school accommodation. The Rural District Council promised to consider the objections, and said they would proceed with twenty houses, to which the Parish Council agreed. The village was growing.

Later in 1952 a letter from the County Surveyor informed the Council that the road through Stockton Park was to be taken over and the footbridge over the river closed. No objection was made to this although regret was felt on the part of some of the older residents- the footbridge had been in use for a long time. Now it was to go.

However, a letter from the Ramblers Association in 1953, objecting to the closure of the footbridge at the ford, occupied the attention of the Parish Council for some time. They had, it was said, approached the Ministry of Housing and Local Government regarding this matter. The Council had accepted the alternative route through the Park, as it was, without any doubt, essential for motor traffic, and the loss of the footbridge was not very serious. The Ramblers were informed of the attitude of the village over the subject, and told they would get no support from the Council – so nothing more was heard of that!

The Coronation of Queen Elizabeth II now occupied our attention and arrangements were made for a day of general rejoicing. Nobody living had any experience of a Queen's Coronation, and as she was young it would probably be the last English Coronation of which many people would have any knowledge- English Queen's have a habit of reigning for a very long time. It must be a day to remember, so our energies were devoted to that end. All seemed well and the day was awaited with keen anticipation. Alas, the weather did not play its part, and though we were much more fortunate than many other places, the afternoon was dull and wet. The procession went well, and had just finished when the rain came down. The evening was finer, and a huge bonfire had been built on Codford Circle which is the highest point in this area. From the top could be counted a dozen or more bonfires, and this fine sight transported us back to the days of the first Queen Elizabeth and the Armada – or so it seemed- we were compensated for our damp day!

The fortunate people who had television sets were besieged by friends and neighbours. For the first time in history, millions of people were able to see the actual coronation ceremony, and hear the inspiring music and singing which was part of it. Truly a wonderful experience.

By 1954 television aerials were a much more common feature of the village, TV had enormous advantage of being visual. It entailed no journeys out of doors; it cost no more than HP than was previously spent on the cinema. What was more important, there were grandstand viewpoints of racing, cricket, football, athletics and current events. It widened our experience of plays and enabled us to set standards of performance. It was obviously going to be a serious competitor to local interests and events.

The weekly cinema which had been held in the Codford Club closed down for lack of support, and the attendances at the Whist Drives declined. Bingo had not yet reached the villages with its heady excitements and jackpots!

The new group of council houses were nearing completion and the last of the squatters moved into proper homes- or so it was thought- but within forty eight hours another family moved into one of the unoccupied huts. However they were moved on and the huts demolished. Most of the disused buildings were now cleared up, but some scars remained to join those left by the 1914- 1918 War.

Of the village activities restarted after the war, the Theatre Club was continuing and successfully producing plays yearly. They had secured a regular producer and the value of this was apparent in the standard of plays being presented. "Rebecca" produced for the Jubilee performance, was perhaps the most satisfying play to audience, producer and cast, that had been done by the Company. Another interesting innovation in the village was the performance of an operetta "True Lovers Knot" by Lionel Crawhall, the County Drama Advisor, with music by Michael Vickers. It was an enjoyable experience and was followed in 1955 by another original operetta "Quack Quack." This was performed in the round in the Codford Club and was the first attempt at this kind of presentation.

1960-1964

The Railway Station which had served the village for a hundred years was closed in 1956 for passenger traffic and in 1960 for freight. Thus the station ceased to function for any function whatever. It was a striking illumination of the change in our way of travelling, that this should come about without any objection from the general public, but the closure entailed no real hardships – the bus service was much more convenient – and many more people had cars.

What did cause concern was the ever-increasing volume and speed of traffic through the village. Twenty years before this, the village street was described as a racetrack and a death trap. The two councillors who made this comment had been gathered to their fathers. Had they lived to see what went by in these days their description of the speed would presumably have been unprintable.

More houses were foreshadowed in 1960 when the Rural District Council proposed to build another twelve and eight flats for old people – the proposal was not welcomed, particular objection being made to building upstairs flats for elderly folk. These protests, however, were not successful in getting any alterations made to the plans.

It is not often in the life of the village that a diamond wedding celebration occurs. Such a one did take place in 1961 when Mr and Mrs Weston who were married in 1901 were generally congratulated on having achieved this rare distinction. The only case recorded in the fifty years of this history.

The Congregational Church also had reason for rejoicing, in that it celebrated the triple Jubilee of its foundation in November 1961. "It is recorded that toward the close of the eighteenth century some earnest Christian workers under the leadership of the Rev. Joseph Berry came out from the Congregational Church at Common Close, Warminster, into the neighbouring villages. The Codford meeting was formed and the Chapel building dedicated and opened for worship on November 2nd 1811."

The great snowstorm of 1962 was, as has been noted, a repeat performance of 1927 and the onset of the blizzard occurred approximately at the same time but in severity it was much worse than in 1927. It persisted for some days with little or much snowfall and by January 1st 1963 the roads were almost impassable. Mechanical methods were used to clear roads enough to allow limited use, but the blizzard was followed by frost and the work of clearing slowed up. Although the countryside was very beautiful, a lot of sheep were lost.

A milestone in the life of the Theatre Club was reached in 1963 when they purchased the Wool Store Theatre. From being probably the first village Theatre Club in the country in 1948, they had achieved the distinction of being the first village theatre group to own their own theatre. Since their formation they have produced some notable plays and "The Diary of Anne Frank" produced in 1959 scored a remarkable success. It was widely reported and marked a highlight of achievement for the Club.

The houses being built in Cherry Orchard came in for some sharp criticism from both the Parish Council and the public who objected to the cramped lay out. It was creating slum conditions in the countryside it was argued, but the protests were unheeded – the work went on.

Similar protest about the volume of heavy traffic and the provision of a bypass were listened to, but with little relief promised.

The Congregational Church which had celebrated its triple Jubilee in 1961 ceased to function as a place of worship in 1964. A sad reflection on the declining attendances at places of worship. The roof had become unsafe and the money to make it secure was not available. The Pastor Mr Farmer Jones carried on for a time in the adjoining schoolroom but his sudden death brought to an end 153 years of the nonconformist church in Codford.

The setting up of an Evergreen Club for older people in 1964 was another sign of the times and a reminder that we are not as young as we used to be.

The last fifty years have been an amazing time. Ours has been a great age of history, perhaps the greatest that the world has ever known. So much that is momentous had occurred. It has not always been a happy time but **certainly a very interesting and exciting one!** Mr Churchill once said that to change was to progress, and can there have been more changes in the short space of fifty years? They have come about gradually and in tune with the trend over the whole country. One result of this was to make us more like town dwellers. We have become more cosmopolitan in type and character which may be a good thing, but we have less sense of belonging to the place than used to be the case; "You must preserve the people of a place if you want to preserve its character." We are courteous to each other, with the politeness which is natural to the countryman, but we do not always know whose greeting we acknowledge. We are in a sense strangers to each other – our interests are not entered or in common as was formerly the case when the only occupation was farming or work connected with it. We seem to have become moulded to a common pattern and have less individuality.

Fifty years ago   there were a number of characters who though often unlettered, possessed a natural culture and store of knowledge. Snakeshole Jack- why snakeshole is not clear, but he did have a wider knowledge of edible fungi and where they could be found. He claimed to be able to find truffles and is on record that a very large one of over 4lbs was dug up in Stockton Park. He was a jovial, talkative old fellow and he certainly knew where to find mushrooms in a bad year, and morels [which seemed to disappear when he died.] Perhaps only he knew where they grew.

Black Jimmy, who lived a hermit's life in the middle of the grove, was another. The children were frightened of him and his wild appearance and black whiskers. He occasionally emerged to go to the shop but he did not encourage visitors to go to his hideout. He was said to have come from a good family and he was well spoken and knew the habits of birds and wild life intimately. It is a fact that since his removal the nightingales, which used to be heard frequently, are now heard but rarely.

Farming methods have been revolutionised and the status of the farm worker has risen. The ploughman with his team against the skyline is there no longer. The shepherds who tended large flocks of Hampshire Down sheep in the locality are now few. The sheep bells are mostly silent. Haymaking and harvesting have lost their colourful significance and excitement. You cannot enthuse over a hay bailer or combine harvester, invaluable though they are in tricky weather- the rick yard has ceased to exist – the water meadows have gone and the drowner no longer drowns anything. Nor does the clang of the anvil bring the children coming home from school to the blacksmith's open door. There is a blacksmith but he comes in a motor van from eleven miles away to shoe the hunters and ponies.

Farming has become big business for the scientist and economist with enormous capital investment in machinery and labour saving devices. Livestock farming tends to assume the aspect of a production line – new feeding methods shorten the life of nearly all our farm animals, they walk in as calves at one door and out of the other as baby beef at ten months – ewes more prolific. Pigs up to bacon weight at five and a half months – chicken by the million. Hens in batteries, heavier crops of corn, milking parlours for cows with the milk handled by machines from cow to consumer- the stepping up of milk yields- artificial insemination- wider veterinary knowledge and practice – antibiotics – injections- elimination of TB and other diseases – the overall urgency to speed things up – earlier maturity – quicker growth- larger crops – these are the slogans of our farming practice – there is no time to stand and stare.

Perhaps the greatest transformation of the last fifty years is in the matter of women's dress. What would have happened in 1914 if a young woman had dared to walk down the street in shorts and a brassiere – she would have been arrested! Nowadays in summer time- but that's another story.

But generally clothes are lighter, and more colourful, and although less durable perhaps and much less voluminous, they make our village women and girls more attractive. Their long hair has gone or nearly so, and there is a freedom of movement which is certainly more healthy. The children too wear more colourful clothes and less of them. Fewer hats are worn by the girls and with their short hair and slacks they often look like boys. Men's clothes have not changed so much, lighter materials, easier to get about in but otherwise much the same. Oddly, whiskers are coming back and longhaired men with side- boards- well! Well!

In the educational field many changes have taken place. Our children no longer stay in the village school until they are old enough to leave and go to work. They pass from Primary to Junior and from there to Senior or Grammar Schools. The extended school leaving age has given more opportunities for advanced education for many promising pupils from the village. One such has indeed become an Oxford Don in her special field- another a doctor- and one a hospital matron. Whether this wider education has led to an earlier mental maturity on the part of our children is debatable but that they are physically mature at an earlier age seems undeniable. What is very uncertain is whether they are as emotionally mature or secure at this earlier age – they often seem perplexed and frustrated by the complexities of modern living.

Political allegiance, once seen in strong expression on the part of supporters, is now no longer such a feature at elections. Most of us do not bother to attend meetings – we get our information, if that is what it can be called, from the turgid headlines of the brash dailies, or from television appearances by our would be leaders – and there seems to be an absence of clear-cut issues.

Our housing situation is very different. Since 1928 nearly 100 houses of one sort or the other have been added to the village. Seventy of these are Council houses which have been built in the last twenty-five years. Many older cottages have been modernised and brought up to date with modern conveniences. Housewives now have houses with bathrooms, electric light and power, running water, sanitation and labour saving devices. The drudgery of household chores has largely gone as many wives regularly go to employment in neighbouring towns, as do many of the menfolk, and there is still an unsatisfied demand for houses.

In matters medical we are enjoying a very different service from that provided in 1914. The advance in medical science, surely the greatest progress in any field in the history of the country has revolutionised treatment for almost every known disease. We are nursed from before we are born to the time when we defy the efforts of all the specialists and shuffle off this mortal coil. We are kept fitter and active to a much later age and so able to enjoy life for many more years than formerly. All this is a reason for much satisfaction, but we do seem to consume an awful lot of nerve pills and to suffer from more neuroses – pressure on the emotions and kindred ailments. I do not think there were many of these fifty years ago.

No longer do we take pride in our allotments – they nearly all disappeared after the last war. The village flower show, an important festival in our lives is no longer held. The gentleman who used to walk solemnly down the main street bearing aloft his huge marrow, with name and date grown into it, has passed away. The children no longer gather wild flowers.

Our interests and amusements have not so much changed as taken on a new form. Radio and television have replaced the occasional evening with the glee singers. The children's entertainments of former days and singing are heard no more. Perhaps there is nothing to sing about!

Our village dances are not what they were. Waltzing is an almost forgotten art, and time and tune have been replaced by what has been described as "spasmodic evolutions of mating cormorants" and much "idiotic clamours of frenetic joy." These are strong terms but the young people do seem to get a kick out of it, so perhaps it's not a bad thing for them to let off steam this way. Yeah! Yeah! Yeah!

The fantastic rise in the ease of motor transport has contributed more than any other single factor to our changed habits. Distance has been annihilated and we walk very much less than we used to. Nearly everyone goes on holiday, nearly always by car, and on Sunday's off to the seaside or some place of interest. The regular attendance at

Church or Chapel with a walk around the countryside with the family afterwards has ceased. The number of regular worshippers is low. There is respect for the Churches and their Ministers but formal Christianity no longer claims our allegiance.

We seem to have become more self centred and are concerned with business of our own living to the exclusion of everything else. We have developed an insatiable appetite for material possessions, easy money, pools, bingo, and short cuts to affluence. The car has become our symbol of material progress. The bigger the better!

The Church is no longer the centre of our village life and if our new found affluence has not brought all the joy and satisfaction it promised, it provides an escape, but at a cost. Although there is less physical hardship, there is probably more depression and dissatisfaction.

Nevertheless, the village though it has grown, stays largely as it was. The land remains. Seed time and harvest, summer and winter, spring days of beauty and autumn days with trees in their coloured dresses come round in their seasons. We have friends we know and love – all these things are ours in the village.

4th Tank Battalion with Churchill tank, Salisbury Plain, 1942

*Grenadier Tank Sergeants at Codford. Second from left, Sergeant Rigley;
Sergeant George with drum*

8

Extract from '6th Guards Tank Brigade: The Story of Guardsmen in Churchill Tanks'
by Patrick Forbes

Introduction- Early Days

During the autumn of 1941, certain battalions of the Brigade of Guards were switched from their traditional role of Infantry to form part of a Guards armoured division. This unprecedented step was dictated by the knowledge that that the German forces which were expected to invade Britain during the coming months contained an alarming percentage of armoured formations. The 6th Guards (Armoured) Brigade started life in the new division and, commanded by Brigadier Adair, remained with it until the autumn of 1942, when it was decided that armoured divisions should consist of one Infantry and one Armoured Brigade instead of two of the latter. As a result of this decision the 32nd Guards {Infantry} Brigade was brought into the Guards Armoured Division and the 6th Guards {Armoured} Brigade, after a few weeks of uncertainty, was put into the 15th Scottish Division, then commanded by Major-General D.C. Bullen-Smith. M.C. Within the Brigade the effects of this reorganisation were that the 2nd {Armoured} Battalion Welsh Guards was transferred to the Guards Armoured Division and the 4th {Motor} Battalion Coldstream Guards took its place. The titles of the Battalions were then changed and the Order of Battle, which was never altered, became:

HQ 6th Guards Tank Brigade   4th Tank Battalion Grenadier Guards
4th Tank Battalion Coldstream Guards   3rd Tank Battalion Scots Guards. The
Signal Squadron, the Brigade Workshops and the Brigade RASC Company all remained with the Brigade. It so happened that just as the changeover was taking place, Major-General Sir Oliver Leese, the Commander of the Guards Armoured Division, was given a Corps at El Alamein and Brigadier Adair succeeded him. A few days later Brigadier G.L. Verney, Irish Guards, was transferred from command of 32nd Guards Brigade to take command of the 6th Guards Tank Brigade. He was to hold this appointment for nearly two years. Although the 6th Guards Tank Brigade was part of the 15th Scottish Division, over six months elapsed before the two joined forces. The Brigade was about to be re-equipped with Churchill Tanks, and it was stationed at Codford, in a camp which was particularly well-equipped with workshops and was on the edge of the excellent Salisbury Plain training areas, it was considered unwise to move to Northumberland, where the 15th Scottish Division was situated until the spring.

The intervening period was well spent. There were still large numbers of men who had to be trained as gunners, wireless operators, and drivers, and the Covenanters with which the Brigade was then equipped were perfectly adequate for the task. The Brigade also had time to accustom itself to the reorganisation which its new role as a heavy tank Brigade necessitated. In future each Battalion was to have 58 tanks distributed in the following manner: 4 in each Battalion Headquarters, 3 in each Squadron Headquarters and 3 in each of the 5 troops which made up a Squadron. In addition each Battalion was to be provided with a Crusader anti-aircraft troop, and, later on, Light American Honey Tanks for Reconnaissance. Few alterations were ever made to this organisation. The Brigade received its first consignment of Churchills in the early months of 1943. These early models were quite unworthy of the great war leader after whom they were named; they were totally unreliable and they broke down on the slightest provocation. Although this was disheartening at the time, anyone who knew the facts could do nothing but marvel that their performance was not considerably worse. Because behind this launching of the Churchill into the armoured life of the British Army lay a story which reflected the very greatest credit on British Industry. It proved a magnificent example of the genius of British manufacturers for improvisation and of their ability to work really quickly in an emergency. The need for a heavily armoured tank had arisen immediately after Dunkirk, when the likelihood of an enemy invasion, supported by a number of well-equipped armoured divisions, had been very real indeed. In France, only a medium and a cruiser type of tank had been used, and the vast majority of these had been lost when France fell. If the British Army was to have any chance of repelling an invasion, it had to be provided in the shortest space of time with a large quantity of reliable machines which would compete with German armour, and with German anti-tank artillery. The War Office laid down certain specifications, based on the experience so dearly bought in 1940. The new tank would have to be capable of travelling at 16 m.p.h. and of climbing a gradient of 1:5; it would have to be narrow enough to be carried by train and light enough to cross a reasonably strong bridge; it would have to be fitted with a certain thickness of armour, and be strong enough to carry a 2-pdr. [1] gun and the maximum of stowage for ammunition. Above all the army wanted the new tank quickly- so quickly in fact it almost amounted to a request for immediate delivery. Vauxhall Motors was chosen for the task. Up to this time they had only produced one tank engine, but they had had years of experience with light commercial vehicles and cars. They already had large commitments manufacturing trucks for the Army, but a whole area of their works at Luton was set-aside for the Churchill and they started work at once. There was no time for experimental work, so the usual method of producing prototypes, testing them out in every conceivable way, modifying and then starting production when the models were eventually proved , was out of the question. It would have taken two or three years to perfect the engine alone, and still the Army would have no tanks delivered because production would not have begun. Therefore, the only alternative was adopted. The vehicle was designed and put straight into production from blue prints. In EIGHTY-NINE days two engines were running on test benches, and in less than a year the first

Churchills were being delivered to the Army. This was a stupendous achievement, but Vauxhalls were the first to admit that it did not make for an effective or reliable tank. It meant that Army units would have to carry out the experimental work which would normally have been done at Luton. Undesirable though it was, it suited the Army; because, even if the new tank went only 50, 20 or 10 miles before breaking down, it would provide a valuable fortified position in the event of an invasion. As soon as delivery started, representatives from Vauxhall Motors were attached to each Army Unit to which Churchills were delivered and gradually the faults were set right. When the threat of invasion diminished, all the early models were called in and the Army received a new Churchill drastically modified and vastly improved. Until this stage was reached, the tank crews were virtually the "guinea pigs" upon which the onus of the experimenting fell. This was naturally discouraging for them but in the long run it turned out to be a blessing, for the Churchill became literally their "baby" and as it matured they acquired a paternal insight into its character which could have been gained in no other way. They gradually learnt what they could and could not expect of it, how to remedy its shortcomings, and how to make the most of its many excellent qualities. A bond grew up between them and their Churchills not unlike that which existed between a cavalryman and his mount in years gone by. To anyone who has not had experience of tanks, it may seem incomprehensible that any such feeling could ever be engendered towards such a mundane and apparently impersonal object as a tank. It may seem particularly incredible about a Churchill as it is an enormous vehicle, weighing 40 tons – a mobile fort bulging with armour and making few concessions to streamlining or grace. Yet if the tank crews learned anything during their years with the Churchills, it was that they were human. Handled carefully and properly looked after, they would respond accordingly. The crews came to know exactly how much maintenance was required to make "their" tank go, and partly because their life depended on it, and partly through a feeling of duty towards "their" tank, the maintenance on it was never skimped. Especially towards the end of the campaign, it became a matter of honour and pride for a crew to keep its tank "on the road." Another factor which helped to foster this intimacy between a Churchill and its crew was the knowledge that it was "home." Its inside might be packed with engines and levers and tubes and petrol tanks, with a big gun, 2 machine-guns, and piles of ammunition, but stowed away in the innumerable bins and ledges were all the things which allow a lull in the battle or a short period of rest to be fully appreciated- food and water, blankets and greatcoats, and the most important item of all, the cooking stove. The fact that this last object alone was always immediately available was a constant godsend.; it meant that however bad a days fighting might be a hot meal could be cooked quickly at the end of it. Finally, tucked away in large bins at the back of the Churchills were the waterproof covers; if these were fastened to the sides of the tank they would make a tent which resisted wind and rain and enabled the crew to spend a fairly comfortable night under almost any conditions. For these and many less tangible reasons the men of the 6th Guards Tank Brigade had an ever-increasing affection for their Churchills. Important though it was, if it had not at the same time led to their having complete and utter confidence in their tanks, little would have been achieved. For if a crew does not have faith- a deep and abiding faith in the ability of its tank to stand up to the stresses and strains of war, its contribution during battle will always be strictly limited. The reasons for this are entirely physical. Of the five men who compromise a tank crew, four know practically nothing of what is going on around them. Once the hatches are closed they are imprisoned in a great mass of metal, and their sole job is to obey the Tank Commander's orders. Unless he tells them, they have little or no idea whether the battle is being lost or won. The driver accelerates and slows down, turns and halts, depending on the orders he receives through the internal telephone; all he can see through his periscope is the ground directly in front. Neither he not the co-driver has any notion of what is happening behind or on the flanks. The gunner is slightly better off because when he revolves his turret he can obtain a panoramic view of the battlefield; but generally his eyes are glued to the telescope and he sees only the piece of ground from which opposition is expected to appear. The wireless operator is so busy relaying messages and loading the gun that he also knows little of what is going on directly outside his tank. Only the Tank Commander, who has a periscope with all-round vision, is in touch with the outside world. Such conditions would make it impossible for them to fight at all if they did not have absolute confidence in their tanks. The Churchills gave it to them and they were fully justified in accepting it completely, for not a single life was lost in training or battle because a Churchill broke down at a crucial moment. That in itself is the greatest compliment which could ever be paid a tank.

Notes
1] pdr. = pounder

Sources
Lieutenant-Colonel (Retd.) C.J.E. Seymour Regimental Adjutant, Grenadier Guards. Taken from *6ᵗʰ Guards Tank Brigade: The Story of Guardsmen in Churchill Tanks* by Patrick Forbes, published by Sampson, Low, Marston & Co. Ltd. London.
At the time of writing this book has been long out of print.

9

Commanding The Welsh Guards
David Greenacre

Walter Douglas Campbell Greenacre CB, DSO, MVO was born in 1900 in Durban, South Africa. (His father was a businessman there and later to become Mayor of the city) WDCG came to England in 1913 to go to The Leys School at Cambridge, which he did not enjoy, although he did acquire a lifelong affection for and skill in Rugby Football. He left shortly after his 17th birthday, and intended to obtain a commission in the Royal Artillery, but found himself being interviewed by an officer of the Artists Rifles, then a Territorial Army battalion of the London Regiment. When it became apparent that the Gunners were over-subscribed he was persuaded by a Captain Ellis (good Welsh name) that he should try for the Welsh Guards. He was interviewed by the Regimental Lieutenant-Colonel in late 1917, followed by an Officer Cadet course of 6 months, prior to being commissioned in June 1918. He did not see service in France before that War ended.

He makes no mention of his military days as a Household Brigade subaltern – I suspect plenty of King's Guards, sport and leave, without much field training. Socially it was an exciting time. His connection with the Royal Family began in 1924 when HRH The Prince of Wales (with whom my father had hunted with the Beaufort) requested the Regiment that he should join him for two years as an Equerry. He accompanied HRH on the tours of West and South Africa as well as part of South America that lasted 6/7 months.

In the autumn of 1926 he became Adjutant of 1st Battalion Welsh Guards, married my mother, Gwendolen Edith Fisher-Rowe, in 1928 and completed his 3-year tour in Egypt in late 1929, subsequently becoming Company Commander of the WG Company at the Guards Depot, Caterham. He rejoined 1WG in 1933. In 1935 he was a Staff Captain to a London Territorial Division where he records "the year ... was most instructive and illuminating but hardly reassuring." He became Regimental Adjutant in 1937, and was initially able to devote some time as Hon Secretary of the Army Rugby Union and a member of the ARU Selection Committee.

His connection with HRH had been continued after 1926 by being appointed an Extra Equerry and that continued when HRH became HM King Edward VIII. In early 1937, in the weeks after the King's abdication, WDCG spent two periods in Austria with HRH Duke of Windsor assisting him with the voluminous correspondence – as well as dealing with the Press – arising from the abdication. He was subsequently appointed Extra Equerry to both of the two subsequent monarchs, and attended the Duchess of Windsor during her visit to the UK from Paris for the funeral of her husband in May 1972.

Historians generally summarise the months leading up to and preceding the outbreak of the 2nd World War as confused, full of obstacles and a period which posterity can only describe as: "making the best of a bad job." My father combined his role as Regimental Adjutant at this time of quasi-mobilisation with that of Brigade Major of a TA formation known as the Officer Producing Group until August 1939. After War was declared he was appointed 2IC of 2WG - which made "a difficulty" as the CO already had a 2IC, my godfather (!!) My father's description of the months from September to Christmas 1939 make it clear how unprepared Britain was at the time , so it was with some enthusiasm that he went to 1WG in France in late March 1940 to be the 2IC. The CO needed leave, so father assumed temporary command a few days after his arrival . He was still in command when Norway was invaded on 9th April 1940 and before the CO returned a few days later. Eventually 1WG was to evacuate about three quarters of its total complement in the BEF and re-form in mid-June as part of 24th Guards Brigade.

Father continued as 2IC but was put in charge of building an anti-tank obstacle round the Northern and Eastern approaches to London, about 32 miles in total. It took 3 months, but in January 1941 he went on an 8 weeks senior officer's course in Wiltshire, got a very good report, and returned to 1WG to be told that he was to command the to-be-formed 3rd Battalion on 1st April 1941. Some weeks later the decision to form a Guards Armoured Division was taken and father went on a series of courses to familiarise himself with armoured tactics during which he handed over command of 3WG in August. He arrived at Codford St Mary in late September 1941 "where 2WG was put in an unfinished camp" , as the 2IC. A few weeks later he took over command and could "safely say I have never worked so hard nor enjoyed doing it so much in all my life" (written in May 1944) .

Twin sons were born in December 1941, but the most major military incident in 1942 experienced by father was the RAF demonstration in April when a pilot gunned all the spectators instead of the target and killed 25 and wounded about 50 more. In October 1942 reorganisation of the Guards Armoured Division was announced and 2WG were to become the reconnaissance element of the Division , which meant leaving Codford and moving to Fonthill Gifford. In February 1943 six Army Corps had an exercise over a large part of England and 2WG was one of only two units to be named (congratulatory) in the subsequent GHQ report. The battalion also moved to Thetford having had a complete issue of Crusader tanks to replace the Covenanters. Some time later in 1943 the Division moved to Pickering Yorkshire and the Cromwell tank became 2WG's operational vehicle .

Father's papers now record an interesting introspection : "I had been in command of 2WG almost two years and that with my previous command and raising of 3WG had begun to make me feel a bit stale. I had lived too long in the (Officers) Mess and as usual 'familiarity breeds contempt'. It was inevitable that I should get a bit slack,

Brigadier W.D.C. Greenacre in the gouache medium by William Dring

and as once it was put to me, I would wake in the morning without a new idea !"

In December 1943 the Guards Armoured Division got a very bad report after a large-scale exercise and the repercussions at more senior level meant that my father was promoted to become the 2IC of the Armoured Brigade.   He expresses his sentiments : "I had served , with a short interval on the Prince of Wales's staff, continuously with the Regiment since I joined it as a boy of 18, 25 years before. The Regiment was my life, my first interest, and without disrespect to my wife, my first love."

At this crucial point in his career (he was now 44 years old) father's memories become less detailed and more reflective comments begin to appear. This was also the time when he first took up his pen to start "Plain Soldiering" . He subsequently brought his manuscript up to-date on two more occasions until its rather tame conclusion in October 1951.   .

He remained 2IC of 5th Guards Armoured Brigade until August 1944, when in Normandy the Commander 6th Guards Tank Brigade, an independent formation, was killed when his vehicle drove over a mine and father was selected to succeed him . His movements and experiences in North-West Europe are evidently recorded elsewhere - they may be in the Imperial War Museum with certain papers donated by the family. Since he had been CO of 2WG before the Battalion's transfer to the Guards Armoured Division he would have known of, and been known by, many of the officers from the other regiments represented in this Brigade.   (Having served myself in the Household Division and the Welsh Guards I have always found it most gratifying over the years to hear of the high esteem in which he was held by these former colleagues.) Suffice to say, that less than a page out of 102 typed pages refer to the remaining 10 months of the War. However his authorship resumed in early 1946 , when there are several pages of comment, often critical of the Allies conduct in immediate post-war Germany .

In June 1945 the Guards Armoured Division was ordered to revert to the Infantry role and 6th Guards Brigade was to rejoin Guards Armoured Division with all four Brigades concentrating in an area from Cologne to the Belgian frontier. In the spring of 1946 the Guards Division (note the change of title) moved northwards, but were widely spread, a brigade in each of Berlin, Lubeck , the North of Schleswig Holstein ,with 6th Guards Brigade in Hamburg. In the autumn of 1946 the decision to disband the Guards Division was taken and by 1st January the Division barely existed. Father was left to wind up the Division's affairs and assume command of an ad-hoc formation known as Schleswig-Holstein Sub Area, but under command of HQ Hamburg District. His Headquarters was accommodated in the very comfortable former German Marine barracks and schloss at Plon, buildings that were subsequently to become and remain for many years the boarding school for Services children of the relevant age in BAOR.

In late 1947 , he was extremely disillusioned by the decision to favour another officer with the appointment of Welsh Guards Regimental Lieutenant-Colonel (a Colonel's post). His memoirs speak of his embitterment, although they also reveal that he did feel partially compensated after his return to the UK in March 1948 by being appointed, within three weeks, to command 128 Territorial Brigade whose HQ was at

Salisbury. (There were many other substantive Colonels/Temporary Brigadiers looking for further employment on a Brigadier's pay) Not surprisingly, he found this to be a very different situation to what he had become accustomed in Germany, and although he "cajoled, wheedled, complained" his memoirs do not show the same pleasure and pride he had acquired when commanding a battalion or brigade within the Brigade of Guards.

In August 1949 he was told that in January 1950 he would command 8th Infantry Brigade District in the Canal Zone, Egypt. Promotion to Major General was by now his ambition, and so on the strength of favourably optimistic comments from senior - to him - officers he accepted the appointment.

"Plain Soldiering" thereafter becomes ever more critical of the decline -as he sees it - of the high standards to which he had contributed in 30 years of military life in the Brigade of Guards. He did not enjoy the Canal Zone and annoyingly the memoirs conclude without discussing an incident near the town of Suez, when I believe he ordered the destruction of some mud huts between the road entering the town and from where some shots were fired at passing troops' vehicles.

Father returned in 1952 without gaining the promotion he sought, but was a beneficiary of a War Office decision actively to recruit potential officers from the schools within each geographical Command in the UK. A new title of Retired Officer with grades 1 , 2 , and 3 had already been established , and Schools Liaison Officers had been placed in grade 1. He filled this appointment with Eastern Command at Hounslow and became well known by the Heads located in that Command and can be credited with persuading young Charles Guthrie, whilst at Harrow School , to join the Welsh Guards. A shrewd selection both for the Welsh Guards and, as we have seen, the nation's Chief of Defence Staff, but sadly not observed by father who died in August 1978.

Welsh Guardsmen, Codford, 1942. Third from left: RQMS Tom Curtis

Sergeant Williams and HQ troop, Welsh Guards, 1942

10

Most Secret: The Welsh Guards in Wiltshire

The War Diary or Intelligence Summary of the 2nd Battalion Welsh Guards offers a rare insight into the timetable of events leading up to the Invasion of Europe for one of the regiments of 6th Guards Armoured Division during World War Two. The following extracts are from the Battalion War Diaries 1939- 1945.

From Hendon
September 1941
5th 'Maintenance party proceeded to CODFORD, WILTS.'
15th 1st W/T Operations Course proceeded to and commenced work at Codford [till 22nd Nov.]
17th 2.W.G. Main body moved to Codford.

Codford
19th Lt. Col. J. Jefferson assumed command of 2. W.G.
22nd 1st Gunnery Course started [till 18th Oct.]
      D/M Tracked Vehicle Driving Course started [till 27th Sept.]
23rd Brig. A.H.S. Adair DSO. , MC. Comd. 6 Gds Armd. Bde. visited 2.W.G.
26th Gds Armd. Div. Intelligence Conference.
29th 1st D/M Tank Commanders Course started [till 25th Nov.]

October 1941
7th 1st Driving Mechanics Course started [till 20th Oct.]
12th 2/Lieut. W. Roberts to Mk V Cruiser Tank Course at Weston [till 18th Oct.]
14th, 15th & 16th Command Troop Training at Tilshead. Attended by Lt. Col. Jefferson, Maj. Greenacre, MVO. & Capt. A.A. Duncan.
17th Inspection of Bn. M.T. Vehicles by Major General Sir Oliver Leese, Bt. CBE., DSO., Comd. Gds Armd. Div.
22nd-23rd Phase I "Cruncher" T.E.W.T. for Bn. Comds.

November 1941
9th Lieut. J.C.R. Homfray to Scout Car Course at Div. School, Weston. [till 12th Nov.]
12th Visit by General Sir Alan Brooke KCB. DSO. C in C Home Forces.
14th Lt. Col. Jefferson appointed Comd. With acting rank of Brigadier with effect

30th Oct.

Maj. W.D.C. Greenacre MVO. Appointed Comd Offr. With acting rank of Lt. Col. pending regrant of temporary rank with effect from 30th Oct.

16th   Capt. O.J. Spencer to Anti- Tank Mine Course at South Petherton.

18th   Visit of Maj. Gen. J.T. Crocker CBE. DSO. MC.

20th   Trade Testing of W/T Operators.

22nd   Maj. J.C. Windsor Lewis DSO. MC. Appointed 2-in-C with effect 30th Oct.

24th   Visit of Lt. Gen. Hon. H.R.L.G. Alexander CB. CSI. DSO. MC. G.O.C. in C Southern Command.

This was also when a Young Officers D/M/ Course on Cruiser Mk. V and the Compass Course started.

December 1941

1st   saw the start of a Gunnery Course, W/T Officers' Rear Link Course and Dr. Mechs. Course. 5th Dec. Maj. Evans-Lomer 8 Hussars visited the Bn to give advice on Troop Training.

7th   Capt. J.O. Spencer to Tactics Course at Tidworth [till 3rd Jan.]

8th   Demonstration by 16 A.C. Sqn. RAF.

Bn. Novices Boxing.

9th   Capt. A.A. Bushall to 1 day Camouflage Course at Old Sarum.

15th-18th   Signal exercise "Hotspur" Bn. Rear Link. – 2nd Lieut. Portal

22nd   Brigade Comd. Visited Troop Training.

29th   G.O.C. Gds. Armd. Div. inspected Training.

30th   Div. Movements Exercise No. 4

Field Firing Imber range [Bren gun mounted in tank.]

31st   Lieut. S.O.D. Bateman to Aircraft Recognition Course at Douglas, Isle of Man [till 12th Jan 42.]

Between 5th September and 31st December 1941 30 Cruiser Mk. V tanks arrived.

January 1942

2nd   Lieut. J.C.R. Homfray attended a one day Security Course at HQ. Gds. Armd. Div.

7th   Two pounder Firing at Redhorn Range.

19th   Capt. R.J.A. Watt to D/M Course at R.A.O.C. Workshops, Tidworth [till 31st Jan.]

20th   Lecture to Bn. By Sir Charles Petrie Bt. On " The Mediterranean."

22nd   Introduction of new order of Dress for Bn.- AFV Training Order.

Lecture to Bn. By Capt. K.R. Johnstone 1 W.G. on "My Recent Experiences."

28th   Inspection of all Bn. Tanks by Bde. Comd. 6 Gds. Armd. Bde.

February 1942

3rd   G.O.C. Gds. Armd. Div. visited 3 & 3 Sqn. Training.

6th   Visit of General Sir Bernard Paget KCB. DSO. MC. C-in C Home Forces.

8th   Lieut. R.B. Sawrey- Cookson to Course au Army School of Hygiene
[till 14th Feb]

12th   Bn. Exercise with tanks. No 1. [First ever held in the Bn.]

17th   Lecture to all officers by Major General F.A.M. Browning DSO. Comd.
Airborne Div.

28th   Annual Officers-v- Serjeants Football Match. Another victory for the Officers.

2nd January–28th February   18 more tanks arrived and 3 departed –transferred to
the 42nd Armd. Div. The first was a Light Tank Mk VI B [A.A.] 14 were III

March 1942

1st   First Officers Photograph wearing Berets R.T.R.

2nd   Permanent Administration Party to Linney Head.

3rd   Visit of Press Representatives to Bn.
Blue denim overalls introduced for officers.

5th   T.C.O. to Linney Head

7th   Bn. Advance Party to Linney Head under Q.M. by road.

8th   Bn. Moves to Linney Head by train with 22 Tanks, 34 Officers and 365 O.Rs.
Detachment remains at Codford under Command of Capt. Sir. A.T.C. Neave
Bt.

10th   Firing Tables and Individual Battle Practice at Linney Head. A.F.V. Ranges
until 14th 42. Bn. Average on practices 7 & 8 was 17.

13th   Firing Tp. Battle Practice until 17 March also Bren A.A. and Ground and
T.S.M.G. 21 Tps fired this practice. Bn. Average 8.5 targets hit. 17 hits on
targets. Leading Tp. No. 10 3 Sqn Lieut. R.B. Sawrey- Cookson.

14th   No firing possible all day owing to fog.

17th   Bn. Return from Linney Head.

20th   3 Sqn to Middle Wallop Aerodrome for Guard Duties.

23rd   Spring Drills start until 28 March 42.
Officers: Capt. A.A. Duncan promoted to Major and becomes Squadron
Leader HQ Sqn to date 2.2.42. Relinquishes appointment of Adjutant.
Capt. R.J.A. Watt is appointed Adjutant to date 2.2.42

28th   2 Sqn carry out Anti Tank obstacle exercise in co-operation with 15 Fd. Sqn.
R.E.

30th   Bde of Guards Gunnery Course starts until 4th April 42.
Visit of Col. A.M. Bankier DSO. OBE. MC. Lt. Col Commanding the
Regiment until 1st April 42.

Between 2nd March–22nd April 16 Covenanter III Tanks and a two Covenanter I
from Northampton [one from 1st Fife and Forfar & the other from 13/18
Hussars.] were received. 3 came from C.O.O. Chilwell, 3 from O.O.
Handforth, 9 from Birmingham , 1 from Leyland Motors Ltd, Manchester .
1 Covenanter III and 4 Covenanter I Tanks were sent away during the period

8th March- 28th April.

April 1942

4th   Final of Crew Drill Competition won by No 5 Tp. 2 Sqn.

7th   Bn Shooting at Imber Range

10th   Demonstration by Gds Armd Div R.E's. of A.Tk obstacles.

13th   Fighter Demonstration at Imber. A demonstration arranged by 5 Corp with extra spectators from Gds Armd Div. 4 Hurricane Aircraft to attack targets with M.G. fire attacked the line of spectators by mistake. Approx. 25 killed and 76 injured. No casualties in 1st Bn. Party under Major Sir W.V. Makins Bt. Brig. W.A.F.L. Fox-Pitt, Comd. 5 Gds Armd Bde. was wounded.

15th   Gds Armd Div. Formation Badge taken into wear on Battle Dress.
          Lecture on German Parachutists by Lieut. Turner- Lashmar RA.

16th   Demonstration by Div. for Prime Minister and General Marshall, Chief of Staff, U.S. Army.

17th   Lecture on Tobruk by Maj. The Viscount Dalrymple, 3rd Armd S.G

21st   09 L.Sjt. Jones to 1day 6-pdr. Course at Lulworth. First course on this new weapon.
          Exercise Dover till 23 April. All Bn. A Ech. Took part. 1st Bn exercise for tanks only.

24th   C.O. holds meting of Div. Tank Users Committee. Lieut. J.G. Jenkins relieves Capt. Sir. A.T.C. Neave Bt. as officer i/c D/M.

25th   Execise Tidworth. All tanks in Bde took part. 36 from Bn.

26th   2/ Lieut. G.B. Gibbon to A. Tk. Mines Course with Div. R.ES. till 28th April.

27th   3 RAAF Sjts. Arrive for attachment to Bn. till 9th May. All 3 are Australians.

May 1942

6th   Q.M.S.I. Duncan ACC gives demonstration of use of Tank cooker.

7th   Harbouring demonstration by 3 Armd S.G. 1 Tank and crew to Southsea for experiment in sea portage.

10th   Lieut. R.J. Whistler to Tactics Course G.A.D. School till 24 May.

14th   Lecture on How to escape when a Prisoner of War.

20th   Bn line route to Stockton Park for visit H.M. The King., H.M. The Queen and H.M. Queen Mary. 2 Tps 2 Sqn took part in demonstration for royal visit.
          Lecture by Sir Charles Petrie on France.

21st   Lecture by Capt. Fielding, Green Howards on War in the Middle East.

26th   Demonstration of Armoured Vehicles crossing a river at Pangbourne.

27th   Exercise 'Maude' starts. Adm. Exercise to test Ordnance and Medical Services.

June 1942

11th   Bn Exercise 'Cardiff' till 12 June. Co-operation with 16 A.C. Sqn. RAF and 4 Motor Coldm Guards.

18th   Demonstration by 1 Sqn made up to 5 Tps and HQ for 32 Gds Bde who have just become part of Gds. Armd. Div.

24th   Col. W. Murray-Threipland DSO. Colonel of the Regiment died.

26th   Visit of new Maj. Gen. Comd. Bde. of Gds Lt Gen. Sir A.F. Smith CB., DSO., MC.

      2 Canadian soldiers attached to the Bn for training.

Between June 19th and July 2nd   6 Covenanter IV were received and 1 Covenanter III. [???C.S. after] 7th - 9th June 5 Scout Cars Mk II [Daimler] were received from Raby Castle V.D.R., R.A.O. C., Staindrop, Co. Durham. On 16th June 7 15cwt 4 wheeled G.S. Morris Trucks were sent to 30 D.C.L.I. , Scilly Isles via Penzance and on 18th June 4 Covenanter I were sent to Allied Power, Galashiels in Scotland.

July 1942

3rd   Announcement of death of 3 O. R's. killed by enemy action while at Div. School, Weston- Super- Mare on 29th June.

16th   A new type of badge for Offrs Berets taken into use.

21st   Sn Comd. Exercise 'Sarum' till 24 July starts. This exercise was designed as first real test for G.A.D. Bn went out with 49 Tanks and returned with 48 in running order on 24 July. Enemy consisted of 20 Armd Bde and units of 38th and 47th Div.

29th   3 J.T.C. Cadets, P.N.J. Ward, P.N. Maas and R. Daly att to Bn. till 8 Aug. First 2 are candidates for Regt, third might be.

30th   Bn. Drill Parade under C.O. at Longbridge Deverill. Band of Irish Guards attended.

2nd 10th & 15th   5 Covenanter IV received; during the month 4 Covenanter I [2x CS] were sent to No 4 Liaison HQ, Polish Forces, Galashiels, Scotland, another Covenanter I was sent to D & M wing, A.F.V. Bovington and a Scout Car Mk 1B to No 15 Field Sqn R.E., Tidworth, Hants.

August 1942

Officers were arriving on attachment and leaving on courses, there was Battalion firing on Imber Ranges and various exercises.

7th   1 Sqn to Camp at West Lavington until 14th August 42.

10th   Lecture on "The American Army" by Col. Gunn U.S. Army.

14th   2 Sqn. To Camp at West Lavington until 21st August 42 .

      Lecture on "German Policy in Occupied Countries" by Count Jan Blinski Jundzille.

16th   Appointment of Col. [hon. Brig. Gen] The Lord Gowrie, VC, PC, GCMG, CB, DSO, LL.D as Colonel of the Regiment 25 June 42.

17th   3 Sqn. Takes part in Exercise 'Agincourt' acting as enemy against 3 Armd.

S.G.

30th   3 Sqn. To Camp at West Lavington until 4 Sept 42.

During August 8 Covenanter I tanks and a Light A.A. tank were sent away to the Ministry of Supply, 5 Covenanters to English Electric Co. Ltd in Stafford the other 3 to C.C.C. Chilwell, Beeston, Nots. Meanwhile 1 Covenanter III arrived from Handforth in Cheshire and 4 Covenanter IV from the Birmingham area.

September 1942

2nd   Lecture on "Campaign in Libya" by Lt. Gen. Willoughby Norrie.

5th   Personnel to form part of Div. Admin. Party leave for Linney Head under the command of Capt. J.O. Spencer.

11th   Visit of Tank Circus of both British and Enemy A.F.V's and also German 88 mm gun.

13th   Brig. A.H.S. Adair DSO., MC., takes over Comd. Armd. Div. from Major Gen. Sir Oliver W.H. Leese Bart. CBE., DSO. who is posted to Comd. A Corps in 8th Army in Libya.

14th   Bn. takes part in Demonstration for Foreign Military Attaches.

15th   Special Order of day on 1st Anniversary of formation of Armd. Bn.

21st   Committee of National Expenditure visits Bn.

26th   Bn. Advance Party goes to Linney Head by road.

On 16th & 17th   6 Carrier Universal Mk I were received from J.I. Thornycroft & Co. Ltd. of Basingstoke while No. T18401 was written off charge of 2 Armd. W.G. while at RAOC Workshops, Tidworth.

October 1942

6th   Bn. consisting of 43 Offrs, 416 OR's and 20 Tanks visited Linney Head during period 28 Sep – 6 Oct 42. On first three days Tables were fired the Bn. average being 41 in practices 7 & 8. Bn. was second highest in Division being beaten by 4 Armd. Grenadier Guards. Last three days were allotted to Sqn. Battle practices and auxiliary weapons. Bren A.A. at Manobier was a failure owing to bad weather. A certain amount of 3" H.E. for C/S Tanks was fired. 10 Battle Practice Runs were done, 3 per 'F' Sqn and one Bn. HQ. Each Run consisted of 2 Tps and 2 Tks on Squadron HQ.

7th   Capt. Sir A.T.C. Neave Bart. To Tactics Course Bulford till 3 Nov.
       Lieut. K.D. Neave to Gunnery Course Lulworth till 25 Nov.

17th   Post of A/Tech. Adjt. Abolished. Proportion of Tech. Adjts duties transferred to QM.

19th   Bde. Comd Brig. G.L. Verney MVO inspects Bn. Camps.

21st   Demonstration for H.R.H. The Duke of Gloucester.

22nd   Exercise 'Sunchariot II'- Rehearsal of Bn. Operational Role took place. All F.S. Caps withdrawn from Bn. Wearing berets became universal.

25th   Bn takes part in Exercise 'Normandy.'

27th   Lieut. D.A. Gibbs to Course at English Electric Co. Stafford till 3rd Nov.

31st Draft of 37 men from Training Bn. to help bring Bn. up to new W.E.

November 1942

2nd   Bn. Individual Training starts to be both basic and to bring personnel up to Trade Test Standard as Dr/Mechs, Gnr/Mechs, Dr/Ops, and Gnr/Ops.

5 D & M, Dr/Mech and Gnr/Mech Squads start under Offr j/c D & M, Lieut. W. Roberts.

4 Gunnery Courses start under T.C.O., Lieut. Hon. A.B. Mildmay

4 w/t courses start under Sig. Offr. Lieut. F.S. Portal.

1 Gas Squad starts under Lieut. J.C.R. Homfray.

7th   Capt. A.H.S. Coombe-Tennant arrived in United Kingdom from captivity. Capt. Coombe-Tennant was taken prisoner while with Bn. at Boulogne in May 1940.

12th   C.O. attends Div. Study Day. Div Comd. announces at Study Day that it is likely that Div will have a Recce B if so it will be 2 Armd W.G. 6th Bde will become an Army Tank Brigade with Churchill Tanks. 2 H.C.R. who, equipped with Armd Cars, have previously done reconnaissance for Div, are likely to become Corps troops. Bn Firing on Imber Range.

Lecture on 'Occupied Belgium' by Prince Arthur de Ligne.

16th   3 Rhodesian Offr Cadets att to Bn till 27th Nov.

17th   Lecture on 'Japan' by Dr Aris

23rd   Lecture on 'The War Today' by Mr Halbrook. This was a very indifferent lecture.

24th   C.O. addresses Bn on its proposed conversion to a Reconnaissance Bn. Conversion only proposed.

27th   Bn moves from Codford to Fonthill Gifford, Tisbury, Salisbury, Wilts. 4 Coldm Gds having been changed from Motor Bn into Armd Bn in 6 Bde move from Heytesbury to Codford to join remainder of Bde in a Camp with Tank standings. 1 W.G. move to Heytesbury which has no standings. Although these moves take place no news has been received as to definite formation of Recce unit and only a very rough draft of W.E. is produced. Bn thus remains on W.E. of an Armoured Bn.

The Welsh Guards period in Codford now comes to an end, but the diaries continue to record the daily experiences of the Regiment at war.

December 1942

18th   Smoke Demonstration supposed to take place, bad weather prevented the aircraft from taking off.

19th   Smoke Demonstration takes place in co-operation with the RAF was not an unqualified success owing to bad weather conditions. Certain lessons were however learned by the RAF and other responsible for experimenting with use of aircraft to lay smoke screens either by bombs or Smoke Curtain

Installations.

25th   Christmas Day celebrated in the usual manner.

27th   Lieut. G.B. Gibbon to Tank Destruction Course.

     5 NCOs to go to Training Bn W.G. for 3" Mortar Course as Bn is now equipped with 3 3" Mortars per 'F' Sqn.

31st   Capt. A. G. Milne, E.M.E., to Waterproofing of Vehicles Course at Inveraray until 6 Jan 43.

Between 2nd-16th December 1942   11 Covenanter III tanks and a Scout Car Mk II were transferred from Fonthill Gifford to HQ Gds Armd Div R.A. C.O.O. Field stores, Aldershot. During the month 6 Crusader III and 1 Crusader II plus a B.S.A. M/C Solo were received.

On 5th January a Morris 8cwt were transferred to O.C. 94 Lt. A.A. Regt and an Austin 30cwt to O.C. 4 Coldm Gds. 5 Morris 8cwt were sent to No 2 VRD. Burnham Beeches on 22nd January 1943 and on 26th and 29th of the month respectively 1 Covenanter III was sent to R.A.M.T. Rhyl and a Norton Comb to No 2 VDR, Burnham Beeches. Between 5th and 30th January 3 Crusader III, a Morris 2-Str., an Austin 2-Str. and a Hillman 2 Str. arrived.

January 1943

1st   New Phonetic Alphabet taken into use. This brings the British usage in line with the USA.

7th   Lecture on 'Tactics of German Inf. Div. by Capt. I.R. Bell R.A. I Staff Div. HQ

8th   Lecture by Major Hawkins [10 Royal Hussars] on 'Desert War.'

13th   Capt. A.H.S. Coombe-Tennant captured at Boulogne in 1940 and since escaped awarded the MC.

February 1943

4th   Lieut. G. Clement-Davies killed in a Carrier accident whilst on a 3" Mortar Course at Netheravon.

5th   Bn moved to Linney Head for Field Firing Practice till 14 Feb 43. Strength 41 Offrs 305 Ors. Rear Party remained at Fonthill Camp under Comd of Capt Watt.

12th   Lecture on 'Battle of Alamein' by Major C.G. Dance, Queen's Bays attended by Offrs and NCOs of Rear Party.

14th   Bn Main body returned from Linney Head.

Notes on Linney Head

The first two days were occupied with individual Table shoots: the next day was occupied by 3" Smoke Firing from C.S. Tks based on a practice suggested by Lt. Col. A.C. Dunn, R.T.R. and sent to CO for his views; also by 3" Mortar H.E. and Smoke firing by Carrier troops. 2pdr & 6 pdr individual practices followed and the CO conducted a T.E.W.T. of the proposed Battle Practice for Sqns combining 1 Tk

Tp and 1 Carrier Tp. The last three days were occupied with Sqn Battle Practices and the usual Shore Range Practices.

18th   Bn takes part in Hants and Dorset Dist. Exercise 'Longford' till 14 Feb 43. This Exercise takes place from Abingdon to Salisbury Plain and was intended as a full dress rehearsal for G.H.Q. manoeuvres to be held in March. Bn, which was really trying out its new role for the first time was praised by Div Comd.

27th   Bn attends combined Church Parade Service with 1st Bn and Div A/A/ Coy to celebrate St David's Day in Salisbury Cathedral. Service was taken by Rev. P.F. Payne and Bishop of Salisbury preached sermon. Service was followed by a March Past , salute was taken by Div. Comd. Maj-Gen Allan Adair. Brig. Fox-Pitt Comd 5 Gds Armd Bde and Brig Marriott Comd 32 Gds Bde attended Service and March Past.

28th   Bn. proceeded to concentration area near Ringwood for Exercise 'Spartan.'

General Notes on Exercise 'Spartan'

28th February-12th March 43

Bn was ordered to take part in this G.H.Q. Exercise as Recce Bn. of Gds. Armd. Div. At the same time permanent location of the Bn was to be changed from Fonthill Gifford, Tisbury to Snarehill Camp, Thetford, Norfolk. This move necessitated the sending of an advance party under Comd. Major A.A. Duncan, and leaving the Rear Party under Comd. Lieut. J.T. Faber, to look after Bn. baggage and take over and hand over Camps. Gds. Armd. Div. formed part of 2nd Canadian Armd. Corps [Commander Lieut.-Gen. Sanson] , one of the three Corps forming British 2nd Army [Commander Lieut.-Gen. Macnaughton]. This Army will pass through a bridge-head previously established by 1st Army [imaginary], and to advance and seize German Occupied Capital of Huntingdon. Bn. started the Exercise with 40 Tks., 40 Carriers, 11 Scout Cars, and full compliment of Transport and arrived at Thetford minus only 5 tks/carriers. A new organisation called a Tk Delivery Sqn was tried out for the first time on this Exercise, Bn supplying 2 Offrs and a number of OR's. 1 Tk from this Sqn. Arrived to replace a casualty and was allotted to 3 Sqn. on 6 March 43. No local purchase was allowed throughout the Exercise with the idea of making all troops rely on the Supply Service and no pay was issued.

Amongst the most notable points about this Exercise was the very short notice at which the Bn. was constantly being ordered to move, this making orders very sketchy and making it quite impossible to put everyone in the picture. Bn. became very quick over the Start Line and was always able to avoid holding up the remainder of the Div. The second feature was the large number of other troops who were constantly being put either in support of, or under Comd. of Bn. These did not always arrive in time and the problem of fitting them into the colns. was considerable. On most occasions Bn. had elements of 55 or 153 Bde. Regt. in support with their O.P's up with the forward Sqn. H.Q. and Fd. Regt. Comd. at Bn.

H.Q.

Troops under Comd. usually included Recce. Parties R.E., Recce. Lt. A.A. Scissors Bridge Tks. And Trackway Bridge. A detachment of G.H.Q. Recce. Regt. was with the Bn. at all times, as also, were elements of the 2 H.C.R. who were acting as Armd. Car Recce. to the Corps.

Third feature of the Exercise was the number of times on which Bn. 'B' Mch., which was working on a double Mch. system, failed to function properly. This being mainly due to confusion in the Adm. Area. Bn., was, however, never short of amm., pet., or food.

28th   Battalion Strength - 44 Offrs. 617 OR's

Bn moved out of Fonthill Camp at 1200hrs without lights, except for undercarriage lights and side lights on the leading vehicle of each block. They went to Concentration Area south of Fordingbridge arriving about midnight. The only difficulty on the road was a very weak and narrow bridge, which was unsuitable for the tanks, which had to cross by a ford set at a very awkward angle to the road. One tank [Capt. N.M. Daniel] broke a track in the ford.

Bn Harboured with Headquarters in Braemore [Lady Normanton], 1 Sqn. in Whitsbury [Mr Jack Scobie], 2 Sqn. in Braemore [Lt.-Col. Stanford], 3 Sqn. in Braemore Rectory [Rev. H. Worleman], all 'B' Tch was with its own Sqn.

This area made a good Harbour, the whole Bn. being under cover in houses, huts or billets, which had been recced 2 days before by a party from each Sqn. Braemore House itself, which was empty, and was requisitioned by the Army, was not allowed to be used. When Bn. arrived, the telephone line from Div. was found to be already installed. Strict wireless silence was imposed during the move, all sets having to Net on to a Wave Meter.

The Battalion tracked vehicles arrived at their destination, Snareshill Camp, Thetford at 1600hrs on 16th March 1943

The Invasion Of Europe

In May 1944 the Battalion were in Brighton making detailed preparations for the forthcoming Exercise 'Channel', the battalion name given to Operation 'Overlord'. This included water-proofing vehicles, stowing all vehicles with loads including ammunition and the preparation of nominal rolls and final adjustment of personnel in their Squadrons. On 15th of the month the weldware was completed on the Battalions 61 Cromwell tanks and on 23rd 11 Stuart VI M5 A1 tanks were received.

The Main Party arrived in the marshalling area on 18th June, embarking by 0230 28th June, the voyage passed without incident and the Battalion landed in France by 1030hrs 29th June.

Postscript

Tempting as it was to follow the 2nd Battalion through Europe from Boulogne to the Elbe, others far better qualified have recorded their courageous fight across the battlefields of Europe. On 4th May 1945 while the Battalion were at Stade when Germany surrendered unconditionally to 21 Army Group, the end of hostilities took effect from the following morning. On 8th May the Lieutenant Colonel Commanding 2nd Battalion Welsh Guards wrote:

> 'An amazing sight on the airfield where the 7th Paratroop Division are paraded for their surrender. All their equipment is piled there. Looked with interest at their guns, which have in the past, given us some unpleasant moments. Monsters, they are, with barrels like elephants trunks. Cuxhaven Harbour is alive with shipping, and well turned out German Sailors lined up for surrender. Saw three U-Boats , and some phenomenally large Field Guns in the docks.
>
> Glorious weather for 'V' Day. Heard Prime Minister's speech this afternoon, and the King tonight. London sounded happy. Can still hardly believe the war is over and that we shan't have to move on somewhere tomorrow morning at first light to capture an area which 'I' Staff assures us contains only weak elements of the enemy, but which actually puts up fanatical resistance all day. But I suppose it must be finished now. Anyhow, WINSTON CHURCHILL says its all over, and that's good enough for me.'

Note

I am indebted to Lt-Colonel Charles Stephens and to Lance Sergeant Mark Morgan of the Welsh Guards for allowing me access to the 2nd Battalion War Diaries.

Rex Whistler's Hudson Terraplane

11

Rex Whistler and the Hudson Terraplane

When the 2nd Battalion [Armoured] Welsh Guards moved to Codford on 17th September 1941 among their ranks was the artist, illustrator and graphic designer Rex Whistler [1905-1944]. Despite being 35 at the outbreak of war Rex was determined to join a Guards Regiment, he was commissioned in the spring of 1940, joined his unit on 2nd June and after training at Colchester was attached to the 2nd Battalion.

Rex Whistler was one of the most outstandingly gifted artists of his generation, dubbed by his Commanding Officer as "one of the most delightful men the Welsh Guards has ever carried on its roll." Rex's prolific paintings, cartoons and sketches from the Codford period display his versatility, including copies of Old Masters and the Colonel Blimp series on wooden hut walls, brilliantly satirical observations of life in the military, Christmas cards, regimental emblems, reversible drawings, likenesses and mundane notices.

Rex's parents were living at this time at the Walton Canonry in Salisbury Cathedral Close; he had numerous friends in the West Country including the Thynne's at Longleat House and the war poet Siegfried and Hester Sassoon in Heytesbury House. During his period in Codford he drove a 1937 black Hudson Terraplane registration number EGJ 581, with tan leather upholstery and a grey hood, he had shipped the parts from America and the car was coach built to his specifications in England. During WWII this unique car became almost better known than its owner, with its open top it was invaluable for transportation and half the Battalion used it at one time or another.

In 1934 when the American Hudson car company found that sales were flagging, they decided to market a "new brand" by manufacturing the Hudson Terraplane as the car that "flew over the ground" in England. Rex ordered his very expensive custom made car early in 1937- parts were assembled in the Hudson factory in London. Salmon and Company of Newport Pagnell in Wales, built the three-position drop Tickford body, Rex's car was the only Hudson Terraplane ever built with this chassis. It took six or seven months before the car was delivered to its owner, in the middle or late part of 1937.

Rex used the car a great deal; from delivery in 1937 until he went on active service in 1944 he had driven 27,000 miles – the engine was remarkably fuel tolerant but greedy, on a good day the Terraplane only travelled 16 miles to the gallon, it was however able to run on tractor or later tank fuel, with access to pool petrol [used by the military and about half * rating today!] it would have been ideal in the wartime conditions where petrol was rationed and for the majority of people unobtainable.

Heytesbury House

When the Battalion left for Normandy of 29th July 1944 the Hudson Terraplane remained in the keeping of Hester Sassoon at Heytesbury House in Wiltshire, Rex left the car to Hester in his will and it remained with her when she moved to the Isle of Mull just after the war. Rex had been killed on the eastern bank of the Orne River on a hot summer day during the battle for Caen. He was a Squadron Commander advancing through minefields when his tank tracks became entangled in fallen telegraph wires. Having evacuated the tank crew they came under small arms fire, Rex ran the gauntlet to his sergeant's tank to initiate radio communication for assistance; as he dismounted the vehicle he was killed by a mortar blast.

When Hester inherited the car in 1944 it would have been a financial liability, there was no petrol so in civilian life it was impossible to take on the road. The Hudson Terraplane was a very fast car, after the war Hester found it intimidating to drive; however she took great care of it, the vehicle was put on blocks and professionally serviced, remaining in Scotland until her death in 1974.

The car was inherited by her son George, who had the car made roadworthy locally and drove it back to Wiltshire. George found the drive alarming despite being an experienced driver, the car could easily reach 100 miles and hour and the brakes were weak, coming on one wheel at a time causing swerves which had to be anticipated.

The car was now housed in a garage or outhouse in Heytesbury until it arrived at the Codford Motor Bodyworks in the late 1970's. Phil West and Charles Sinclair Sweeney had opened the Bodyworks in New Road on the site of a WWII Motor

Transport Section around 1968. Mike Prince worked as a mechanic until he was made a Director; later in the early-mid 70's Mike Prince and Mick Godfrey bought the business, at this time employing a dozen men.

Mike Prince clearly remembers collecting the Hudson Terraplane from a stable at Heytesbury House – by now it was in an extremely dilapidated state, rats had eaten away the leather upholstery and the exterior was in very poor condition. This was a standby job, done for a split in the profits on the sale, it took three years to renovate and restore the vehicle. While it was being worked on Rex's brother Lawrence Whistler, an artist in his chosen field of glass engraving, came to Codford to see the car and was taken for a spin through the Wylye Valley. Another visitor was a veteran of the Welsh Guards, a Sgt. Major from the Museum who desperately wanted the car for the Regimental Museum but was unable to afford the asking price.

Mike Prince outside the Codford Bodyworks in New Road, circa 1980s

A friend of George Sassoon's, known locally as 'German Willy', collected the car on a trailer, supposedly to be taken for auction to Sotheby's. However it appears while Sotheby's was interested in the car- not because of its classic status but because of its famous owner, there is no record it was ever entered for sale. There is the suggestion it may have been withdrawn because of contested ownership or it may have been sold privately by the family or Sotheby's, for the next eight years the whereabouts and the ownership of the Terraplane is a mystery, during this period no mileage was added to the clock; it may have been in the keeping of a family friend of the Sassoon's or with an owner who made no entry in the log book.

The story now takes another puzzling turn, for some unspecified reason the Hudson

Terraplane was sold to the Sassoon family jeweller who owned the car for nine years and drove a total of 900 miles during this period. The DVLA have no record of the car being registered prior to 1984.

The story of Rex's car came to my attention while I was researching the Welsh Guards in Codford. In the Regimental newsletter of September 2002 2734610 Cyril Williams of Port Talbot said that while he was in the Welsh Guards, during 1942, he was stationed in Codford, 3 miles from Heytesbury. After he was demobbed he and his family used to return to Heytesbury for weekends and stay in the Red Lion; it was the landlord who told him the story of the car. During the period the Hudson Terraplane was in the Codford Bodyworks my husband John, who was the local police officer at the time, often helped out at the Bodyworks on rest days and so worked on the car. I was intrigued and determined to discover the history of the car and the present location.

I was fortunate in being able to contact the present owner of the Hudson Terraplane, Mike Taylor who lives in East Sussex. I wrote to the DVLA and established the car was still registered but had no idea where it was, a second letter asking for my request for information to be forwarded to the registered keeper filled in many of the gaps. Mike Taylor bought Rex's car from the jeweller, it had been in the garage for three years and lack of use had all but destroyed everything mechanical, he drove the car home and recalls it was a horrible car to drive, the best and the worst ride of his life; the worst because of the condition of the engine, the best because the car is unique and the quality design superb. The total mileage is just 30,000 miles, since Rex Whistler died the car has only travelled 3,000 miles; in recent years it has been in the process of being painstakingly restored with restoration completed by the end of 2006.

Rex's car had two large chrome external horns, at some time since his death these have disappeared- the Codford photo does not show them so presumably they disappeared prior to this first restoration! Mike Taylor has managed to find a pair of horns so that when the car is rebuilt it will be as good as new -70 years after Rex Whistler took delivery.

It is comforting to know that the Hudson Terraplane has at last found an enthusiast to cherish it, not for its connection with Rex Whistler but for its own sake. To a historian though the excitement of detection, following the trail from Rex Whistler through the Sassoon connection to Mike Taylor has proved a fascinating journey of discovery. All because of an obscure question on a Guard's website that posed the question "What happened next?"

Sources
Mike Taylor
Mike Prince
Welsh Guards Association Newsletter September 2000
Swansea & West Glamorgan Branch Welsh Guards Newsletter March 2001

12

A Wartime Childhood: 1940-1944
David Frostick

My first recollection of how the war would affect me was on a sunny afternoon in September. My father was teaching me to ride a bicycle, when the air raid siren went off. His immediate re-action was to put me on the cross bar of the small bicycle that I was riding, with my legs over the handlebars and peddle for home.

My first school, when I was not quite five was a local day nursery at the top of the road where I lived at 94 The Street, Fetcham, in Surrey. It was only a play school and I have no recollection of learning, only playing. My mother was working part time at a local garden centre pricking out bedding plants for a family friend called Dobbie. I recall, that while at the nursery school, when the air raid siren went off, we assembled with our gas masks and walked across the road to the underground air raid shelters that were adjacent to the local main school. During the time spent in the air raid shelter, we passed the time by singing songs such as 'Ten Green Bottles Hanging on the Wall' and 'One Man Went to Mow, Went to Mow a Meadow.'

During this period my father, with his relations, who were self -employed builders before the war, was working in the London area clearing up bomb-damaged buildings, having been co-opted by the Government. Eventually they were all posted to the Salisbury area, to help with the construction of extending the Larkhill and Bulford army camps. They lodged with a Mrs Horner at Harnham, Salisbury. Following this, they were then sent to Corsham to work on the underground town, then being constructed in the event of a major development of the war.

Meanwhile for a short period, life at Fetcham continued. As a safety measure, my father had constructed a protected area made of scaffold pipes and planks over our beds, in the event of us being bombed and unable to get to the air raid shelter.

I recall that a Messerschmitt fighter plane was shot down and crashed at Leatherhead, a town near us. As a young boy I was quite excited to go and look over it. On more than one occasion, in the company of my father, who came home from his job on the army camps, we would go outside when it was dark, at a time when London was being bombed and you could see the sky glowing red from the fires that the bombs had caused. Eventually the terror of war caught up with us, one night a German bomber bombed the whole of the street, fortunately when my father was at home. Destroying one house belonging to a friend of my father's a Mr Hart and leaving a bomb crater in our next door neighbours garden large enough to accommodate a double-decker bus.

In response to this my father decided that it was time for us to evacuate Fetcham. Before we left, a decision that would eventually change the Frosticks direction in life was taken; arrangements were made for our house to be let to Mr Hart, the friend of my father who had been bombed.

So the day arrived when we were to leave, all of our furniture was stacked into one room of the bungalow ready for our return after the war. The car, a four-seater 1937 Black Morris Minor with green leather upholstery, was packed up, with things tied to a carrying frame on the back of the car and also on the roof. Inside there was my mother and father, my sister Cynthia, Tibby our white tomcat and me. Our next home for a short period would be Saracens cottages at Corton where we shared with another family who left Fetcham at the same time as us, a Mr and Mrs Martin with their daughter. The arrangement of two families sharing did not work out, so in 1940 my father rented another cottage at Albany cottages near Stockton and we moved on. From memory I believe the Martin family returned to Fetcham.

The cottage accommodation was very basic. The toilet was a shed in the garden, when the bucket was full you had to dig a hole and bury the contents. The water supply came from a pump that had to be primed by hand and then you pumped up and down until the water flowed out of the spout. There was no electricity; food was cooked on a range that was kept alight all of the time. And at night we had oil lamps. As you can imagine this was quite an experience for my mother and for us, as in Fetcham we had electricity, hot and cold running water and a flush toilet.

I now started primary school at Stockton, I was five and had to walk 3 miles to and from school, I went with another boy called Eric who was an evacuee and lived less than a mile from our house on a farm with a family called Poole. We went on our own without adult supervision, winter and summer. When I first started at school, I recall that I was the only boy wearing shoes, all of the others wore boots, and so I pestered my mother to buy a pair of what, don't ask me why, I called 'Tock Boots.' The boots were fitted with studs all over the bottom so that they would last longer and of course in icy weather you could slide along on the studs just like skates.

I cannot remember much about the school curriculum but with all of my friends we enjoyed it. One of the girls in my class was called Christine Bryant and we are still friends, in fact when I was working for John Wallis Titt & Co. Ltd., she became my secretary for

David Frostick on right

162

almost ten years. I can remember the schoolteachers name, we called her Miss Bosworth, but in later years I learned she was a widow whose husband had been the first Codford casualty of the war. Charles Homer Bosworth, a Flight Sergeant in the RAF, seconded to the Royal Navy Fleet Air Arm who died two weeks after war was declared. He was aboard the first aircraft carrier lost in WWII, HMS Courageous, when she was sunk in the Atlantic by a German submarine, U.29, commanded by Lieutenant Schuhart.

As most of the children lived in the village of Stockton and Bapton they went home for lunch. However, as it was too far for me to walk home, I had my lunch with a local old couple called Mr & Mrs Grant. As a boy I did not like meat, but I will always recall Mrs Grant's stews, a mixture of vegetables of the season plus potatoes and large onions that had been cooked whole, with dumplings.

My father was at this time working on the underground construction at Corsham and cycled every day from Stockton to Warminster, to catch the coach that took him and others to their work. The car by this time was garaged at a farm at Boyton. My father had jacked it up so that the tyres were not supporting the weight of the car, as he did not know how long the war would last or when we would be able to use it again. Petrol was now rationed and only available for emergency use. We used bicycles, the bus, the train, or walked.

A cottage became available to rent at Boyton in 1941/42; it was on the bridge near the main entrance gates to Boyton Manor, as it was closer to Warminster, it made my fathers cycle journey easier. This era was to be the greatest enjoyment of my life and quite an adventure as a young boy.

My playmates living in the village during this period were: my sister Cynthia, Olive Foggin whose father worked in a post office at Sturminster Newton, cycling home at weekends; Reg and John Pill, who lived next door, their father worked on the railway; Peter Crawshaw, he lived with his grandparents and never spoke about his parents; David and Nigel Manning, sons of the local vicar who lived in Boyton Rectory. Edmund Fane, a year older than I was, his father was an invalid wounded in the First World War, they lived at the Dower House and he went to a private school at Codford called Greenways now Ashton Giffard House. Edmund's nanny went everywhere with him, she was quite old, but great fun.

My sister Cynthia, Olive Foggin, John Pill, and I went to the schools at Codford, apart from the time that I spent at the Common Close, at Warminster. Reg Pill and Peter Crawshaw went to a Secondary Modern School in Warminster, I believe it was Sambourne while David and Nigel Manning went to a boarding school at Leatherhead in Surrey, about three miles from Fetcham where we left in 1940.

Our cottage at Boyton was rented from the Estate and the manager at that time was a Mr Jakins. He wore a Trilby hat, leather gaiters and had a glass eye. His son Peter was in the RAF and he was very proud of this. Unfortunately, although he survived the actual war, he was killed in an aircraft accident on 19th September 1946.[1]

My parents had rented the cottage from the estate, on the understanding that after the war we would vacate it, as the cottage would be required for an estate worker. Once again this would have some bearing on why the Frostick family lives locally and not in

Fetcham.

Our house at Boyton still had only basic amenities. An outside toilet, we still had to empty the bucket and bury the contents when it was full. Our water came from a well. We had to use a bucket on a rope for every drop of drinking water. Water for washing clothes and baths could be taken from the river, it was quicker as the river ran through our back garden, there were stepping-stones originally, so that you could walk across. My father eventually built a lightweight wooden bridge. We had electricity, so this made things easier for my mother when cooking; she did not have to rely on the old range.

To heat water for the weekly wash and bath, we used what was called an out house boiler, it was a solid fuel fire with a large half oval shaped copper bowl housed above it; the whole unit was encased in a brick construction with a fire door, where we put the wood in to feed the fire.

Monday was usually washday, it was our job as children to collect wood from the local woods on Sunday, enough for our mother to heat the water for the washing and at sometime during the week heat water for our once weekly bath. There wasn't a bathroom in our house so we used a long tin bath that was usually put in front of the living room fire and then filled up with water from the copper, this had to be carried in by the bucketful. When we had finished, the water had to be removed by the bucketful. After a short time however my father bought a second-hand enamelled cast iron bath and installed it in the outhouse. There wasn't anything like central heating, in winter it was into the bath a quick wash and then out, to stand in front of the living room fire to dry off. Now the water could be easily transferred from the boiler to the bath and when we had finished we pulled out the bath plug and the water flowed away into the river, as this is how my father had plumbed it up.

During my time in Codford I attended three schools, Codford St Peter's, the Common Close School in Warminster situated in the Close next to the old fire station adjacent to what is now called Kyngeston Court, and Codford St Mary's. We travelled to and from Boyton to Codford by the school bus, driven by a man that we called 'stubbles,' he had dark hair and always looked as if he needed a shave, his name really was Mr. Ploughman; he was quite a laugh always joking. The buses locally were run by Mr Couchman who had his depot was at Codford.

My first school at Codford was St Peter's; we had two teachers Mrs Cuff and Miss Cole. Every morning after assembly, we all lined up for medication, a spoonful of a sweet sticky concoction called Virol. There were no health precautions, everyone used the same spoon, the medication was a supplement to our diet as we were all on rations. At this school, we were taught the usual reading writing and arithmetic, together with handicrafts, this included knitting and sewing, more of a type of embroidery. We got quite good at knitting; in fact we graduated to four needles and even knitted gloves, as children this seemed to take forever. At Christmas time there was a local lady, Mrs Houston lived beside St Peter's Church, to us she seemed quite well off. She gave presents to all of the children; they were distributed from the school just before we broke up for Christmas.

For some reason not known to me, my parents, probably my mother, decided to send me to the Close School at Warminster. This entailed a daily return train journey to and from Warminster, from the railway station at Codford. This was about _ mile from Boyton and in fact was nearer to Boyton than Codford. The train had two carriages, one either side of the small steam engine, it also stopped at Heytesbury to pick up other school children, who either went to school in Warminster or Trowbridge. Some mornings when we were waiting for the train we would place a halfpenny on the line and when the train ran over it, it was squashed to the size of a penny. We were caught on occasions by the stationmaster, a Mr Bunce and told off politely. He lived in a pretty little cottage right next to the railway station, everything now has been demolished and an automatic barrier fitted to control the crossing.

Again, I cannot recall very much about what we did at school, there were no school dinners, we took sandwiches. I believe the headmasters name was Mr Fred Watkins, our teachers here were called Miss Pretty, Miss Petty and Mrs Watkins.

At St Mary's we once again we had two very kind teachers, Miss Scull and Miss Carpenter, Miss Scull, the eldest and more senior, kept us in line. At this school, I travelled to and from Boyton by bicycle. This enabled me to go home to lunch and if need be use the toilet. I could not face the school toilets. My journey took about 10 minutes each way, I went past the railway station at Codford and then took a short cut through the grounds of Greenways School.

Again, I have no recollection of reading writing and arithmetic, but will always remember the large hand made carpets that were made in the handicraft lessons. They were so large that there would be about three children at each end, three girls and three boys. We competed against each other to see who could make most of the carpet. We used short tufts of wool and a carpet hook. You pushed the hook through the special carpet canvas backing, looped the wool in the hook and pulled it back through and made a knot.

We were never bored, in fact there was never enough spare time, in the holidays and when ever we were free, we went on extremely long walks or 'explorations' as we called them. Our legs took us to Stockton Woods and Great Ridge, it would take all day. Our packed lunch or picnic was usually pretty basic; jam sandwiches or bread and a hard-boiled egg, no lemonade, just a bottle of cold water. On these walks and when in season, we would collect wild strawberries and hazelnuts. As boys, we were never without our sheath knife, string and a catapult. They were very important to us we did not consider them dangerous as we treated them with respect. The knife was a tool, the catapult for amusement only, not to kill animals with, or harm one another. I also had an air rifle we used this just for amusement, firing at empty cans etc., not living creatures.

When we were not walking, we were construction engineers. Our first effort was a hut, built in the withy beds and later a more permanent hut or house in the woods. This was constructed from items that we salvaged from the dump. This was a rubbish tip established at Chapel Hole just off the road between Corton and Boyton near Suffers Bridge at the turning to Upton Lovell. At this tip the American army dumped all sorts of interesting items that we were able to use, empty 5-gallon oil drums, large cardboard and wooden boxes etc. We were lucky enough to find a hammer one day and this increased the size of our tool kit, which I still have today, more than sixty years later. We built a trolley using three large ballraces [encasements of ball bearings held in place by two steel rings], for the wheels found on the tip; two were fitted to the front axle and the other at the rear.

We constructed a raft and a jetty with a diving board, this lasted for more than one summer season, in fact we used it all the time. The raft was constructed of logs cut from fallen trees in the woods. Our first attempt was not successful; it sunk when we climbed on board. However we were not put off, we persevered and fitted empty 5-gallon oil drums underneath the log construction, held in place with thin metal banding removed from a wooden packing case. This again came from the dump. All nails and screws etc were salvaged items, as we were not able to buy new.

In winter we had of course our sledge this was an item constructed by my father it had a steering bogey on the front and was quite fast. We used it down the cut, a place in the woods near Boyton Rectory. By this time my father had received his calling up papers and was deemed medically fit for the Royal Navy. He was sent initially to great Malvern and then to Dartmouth in Devon. His rank was First Class Stoker; he wore a propeller insignia on his arm. His duties at Dartmouth were to maintain the engines on the motor torpedo boats that operated in the English Channel.

As I have mentioned earlier, the Americans were now stationed at Codford. Boyton Manor had been requisitioned as an American army officers quarters and the entrance gates near our house were guarded by the American military police. As everything was rationed including sweets, we were always asking the American soldiers if they had any and more often than not, we were given chewing gum. I recall on one occasion, that the officer we approached didn't have any gum, so he gave us a large cigar. As boys we were delighted, we went off to our raft, lit up, laid back and prepared to enjoy it!!!! What a surprise, within minutes we were all violently sick and to this day none of us ever smoked again.

Needless to say, as the weeks went by, we became very friendly with the American soldiers, they were only young men and away from home. In their spare time they came to visit us and talked about America and how they lived. In particular one called Joe Triano, he was Mexican and came from a very poor background. His speciality and quite a marvel to us boys, was his ability to catch fish with his bare hands, 'tickling' them is the phrase. During his brief fishing trips in summer, he emptied the river of trout.

In summer we lived for the woods and the river, we spent all day on the raft or swimming. Edmund, who was a descendant from the local Fane family, was quite a character; he was only allowed to mix with us if his nanny came as well. On one occasion I can recall that she was standing on the jetty shouting to him to get out of the water, as he had gone into the river fully clothed. He got out and then pushed her in; she took it very well and laughed it off. We spent many hours at the Dower House where Edmund lived, there was armour in one of the outhouses and we used to dress up in it. When he had a birthday party or a Christmas party we were all invited. Although there was rationing, at his house they seemed to have plenty. There was always entertainment laid on, usually a magician. We thought that this was great.

Joe Triano, Cpl. Dippary and the boys after an afternoon of trout tickling at Boyton, 1943

Fred Carpenter was the estate agent and water bailiff who lived in Corton and travelled his rounds in a pony and trap. Quite often, as the pony only walked very slowly, Fred would fall asleep; the pony knew exactly where to go. When Mr Carpenter was awake, he kept a watchful eye on us but we were always one jump ahead. Whenever he saw us near the river he would say, " Hope you boys aren't catching my fish" and our reply was a polite " No Mr Carpenter" lying through our teeth. Little did he know that we had our secret weapon - Joe Triano!

The gamekeeper Mr Noakes was a different type of person, he nearly always carried a gun in the crook of his arm and gave the impression of being a typical miserable gamekeeper. On one occasion, when we had been on a gin trapping mission, setting off all of the traps set by the game keeper with a thick stick, he caught us in the act. We also had my dog Judy with us and this did not help matters, as he accused us of poaching. He said if he caught us again he would shoot the dog. Our polite reply to this was, "If you do, we will let all of your pheasants and partridges loose." He was quite taken back as the breeding of those birds was quite important to him as a gamekeeper.

All food was rationed including sweets and clothes, as an example we were allowed 2 ozs of sweets a week, this represented about six sweets or six squares of chocolate, that was, if you could find a shop that had sweets. Even rationed, they were a luxury.

Each person, including children, was registered and had a ration book.

As we lived in the country, we could supplement our diet, we kept chickens and sometimes rabbits for meat, we also ate the fish that we caught in the river. The chickens were free range and were fed also with scraps of food left over from our meals, nothing was wasted, even the potato peelings and any of the waste that was left over when the vegetables were prepared, were boiled up and used for chicken feed. The chicken's laid their eggs in the hen house, where they were shut up at night to protect them from the foxes. They also laid eggs in the hedgerows of our garden when they were broody and if left, they would sit on them for about three weeks and hatch out the eggs into little chicks. When we were aware that a hen was doing this, she was put into a special little hutch so that she could be looked after safely, until the chicks hatched.

The moorhen and the pigeon were wild birds that laid eggs that could be eaten provided they were fresh. A pigeon usually laid two eggs, if you found a nest with one egg it was usually fresh and we would take it, as the pigeon would lay others. However if there were two we would leave them, as there was every possibility that the pigeon was sitting on them to produce chicks. With the moorhen, this was a different story, as she would lay quite a lot of eggs, sometimes as many as ten or more. So provided there were no more than about six then they were fairly fresh, possibly only a week old.

Apart from the eggs that we collected from the pigeon and the moorhen, we also collected other wild bird's eggs, which is now illegal. We were always very careful how we took the eggs, never more than one. As children growing up in the country, we were always very aware to conserve nature. We would spend hours watching birds to establish where they were building their nests. A bird is a very wary creature and if they know that you have knowledge of their nest, they will desert it and this could be disastrous if there were baby chicks. So the secret was to observe, but don't be noticed by the birds.

As well as the American soldiers stationed at Codford, we also had Italian prisoners of war. They worked locally on the farm and were very friendly. They were dressed in a maroon coloured uniform with yellow circles stitched on the back of their jacket and on the knee of their trousers. In their spare time they collected withies from the withy beds in season and made baskets. They also made rings from the old imperial multi flat-sided three-penny pieces and mugs from small empty bake bean tins. One of the prisoners showed me how to make a whistle from a willow stick and it is something that I have never forgotten. I am still able to make a whistle from any green twig when the sap is rising in the spring.

The only wartime holiday that I can remember was spending a few days at Weymouth. We went to see my father who had been posted there with the Navy. I remember that the beach was protected with steel scaffold poles and barbed wire and that you could not play on the sand.

One Christmas with my father still in the navy and unable to come home, we returned to Fetcham. We stayed with my mother's old friend, Mrs King. It was to us quite exiting, there were no elaborate gifts, just simple things like second hand toys and home made Christmas crackers. The crackers did not make a bang and contained only home made sweets.

Finally war in Europe was over and there was a large celebration at Codford. My father was medically discharged from the Navy and returned home to start up his own business as a Builder and Decorator. Our tenancy at Boyton was terminated and we were given notice to leave. Life is not always straightforward, Mr Hart who lived in our house in Fetcham would not move out, he was protected by the laws that were in force at that time. We were fortunate however, as a Mr. Campony, the gardener for the Boyton Manor came to our rescue, he had always been a good friend of the family one way and another and offered to buy the bungalow at Fetcham with a sitting tenant. In his words, "an investment for his old age." An income on the rent to supplement his pension when the time came. My father purchased the 'Cotsmere' in Chitterne in 1944, I believe for about £700, so we moved. Quite a sad day, as we said goodbye to all of our old friends.

Note

1 Peter Jakins. According to a newspaper cutting twenty-five RAF men were reported missing, believed killed in an air crash the Air Ministry kept secret for four days. In 1946 Peter Jakins was a passenger in a Lancaster bomber on a night flight from St Mawgan, Cornwall to Egypt that crashed near Homs, near Tripoli. Homs is a coastal town on the route the 8th Army used when Rommel was chased out of Tripolitania. Seventeen passengers and eight crewmembers perished, in the accident presumed due to "loss of control." The Air Ministry [Casualty Branch] stated "The aircraft was broken up by an explosion, and in consequence none of the bodies afterwards recovered could be identified, but there can be no doubt that all the occupants of the aircraft were killed. Their remains were buried on 23rd September."

Peter was 22 years of age, with a lively nature and friendly disposition. A pupil of the Trowbridge Boy's High School where he once created something of a mild sensation by winning both the junior and the senior Cricket Ball Throwing event in the same year- he left in 1940 to assist his father, a well-known local farmer. Always keen on flying, he was one of the original members of the Warminster ATC Unit, in which he held the rank of Warrant Officer. He joined the RAF in April 1943, and early the following year he was commissioned as a signaller and posted to the Middle East and after further training. He did tour of operations against the enemy from Italy, the completion of the tour, for which his pilot was awarded the DFC, almost coincided with the conclusion of hostilities in that theatre. He remained in the Middle East after the war had ended, but was able to return to this country on a number of occasions. It was whilst he was flying to Cairo from St Mawgan, in Cornwall that the 'Lancaster' in which he was a passenger crashed."

Rita's father (top right) and Wylie Railway Station

13

After The War Was Over:
Rita Chapman's Story

I was born at 3 Council Houses, we called it Green Lane but today the houses are in New Road, Codford in 1943. My dad was born in Pembroke in 1906, he came to the area with his parents, his father was the Station Master at Wylye for many years. My mum was Ellen Gurd, she had been the personal dresser/ ladies maid to Lady Bonham –Carter before working at Stockton House, she was there when she met my dad, they married and had four children, and I was the youngest. Dad worked on the railway, he had to walk to Salisbury and back to Wylye lighting all the oil lamps in the evening, and go back the next morning to put them all out, the next day he had to start all over again.

My dad had two sheds, one was full of junk, dad would collect anything he could get his hands on. The other one was MINE to do what I wanted to do in it. I had an old stove that had an oven on the side, me, Barbara and Christine would make mud pies and put it in the oven and hope for the best. We would play mummies and daddies till we had an argument about something then one of us would go home crying.

Before the old range was taken out my mum would black lead the range every morning before she lit it. It had a side oven where she would cook a big stew that would last about four days, and a spotted dick or jam roly-poly. There were two brass boxes on each side of the hearth where you put your shoe polish and cleaning rags. In the recesses by the fire dad would put eggs under a big lamp to hatch the chicks. I would sit for hours waiting for them to hatch out. When they were large enough to go outside I would feed them in the morning before school and when I came home. We had a very tall jug to put the water in, one day I filled the jug and slipped on my way to the chicken hutch and broke my wrist. It was in plaster for six weeks, two weeks after the plaster came off I did it again and was in plaster for another six weeks. After a few months the chickens were ready to eat- what a treat!

We had a toilet in the back garden, it was OK in the summer but in the winter it was very cold and would freeze up, not very nice! There were always spiders in a big web in the corners. We never had toilet rolls, we had to cut up newspaper on a piece of string and hang it on a nail- you would end up with newsprint on your bum. The toilet had to be emptied every two weeks; dad would dig a big hole and try to remember where he dug last time. We had some lovely rhubarb come up!

I don't remember anything about the war; I was only two when it finished. My mum told me Vera Lynn came to entertain the army in a large hut at the top of the hill (where Bury Mead is today] My brothers and sister were much older than me, Vera was fifteen years older, she would take me up Malmpit Hill on the Salisbury Road for walks in my pram. My brother Den went into the Navy in 1952, he looked lovely in uniform, when he came home on leave he would whistle "Stranger in Paradise" as he came along the lane. He would be in the kitchen doing his washing and I would say to him "Can I wash your bit of string?" He would answer, "It's not a bit of string, it's a lanyard." I would only do it to wind him up! Our Bob worked at the Creamery in Warminster while Vera was working in the NAAFI at Larkhill.

The Chapman family at Weymouth in the 1950s. Rita far right.

In the summer my dad would hire a charabanc from Mr Couchman. On Saturday morning the day of the annual seaside trip we would all meet outside on the road with our buckets and spades, walk up the hill- all thirty of us, to catch the bus at the village pub. We all piled on the bus and headed for Weymouth. Mum made tomato sandwiches from home made bread, I had a bottle of pop and there was a flask for mum and dad. We would all fight for the seat in the back seat of the bus, waving to the people behind us in their cars.

When we got to Dorchester we would all shout "HOW MUCH FURTHER." Weymouth was just over the hill; we would see it, all laid out in front of us, lovely calm blue sea. What a thrill when we saw the sea and the sand, the sun would be out, there were rowing boats and pedalos bobbing about on the water and we would be ready to go. I would dig into the sand and fill my bucket with my red, yellow and blue tin spade. When the digging was finished we went for donkey and swing boat rides, then it was time for dinner. Mrs Whatley would shout "Anyone for fish and chips?" All the mums would go and get them while the dads looked after the kids, didn't fish and chips taste lovely out of paper!

A man with a megaphone would walk along the sand and shout "Punch and Judy in half an hour and don't forget your sixpences." We would all run to the Punch and Judy show to get in the front before the rest could get there. What great days we had, all too soon it would be over and we got back on the bus to go home. On the way we would stop in Blandford at a pub, we would head for the garden and have lemonade and a packet of crisps with a blue bag of salt inside. We headed for home tired but very happy!

In the summer I used to go for holidays to visit my two of mums brothers and play with my cousins. Uncle Perc was a gardener at Sutton Parva near Warminster. He lived with his wife Lillie and daughter Lavinia in a little cottage down a very dark lane next to the big house. It was very creepy in the winter evenings. I would help uncle Perc in the greenhouse and the garden; my job was to wash the stone flowerpots ready for the planting. I thought it was a very important job for a little girl. Even now, when I smell cucumbers and tomatoes my thoughts go back to the greenhouse, when you open the door in the morning.

Uncle Joe worked on the land most of his life, mostly in Wiltshire. Whenever we went anywhere in the car we would say Uncle Joe lived there.... and there.... and there.... it was a standing joke! His wife Nora came from Liverpool, they couldn't have children so they adopted John. He was a lovely person to grow up with, he would stay with us in Codford in the summer and we would have so much fun. Aunty Nora was a cook. I remember Uncle Joe and Aunty Nora got a job at Longford Castle near Salisbury. I stayed there in the summer as well. We found a secret garden; it was magical for kids nine years old. We played there for hours, eating apples, plums and strawberries. We would go back into the kitchen this enormous table in the middle of the room. It was covered with home made pies- the smells were wonderful.

The winters in Codford were very cold and windy; as we lived in a house in the middle of a field the wind would sweep around the houses. When the snow came we were often snowed in until the tractor came and cleared the lane. Dad made me a sledge and all us kids would go up on the hills with tin trays and planks of wood, great fun for hours, returning home with red noses, wet gloves and feet. We couldn't wait to go out the next day and do it all over again!

I can't remember having a tree at Christmas, I suppose we did, we had lots of decorations to hang up. We had huge paper bells we hung up year after year, and Mum got sticky strips of paper of different colours and we made paper chains that reached from one side of the room across to the other. I always had two stockings, one hung by the fire and another on the bottom of my bed. Mum and dad couldn't afford much so they gave me lots of love to make up for it!

Christmas came and went, and then spring came bursting out all over the place. We lived a few yards from the Chitterne Brook; I would go down and sit on the stone bridge with my jam jar tied with string around the neck and fish for minnows, catfish and tiddlers. It was so quiet and wonderful to paddle in the clear stream. When my jam jar was full I would leave it on the bridge and go for a walk along the hedgerows, picking violets, buttercups, daisies and a grass I could wiggle-woggle, I think the proper name is shepherds purse!

With Christine and Barbara my next-door neighbours I would take a bottle of lemonade and some sandwiches and go to the hills for a walk. We'd pick cowslips and lie in the grass, listening to the bees and the skylarks. Childhood pleasures were so much simpler then, the days always seemed to be warmer and the summers longer. I would love to go back to those carefree days in the late forties when I could do handstands all over the lawn, go upstairs two at a time and run like the wind!

The people who lived in our road went about their days so peacefully; everything was at a slower pace. People had time for you then, if you were in trouble they were there for you. We never closed our doors; neighbours would just knock and walk in for a cup of tea and a chat anytime, day or night. Mr and Mrs Tigg with their children Walter, Mary and Ethel lived in no.1. In no 2 were Mr and Mrs Whatley, they had two boys, Kenneth and Patrick * who died when he was sixteen, I can't remember how. [* Patrick died in a car accident on the A36?] We lived in no.3, I had a sister Vera and two brothers Bob and Den, next the Collier family with Brian, Joyce, Don, Terry and Christine. The Fry family lived in no 5- they had four children Jack, John, Stella and Kath. In no 6 Mr and Mrs Whatley, Lesley and David, in 7 Mr and Mrs Dawson with a large family whose names I can't remember. Mr and Mrs Davis, Dick and Celia lived in no. 8.

We all shared one water pump, it was in the middle of the rank. Every winter it would freeze up, we would have to light a fire around it to get water. Doing the washing was hard work for poor old mum, she would have to chop wood to light the boiler in the corner of the bathroom, the water took about an hour to boil. There was always a race who would put their washing out on the line to blow in the breeze first .

In the fields all around us were the army camps, as the war was on. Mum would do all the khaki uniforms for the Americans and the Italian POW's. I would help with the mangle, mum would rinse and I would turn the handle, it had two big wooden rollers and a tin bath to catch the water.

At the top of the village, the St Peter's end, on the Warminster side was a private

Rita

school called Greenways, run by Mr and Mrs Hathaway. My mum worked in the kitchens there, sometimes in the school holidays I would go to help her. Maurice and Mary Cole lived with their three children and a dog called Pucky in the house going down to the school.

Crossing over the road was the garage that was owned by Mr and Mrs Bee, they were very large people, so they would look big to a small girl. I would get my sweets in the shop, from the large glass jars filled with humbugs, sherbet dabs, penny chews, liquorice shoelaces and gobstoppers before I went to school. I started school in St Peter's in 1948 when I was five years old, I remember it all so clearly, me and my mum holding hands, walking up the hill, me with my satchel on my back, my hair in pigtails, I always had ribbons in my hair.

St Mary's School and Chitterne Brook

The school had only two class rooms and a kitchen, the porch door was in the shape of an arch and very wide, the cloak room had rows of little pegs for us to put our things on. When we were all settled at our wooden desks with empty ink wells, Mrs Cuff the teacher, she was lovely, all round and cuddly, would come round handing out big white cards with a big red A and the outline of an apple. This was how we learned the alphabet- A is for apple, B is for ball, C is for cat and so on. We had small wooden trays with sand in it and a small stick to write our names, I had three happy years at St Peter's school before going to St Mary's at the other end of the village.

The boys and the girls had separate toilets in the playground, each toilet contained a long plank of wood with four holes cut out so four children at a time could use them.

Under the holes were buckets that were emptied each week by a man with a lorry. One day I was having a wee when I felt cold all around my bottom. The man had opened the back flap and taken out my bucket while I was using it.

St Mary's was a big shock- the Head Master, Mr Mein was a very nice man who lived opposite the school. [He died on 13th March 2001 at the age of 84.] He was very strict and if we were naughty we would get hit with a ruler or shut in a cupboard! The school had two rooms and a kitchen, and a big bell that hung between the class rooms, rung at nine o'clock in the morning and again at three fifteen when it was time to go home.

I don't remember much about the lessons there only the day we had prunes for pudding. I hate prunes so I left them in the dish, Mr Mein came in and said, "Eat up your prunes or you don't go out to play until you have." So when he had gone I put them in my hanky and put them in my knicker pocket and by the time I went home the prune juice had run all down my leg and into my sock. I got a good slap from mum! I had another three years at St Mary's before going to the Avenue School in Warminster in 1954

On the way to school in the village the pig farm was the first thing you could smell as you walked past, it belonged to Mr Cole. A bit further along his father lived in a corrugated tin bungalow, painted dark green.

Over the road, next door to the Bee's lived Mr and Mrs Phelps with their four children, Jean, Maureen, Robin and Margaret. The Dyers and their daughter Helen lived next to my school. On the other side of the road towards the village were two Nissen huts left over from the war, I think Mrs Pothercary lived there. Mr Wheelers shop was at the top of the hill.

On the other side of the road was a lane that went to Green Lane by Bury Camp. My nan and aunty used to live in one of the tin huts that were left on the site after WWII. There were about thirty huts the army had left there. My nan had three rooms, two bedrooms and a kitchen/dining room/ sitting room. It was very cosy and warm in the winter, and very hot in the summer. I can still picture the path that led up to the front door, each side had lavender bushes and boy's love right up to the front door. When Cherry Orchard was built in the 1950's they moved there.

I was in the choir at St Peter's Church, I had to go twice a day, morning and evening and I was paid two shillings. My great nan and my aunty Daisy were buried there and it's where I was married in 1963. Down the road from the church on the right was the butchers shop, run by my best friend Christine Blackwell's dad. We went to secondary school together in Warminster. From the time I was eleven I used to walk about half a mile to Station Road outside the cafe to catch the bus. Christine and I left the Avenue school in the summer of 1958, FREE AT LAST, we worked in the same place.

My aunty and my nan lived in the council houses at no. 9 Cherry Orchard. I used to stay there during the summer holidays. Nanny Gurd was born in 1880 in Hampshire. She was a small, plump lady who had ten children, a lot of kid's to feed and clothe in those days. Her husband worked on a farm with horses, while ploughing the fields the horse reared and kicked him in the chest. He had very bad internal injuries and died shortly afterwards. The thing I remember most about nan was that she had very swollen legs, she had to have Germalene cream and bandages on them every day. She must have been in a lot of pain! Mum and I would go to tea on Sundays, she always had seedy cake, which I hated.

The village hall, across the road, was used for weddings, village meetings and as a bank. Mr and Mrs Legg ran it; they had a son David and a daughter Catherine. Mr Legg used to deliver the papers round the village. On the windows of the hall there were shutters painted with regimental cap badges. Beside the hall was Paul Cole's garage.

The doctor Houghton-Brown lived opposite the hall, he had a surgery on the side of his house. Next to the doctor's was the drapers belonging to Mrs Knight, then a hardware shop owned by Paul Cole's wife, then the chapel where I was christened. The hub of the village was the bakers shop; you could smell the bread up the road. Along the row was the Greens Grocery shop, the Post Office run by Mr and Mrs Watkins, across the High Street was The Snobys, a shoe shop run by Mrs Snailgrove, the hair dressers run by Mr Black, then a side alley where Mr Simper had a clock and radio repair shop. Close by Mr Couchman had a coach business, he picked people up through Codford and the back villages on a Tuesday and a Saturday to take them to Salisbury shopping or to the market.

The Dairy was just down from the Post Office, then Mr Vines shop. On the corner of Chitterne Road was the café called the Milk Bar, owned by Miss Sparey. She had a Polish chap who worked for her and he made Bread Pudding in a pee-pot, I never knew this till years later, my brother in law knew him and was told how it was done.

Beyond the Milk Bar St Mary's School was run by Mr Mein. Going up Chitterne Road on the left was Mrs Weston's house, she was a lovely old lady, I would go and see her on my way home from school. She would show me round her garden every time I went there, be it twice a week or four times, she was very forgetful, bless her.

Opposite in the big house lived Mr and Mrs Pers Jensen, he owned the Flying Goose. His cousin was the 1960's Danish duo Nina and Frederick. Further up the road the house on the corner of Cheapside used to be a fish and chip shop, I don't know the name of the two ladies that ran it. The only people who I know there now are Brian and Barbara Collier, they lived next door to me in the Council Houses in Green Lane.

In Dairy Cottages Mr and Mrs Bundy lived. He was a shepherd and had been in the Home Guard with my dad. The last house up the hill belonged to Mr Rasputinski, he had a gorgeous son. Back down the road was the Police Station, along Benis path lived Pauline Spruce with her mum and step-dad. At the end of the path is the cemetery where there are graves of the Australian Army boys that died in the Great War.

In the 1950's, '60's and '70's you would know everyone in the village, I grew up and went to school with them, in some cases married and had children at the same time. Now when I go back to visit my sister-in-law Joyce Green, I know hardly any one. Over the last twenty years a lot of new comers have arrived, they live in the big houses where Bury Camp used to be.

Every year the village had a fete, it was a great event for the villagers to get together and have fun. They had skittles and the prize was a pig, my brother Bob won it four years running, it kept us going in meat for a bit!

Things I remember: The nit nurse, ration books, farthings and thruppeny pieces, white five pound notes, sit up and beg bikes, blue bags, Rinso washing powder, calor gas, Red Cardinal polish, old Smiths crisps with blue bags of salt, Cod Liver Oil, Grampian TV, half-a-crown, sixpence, ten bob notes, one pound notes, Eiffel Tower Lemonade, Five Boy chocolate, Watch With Mother, Cracker Jack, Dick Barton- Special Agent, In Town Tonight, Black and White Minstrels, Pogo sticks, jacks, skipping, rounders, Morris Minors, picture tickets for two shillings, hay making, village fetes, woollen swimming trunks, rubber swimming hats, elasticated swim suits, gymslips, dirndl skirts, ribbons and slides in my hair, Alice bands, white knee length rubber boots, out side larders, beaded jug covers, washing boards, liberty bodice with rubber buttons, pan stick make up, parma violet sweets, 4711 scent, woodbine fags, cross over apron, milk churns, bucket bags, out side toilets, toilet paper on a string, mangle with wooden rollers, copper boilers, tin plates, black and white TV, tin baths, beehive hairdo's, mobile fish and chip van, Carbolic soap, yo-yo's.

I always felt safe living in Codford, you never heard of anyone getting hurt, I loved the place and am still very passionate about it, it was a very big part of my life and it still holds something magical for me.

14

The Search For the Codford Spitfire

Early in August 2004 I opened the door to two young men from Cardiff on a quest to discover the location of a Spitfire that crashed in Codford on 6th November 1943. Ian Hodgkiss and Gareth Jones are among a band of dedicated volunteers of the Marches Aviation Society, individuals who give time to piecing together the tangible history of the air war over the United Kingdom under the overall management of the British Aviation Archaeological Council.

Planes that crashed with a loss of life are classed as War Graves and must remain untouched, but in the instance of a crash without a fatality it is possible that if the site is identified and the landowner gives permission the site can be excavated, investigated, recorded and a memorial erected. A common problem with the type of accident the young men were interested in is that it was not very memorable; a smoking crater left by a deeply buried aircraft does not leave the same impression as a force landed Spitfire on its belly on pasture land or a crashed German fighter plane with a dead air crew and twisted metal wreckage.

My previous research into village history made me certain that the Spitfire had not crashed close to the settlement, it was hardly something that would have passed unnoticed. The military records show that the Spitfire VB [5B- in WWII Roman numerals were used to denote numbers], piloted by an American aviator, 2nd Lt. Robert P. Humphrey serial number 0-885583 was attached to the 12th Rec. Fighter Squadron, 67th Recon. Group, IX Fighter Command of the USAAF. Lt. Humphrey was probably one of the 6,700 American pilots who volunteered for the RAF between 1940-and October 1942. Privately recruited by Clayton Knight these pilots came from private flying clubs and airports from across the United States. The American Air Force mainly used the Spitfire, a far superior aeroplane to the American planes of the period. Lt Humphrey would have spent at least 3 months with an Operational Training Unit learning to fly the Spitfire before being posted to an RAF Squadron- possibly one of the 'Eagle Squadrons' made up entirely of Americans.

In 1942, with the United States now in the war, American pilots transferred from the RAF to the U.S. Air Corps. Lt Humphrey served with the 153rd Observation Squadron of 67th Observation Group based at Station 466, Membury. The Squadron was spread across the surrounding countryside; one of the nearby satellite airfields with 153rd was Station 471 at Keevil.

Lt. Humphrey's account of the accident was written on 11th November 1943:

"I took off at about 1415 in Spitfire VB ZMK on a test hop. (Engine had 30 minutes flying time). After climbing to 7,000 feet at plus 4 boost and 2400 RPM I levelled off. Rad. Temp.110, oil pressure and temp normal. I did some steep turns to right and left and the engine became excessively rough and glycol temp increased. I decreased the RPM and made matters worse. Upon increasing RPM to 2600 engine smoothed out a little. I decreased RPM again and engine got rough, missed and quit. Fearing an internal glycol leak and the consequent danger of fire I abandoned the aircraft.

The description of the accident signed by three 1st Lt's Saunders, Ware and Symes, dated 12th November 1943 states:

The pilot took off in Spitfire VB No.BM-540 on a local slow time mission at about 1415 hours. He climbed to 7,000feet at plus 4lbs. manifold pressure and 2400RPM. At this time he noted that the glycol temperature was 110C and the oil temperature and pressure were normal. After the pilot had done several steep turns he noted that the engine was getting very rough and that the glycol temperature was increasing to 115C. He tried decreasing his RPM but that seemed to aggravate the situation. By increasing his RPM to 2600 the engine smoothed out a little. He decreased his RPM and this time the engine cut out completely. The pilot bailed out at 7,000 feet. The accident resulted in the complete wreck of the aircraft.
RESPONSIBILITY: lies with material failure.
RECOMMENDATIONS: none in that cause of accident is undetermined.

That same day from Headquarters of the US AAF Station G-446, Office of the Station Commander APO 638 - US Army to Commanding Officer IX Fighter Command, APO 638, U.S. Army the Report of Aircraft Accident was forwarded.

From Headquarters, IX Fighter Command, APO 638. U.S. Army 17th September 1943 to Commanding Officer, USAAF Station 466.
1.   Form 14 covering accident of Spitfire No. BM-540 is returned for additional information as follows:

a] The cause of the accident will be as fully determined as possible. Memorandum No 55-1 Headquarters, Ninth Air Force, 31st October 1943 recommends that an RAF Inspector be called in to assist in the investigation of material failure.

b] A complete explanation as to why it was necessary to abandon the airplane in flight at 7,000 feet of altitude and why an attempt was not made to land at one of the airdromes which could be reached at this altitude.

2.   The possibility of a glycol leak is not considered an adequate reason for

abandoning the airplane before actual evidence of fire and considering that the indicated engine temperature was below the ignition temperature of glycol.

3.   AAF Regulation 62-14 requires the accident investigation to be made of the three most experienced pilots available. Indicate if the investigating committee conforms to this requirement.

By Command of Brigadier General Quesday
Henry L. Taylor Lt.
Col. ACD,C
Adjutant General.

At the time of the crash Lt. Humphrey was not flying on instruments and the weather was good; he had a total of 512.50 flying hours, with 181.20 hours on this particular type and model airplane but appeared to have had neither instrument nor night time flying hours in the past 6 months.

The initial reaction from the Commanding Officer of the Air Corps on 21st November 1943 was that:

1.   The purpose of the AAF Form 14 is to report the type of accident and the basic cause, and to submit recommendations for the prevention of similar accidents in the future. The basic cause of the accident in question was engine failure. The engine in this case was completely destroyed, making it impossible to determine the cause of the engine failure.

2.   Lieutenant Robert P. Humphrey was transferred from RAF to US AAF 27th November 1942 and assigned to this Group. He had three (3) accidents prior to 16th April 1943, when he was ordered before a Flying Evaluation Board. The Board found him qualified and he was continued on flying status. When this accident report reached my office, I immediately called for an investigation. The officer was on leave at the time, and the investigation was delayed until his return.

3.   In my opinion the officer used very poor judgement in abandoning the aircraft at 7,000 feet under circumstances described and weather conditions existing at the time. No satisfactory reason for his action has been received.

4.   Lieutenant Humphrey has been suspended from flying status by order, and his commanding officer has been directed to order him before a Flying Evaluation Board to determine his fitness for continuing on flying duty.

5.   The officers currently detailed to the Aircraft Accident Committee at this station are officers with an average of seven hundred hours flying time, and include the assistant group operations officer, a squadron operations officer, and a pilot who is considered above average.

Frederick R Anderson
Colonel, Air Corps Commanding

This action was approved on 25th November 1943.

The Accident Report was intriguing- while it documented a single incident it instigated a desire to know more about Lt. Humphrey, his earlier accidents and what happened to him after. With the help of Craig Fuller of Mesa, Arizona who runs Aviation Archaeological Investigation & Research, I was able to obtain Lt. Fuller's confidential accident reports.

Lt. Humphrey seemed to have been a lucky pilot with a Jonas touch where Spitfires were concerned, by the time he left Keevil he had an intimate knowledge of the soft earth at the edge of the runway, of the experience of having a Spitfire go nose up, had damaged three aircraft, accounted for several propellers, and had, remarkably, walked away unscathed. Lt. Humphrey crashed his first Spitfire on 28th December 1942 at 1700 hrs., he had a total of 328.5 pilot hours, but only 4.45 on the Spitfire VB; he had taken off from Keevil where he was stationed at 1600 hrs, the visibility was 4 miles with clouds at 1500 ft and 9/10 cloud cover, the wind was from the South East and the velocity 10 – 15 mph.

Lt. Humphrey's version of events is on record- he stated, "I made my approach to land much faster than normal due to engine overheating. I levelled off and flew down the runway with the intention of getting as near as possible to the parking area to avoid having to taxi far. The plane touched the ground past the halfway intersection and continued to roll on off the runway. Due to the soft earth and hitting a pipeline which circles the edge of the perimeter strip the plane nosed up breaking two blades off the propeller."

Flight Control Sgt. John W. McCorkle witnessed the accident. "As enlisted man on duty in Flight Control Office, I was present in Control Tower on Monday afternoon, December 28th, when Spitfire No. EN-945 cracked up on landing. Pilot, upon receipt of signal light from Tower, made first attempt at landing and, when nearly on the ground, apparently decided to take another circle of the field and come in again. At his second approach he came in high on 6,000 feet of runway and seemed to have covered 3,500 or 4,000 feet of this runway before cutting his gun. About 200 feet further along he put the ship down and his speed indicated that he would roll past the end of the runway. Just before reaching end of runway he evidently applied right brake which resulted in swerving ship sharply to the right as it rolled off end of runway onto grass. Left wing touched or almost touched ground and ship nosed up on its prop and spinner."

A further statement comments that Lt Humphrey did not "cut the gun" probably meaning close the throttle until two thirds of the way down the runway so as to get as near as possible to the parking area because of an overheated engine. The result of the crash was two broken wooden propeller blades and possible major damage to the propeller shaft and gear reduction box, this could only be determined by the use of proper adjustment equipment.

The Investigating Officer of the Accident Classification Committee findings, 2nd Lt. Francis J. Dillon Jnr., concluded that: "The accident occurred when the pilot was landing. He believed that he could fly the plane down the runway and decrease his taxiing time. This shows very poor judgement, as it was impossible for him to stop the plane before coming to the end of the runway. Therefore I believe that this was complete pilot error." The recommendation was that there should be intensive training in the intricacies of the type of plane.

Two days later, on 30th December now with 5.45hrs flying time in the Spitfire VB, Lt. Humphrey in the same type of plane, same place, did it again! This time the right tyre blew out on landing, the plane turned off runway to the right about 60 degrees and nosed up when it hit the soft earth and mud, damaging one wooden propeller, the right landing gear casing and inner tube.

The landing was logged as a perfect three-point landing with no tendency to bounce, immediately on landing the tyre began flapping while the aircraft was rolling at a very slow speed. The conclusion was that the accident was entirely due to structural failure; before take off the left tyre had been replaced; the recommendation was that instructions were issued to inspect tyres carefully prior to every flight.

By the time of the third accident Lt. Humphrey had logged up 43.20 hours in the Spitfire VB- this time it was not ill judgement or structural failure but the weather that caused his undoing! As he landed his aircraft at 1030 after completing a local training mission, Lt Humphrey taxied about 300 yards to and area of the perimeter strip that was crosswind. The wind velocity was 25 –30mph in gusts, a sudden gust weathercocked the aircraft towards the end of the strip, the air pressure became low and the brake overheated, so that despite full application the brake was insufficient to stop the aircraft, it struck the soft shoulder off the edge of the strip, tipping into a small ditch sinking two propeller blades into a mould of soft dirt as it nosed up. The damage to the Spitfire this time was to the landing gear fairing, the propeller, possibly the crankshaft alignment and the motor mount was distorted.

Perhaps his luck ran out the year following the Codford crash, a Lt. Robert P. Humphrey serving with the 364 Squadron of the 357th Fighter Group [nicknamed "The Yoxford Boys"] was killed in action in a P51 B Mustang on 23rd March 1944.

The story moves on to the summer of 2004- no one remembered a Spitfire crash in or around Codford, it was obvious that the plane crashed somewhere in the downland away from habitation. A story in the local paper, "The Warminster Journal", brought forth a witness able to pinpoint the crash site on a steep hillside to the north of Codford across the parish boundary at Knook. When David Williams wife read the report she told her husband someone was looking for 'his Spitfire'!

In WWII Jack and Blanche Williams lived a 1 Down Barn, Chitterne Ansty with their daughter Bess and their six sons, Ben, Bill, Jim, Jack, David and Harold. The family had moved around following the work, living in tied cottages in the countryside. 1 Down Barn had no running water or electricity, Blanche cooked on an open coal fire or on a three- burner paraffin stove, the boys walked to the Prince Leopold public house in Upton Lovell each week to collect a gallon of lamp oil. During the war years with rationing in force the family lived on a supply of rabbits snared using a wire by their father, Jack Snr sold his surplus to the local butcher 2/- for a small rabbit and 2/6 for a large one.

The Williams's cottage at Chitterne Ansty

Blanche with Harold;
Jack with David

Jack Williams Snr. was a veteran of the trenches in the Great War, he had been seriously wounded at Ypres and still bore the scars of the earlier conflict. In 1943 he worked at the REME workshops, also a Prisoner of War Camp, as a boiler-man. Blanche Williams, like most married women of the time, stayed home to take care of her family, she was a prudent housewife, the family wore old clothes to eke out the clothing coupons while she earned extra income by taking in washing from the American troops stationed in the immediate vicinity.

At the time of the Spitfire crash Jim was serving in the Royal Marine Commando's in Belgium and Holland; Ben was working underground at Corsham for the Ministry of Defence; Bill was working on a farm at Upton Lovell; Bess was living at Woodyates taking care of her grandmother; Jack had just started at Sambourne School in Warminster while the youngest boys David and Harold were at primary school in Heytesbury.

On the afternoon of 6th November 1943 nine year old David Williams was walking along the road with his brothers Jack and Harold, when from the direction of Codford the Spitfire, at full throttle with its engine spitting and spluttering, went straight down into the hill. They saw the pilot bale out and the parachute open, racing towards the crash site they saw an enormous smoking crater, the plane was completely buried by the impact. The military were camped all around the area, it took only minutes for RAF, American military and civilian police to congregate at the site together with a lorry, presumably to collect the plane.

Lt. Humphrey's parachute landed at Lavington, he was picked up and arriving at the scene accosted the youngsters with a cheery "What have you done with my plane boys?" The youngsters were soon shooed away from the crash site as the military congregated on the steep hillside.

On 21st August 2004 David Williams returned to Knook Down with Ian Hodgkiss, Gareth Jones and a metal detector, he unerringly located the spot where the Spitfire had lain hidden beneath the chalk for more than sixty years. Field walking with metal detectors revealed a scattering of random structural remains over an area of approximately 20m diameter. A flux gate magnetometer was employed to locate more deeply buried wreckage, this pinpointed a strong steel reading, suggesting engine remains in the centre and armament remains in the corresponding wing locations. A shallow excavation down to 30cm bore this out with two concentrations of burned and exploded .303 ammunition and magazine components. In the centre a number of fuselage parts were found including fragments of rear frames, part of the door latch mechanism and the gun-firing button. Nodules of once molten aluminium were also found indicating a fierce post crash fire.

The landowner had given permission to excavate, so once the licence was obtained from the RAF the painstaking work to recover the Codford Spitfire could begin. On 10th September 2005 the remains of the Spitfire were excavated using a wheeled JCB digger. The soil at the site consisted of a dark friable topsoil with considerable hard flint deposits of varying sizes extending approx 0.3 meters before giving way to hard chalk. It had been estimated that the nature of the soil it was unlikely that the engine

Cuckoo Pen crash site

Ian, Gareth with metal detector and David Williams

Excavation site

*Work begins; Ian, Gareth and David
Williams*

Part of engine

John Wyeth and Ian

*Romy Wyeth, Andy Webb, Don Bartlett,
Louis Hoareau and Ian Hodgkiss*

and propeller boss would have penetrated more than 2 meters. The area of the wreckage was indicated using a spray marker, laying out the wings and fuselage relative to magnatometer and deep scanning metal detector readings.

A number of pieces of aluminium wing structure and skinning were unearthed, then a deeply buried item at 0.5 meters was found, the steel cannon mounting plate from the wing leading edge. A discovery that interested the excavators was a hole left by the removal of one of the aircrafts guns from the chalk, the vertical hole was the correct diameter for a 20mm Hispano cannon barrel. The remaining 1-meter of the breach of the cannon may well have been sticking out of the ground at the time of the crash and would thus have been easily winched out.

Digging in the center section revealed the remains of the aircraft compressed into a 1.5 meter bowl in the chalk. The most deeply buried item was the DeHavilland three blade propeller boss and final reduction gear. All three aluminium blades had been sheared off at the base. Above and slightly north was the badly distorted compressed Merlin engine crankshaft, with the rear half missing. Alongside and above this were 5 flattened piston liners of the 12 in the engine, as well as the armour plate from the engine oil tank and a number of stainless steel valves and hold down bolts. The chalk above contained a disarticulated assortment of mainly copper, bronze, and ferrous remains. Almost no aluminium structure had survived the impact crater although there was considerable evidence of corrosion.

Having remover the larger items from the crater with the aid of the mechanical digger the spoil heap was searched thoroughly before the site was reinstated- the area around the north wing was not excavated.

The hard chalk had clearly prevented the aircraft from penetrating deeply and the sudden deceleration had caused unusually serious damage to the remains, with even small pieces such as the gun button and starter switches from the instrument panel being heavily deformed. The aircraft clearly burned in the crater, as witnessed by the melting aluminium. This accelerates corrosion in the structure and if fire-fighting foam was used to extinguish the blaze this would have further instigated corrosion in the aluminium alloys. The aluminium pistons had been almost entirely reduced to oxide inside the stainless steel cylinder liners.

The shallow crater would have presented little difficulty to the recovery crew in removing the remains with only the firmly embedded engine parts being abandoned. Large parts such as the tail wheel, cockpit armour plate and undercarriage hydraulics which are often found were not present. Many of the smaller items were probably thrown into the crater when clearing up the field.

Evidence of the aircraft armament was found in the form of mounting brackets for the .303-inch calibre guns and exploded ammunition. No trace of ammunition for the 20mm cannon was found which suggests that none was carried on this training sortie.

Examining pieces of the outer skin shows the aircraft to have been painted in standard dark green, dark grey camouflage with a light grey underside. Some black stencilling was also found but in too small pieces to read.

The conclusions were that the US Airforce were diligent in removing the majority of BM540 at the time of the accident. The vast majority of the aircraft aluminium structure which remained buried in the crater had been degraded or destroyed by corrosion. Fragments which avoided the post crash fire for were less deeply buried have survived much better. There are still quantities of these fragments on the field but they are being dispersed by ploughing. Sufficient wreckage was recovered to allow positive identification of the Spitfire. These can now be preserved.

From such small beginnings, a knock on the door and a tentative inquiry, a journey back into recent history began. In the autumn of 1943 for one brief moment in time, an American pilot and a small local boy met at the site of a Spitfire crash- the pilot may not have survived the conflict, the small boy grew to manhood and never forgot the incident. David Williams has at last told his story; Robert P. Humphrey can only be reached through the accident and military records available; the Spitfire resurrection focused on one small pinprick of eternity and has ensured that in some way their meeting will be encapsulated beyond both their lifetimes.

Sources
Craig Fuller: Aviation Archaeological Investigation & Research, Falcon Field, Mesa, Arizona.
Ian Hodgekiss
Gareth Jones
Christopher Green
Tim Woods
David Williams

For technical details 'Excavation of Spitfire BM540., East Farm, Knook, Wilts September 2005.' Compiled by Ian Hodgkiss MA, Beng, PGCE for the Marches Aviation Society.

Olympic wrestler

15

The Oldest Living Commando

Stanley John Bissell, known to his family and friends by the nickname given him by his older sister Leah, as 'Sonnie,' was born on 26th October 1906 in Dulwich, South London in a city of 4.5 million people. His first birthday saw the establishment of the Territorial Army; he was two when London hosted the Olympic games, and eight when the first Zeppelin attack on London took place.

Stan was a remarkable man, who bought a cottage in Cheapside, Codford from Mrs Lock in 1964, living there full time after finally retiring for the second time from the Metropolitan Police in 1975, remaining in the cottage until his death on Saturday 2nd January, 1999. His life story spans almost the whole of the twentieth century reading like a film script, an all round sportsman, Olympic athlete, police officer and, at the time of his death, the oldest surviving wartime Commando.

"On looking back at my early childhood days it would appear that there were several motivating forces in my life which helped to shape it's course. Unfortunately, I lost my father when I was two years old; this meant that I missed the male influence of family life in the early days of my childhood. It also, very much, affected our standard of living, we were at workhouse level! My mother, although frail, kept us by scrubbing the local church hall floor and everything else of similar need. The proceeds enabled the family to rent a small upstairs flat, consisting of two bedrooms and a kitchen, in Pilkington Road, Peckham. I lived with my mother who was christened Alice, and my sister Leah, who was three years older than me. Presumably our previous address was Bawdale Road, Dulwich where I was born.

Both Leah and myself attended a small church school, St. Mary Magdalene, which was opposite where we lived and across from the local church, of which my mother was a staunch member. As a child most of my spare time was spent playing in the street, which was my playground, football in the road and cricket with the iron base of a lamp standard as the wicket. We were often chased, but never caught, by the local policeman.

I was an avid reader of most sporting news plus adventure novels of a military nature. A hero of mine was the Russian George Hackenschmidt, a professional wrestler who toured the world on the stage and in the wrestling ring. In no way should he be linked with the present day set up of farcical wrestling 'professionals!' A long article written by him was published in the Times, he had written several books on wrestling and 'Way To Live,' and was considered to be a great philosopher.

My interest in wrestling, was thus, well stimulated and established. In those early days I had little idea that subsequently he would become my good friend and wrestle in my gym at the age of seventy. We remained firm friends until he passed on at the age of ninety. The interest having been well established I was naturally one of the first volunteers for a class at scouts which was run by 1908 World Champion wrestler Stan Bacon. He was the eldest of three brothers, his siblings were Ernie and Edgar, all very famous wrestlers, I beat the latter when he retired injured at an elimination trial for the 1930 British Empire Games in Hamilton, Canada.

I was greatly encouraged and influenced towards gymnastics by visiting an open-air playground in Peckham Rye Park. It was a small area of fixed apparatus set on a solid base. It consisted of parallel bars, a horizontal bar, a hand swing for about six and a few other items. As a youngster I visited the gym whenever I could, which was mainly in the evening. There was no instructor, but one night a man visited and performed a variety of exercises on the horizontal bar, which included long arms on the parallel bars. Cheekily I went up to him when he had finished and said "Will you teach me that guvnor?" From that day Frank [Stormy] Nash became a father to me. He taught me various tricks and also introduced me to a scout troop in the Arches, Albert Road, which I subsequently joined. Stormy was an engineer in the Navy, he introduced me to an open-air life, and took me to camp on the back of a Calthorpe motorcycle. Eventually I secured a cycle and joined the rest of the scouts at their various camps. When I reached the age of fourteen I became an assistant gym instructor to Stormy and we visited three scout troops. My interest in gymnastics thus became firmly established, as was the urge to help others. Eventually I joined the Regent Street Polytechnic and another leading gymnastic club."

Stan was nine years old when he joined the 34th Camberwell Scout troop, by this time his ambition was to emulate his hero's and to wrestle. Meanwhile his religious education was being addressed, on April 15th 1917, aged eleven, young Stanley Bissell signed the Gospel Temperance Pledge promising with Divine Assistance to abstain from all Intoxicating Liquors as beverages, and to encourage others to do the same. He appears to have attended the Reverend Ernest Thorn's Great Popular Meetings at the Church of Strangers, High Street, Peckham. In the following three years he passed a creditable examination in Religious Subjects while at St Mary Magdalene School, Peckham, receiving a certificate from the Diocese of Southwark.

The family stayed in Peckham until around 1932, when Leah obtained a job at County Hall. Before joining the Metropolitan Police in 1926, Stan had worked for six years as a mortuary attendant in the Pathology Departments of the Charing Cross and Bromham Hospitals.

When Stan met Helen Sirett is uncertain. It may be that they met in Peckham in their teens or possibly earlier, Maurice Cole has a vague memory that they could have been introduced when Stan was a young PC and Helen worked in his area, perhaps in a theatre. Their eldest son Geoff remembers his mother saying her mum thought that Stan was a bit of a cheeky young lad, not to his detriment but rather admiringly. They married at Camberwell Parish Church on 4th April 1931, Geoff was born in 1934 and Denis in 1948.

Around 1931 Stan was selected as a self-defence instructor at Peel House training school for police recruits. He taught 'police holds' and various methods of arrest, consisting of a set pattern of about thirty methods of detention and self-defence. Stan's syllabus of self-defence consisted of around thirty odd half-hourly periods, with the self-defence taught in the latter few periods. He preferred the terms 'hammer-lock and bar and wrist locks' to 'police holds.'

"Although during my working life- war service apart- the uniform which I have worn has been blue and not khaki, I must at the outset 'come clean' and confess that I have been an intermittent attender at the Army School of Physical Training at Queen's Avenue, Aldershot since approximately 1930/31. The School was therefore no stranger to me, nor was it when I came to the Corps during the last war from the Commando Basic Training Centre at Achnacarry near Fort William in Invernesshire, Scotland, where I served as a staff instructor. The forging of this link was a great thrill to me, as I have always held the Army School of Physical Training in great esteem; indeed if my home circumstances had been different, I would undoubtedly have joined the Army with the hope of 'making' the School of PT.

As it was, on 1st March 1926, I joined the Metropolitan Police and entered Peel House, the recruitment-training centre at Regency Street, Westminster. After passing out and serving as a police constable in 'N' & 'P' divisions, I applied for the post of 'self-defence' instructor on the staff at Peel House. Competition for the post was keen, one of my chief opponents being a 1st Dan [black belt] judo exponent. I knew nothing of self-defence and my only claim to fame was that I had just returned from the Canadian British Empire Games where I had managed to obtain a silver medal in the middleweight freestyle-wrestling event. At the same time I was left in no doubt by the then Superintendent George Abbiss [the late Sir George Abbiss, Assistant Commissioner 'D' Dept.] that a condition of my appointment was that I must earn my judo black belt 1st Dan, which in those days was considered as being the instructor's qualification, and that I must also pass my sergeants' examination; apparently no one of constable rank had ever before been appointed as an instructor at the training school. This I promised to undertake.

In the event the post proved to be one where I was also expected to stand in for physical training and foot-drill classes when other instructors were away sick or absent for other reasons like annual or weekly leave. Because of this required qualification I was sent to the Army School of PT for a two weeks initial PT course and was housed in the old Hammersley Barracks in one of the staff bedrooms at the end of the dormitory. This was my initial course and the primary purpose of my instructor was to see that I got enough P.T. leadership training and theory. Most evenings I attended voluntary gymnastics and recreation.

After attending this first course, which left a lasting impression on me, I realised that two weeks were all too short to consider myself a physical training instructor. Happily, however I was no newcomer to gymnastics as I had been running three youth clubs and was also a member of the Herne Hill Harriers and Orion Gymnastic Club. I became a member of Herne Hill after having won my first novices' one mile race at Herne Hill track and having been presented with the 'News of the World' silver medal by Joe Binks.

On looking back over these years I think I was probably better qualified in the physical training field than I was in that of self-defence. Then followed two years of hard 'slogging' at the Budokwai Judo Club where I qualified as a 1st Dan [black belt] under the late G. Koizumi. He was a great teacher and friend and founder of judo in this country. I often wish that G.K. could be alive today and see the progress made in the sport of judo in the Olympic games and internationally. Maybe we shall see judo included in the Commonwealth Games, but I sincerely trust not at the expense of my first love, which is free-style wrestling. Over the years I have watched with interest the progress made in judo in the army. The initial courses, I believe, were started by that enthusiastic judo exponent C.S.M.I. Mitchell at the Army Physical Training School. I last saw him in Munich at the Olympic games when Dave Starbrook won a silver medal. He was a judo international judge and officiating.

Following the initial course at Aldershot I felt there should be some follow up in the shape of refresher courses. On my return to Peel House I discussed the matter   with the physical training instructor, twice Olympic undefeated middleweight boxing champion, the late Harry Mallin. We both agreed it was desirable that there should be regular refresher courses, ideally every two or three years, held at the Army School of PT for Police instructors at Peel House. This is how I kept in touch over the years with the ASPT and remained abreast of various changes in the physical education system. By way of a bonus I was also able to make and renew friendships struck up whilst on courses. I remember with affection my old friend 'Dusty' Miller and the martinets of those days who maintained discipline of the highest order; the school of PT was never the home of weaklings! I was determined that, when the opportunity arose, I would recommend the Assistant Instructors' short and long PT courses for our own training school staff and this, I am glad to say is what now happens!"

On 21st November 1932, Stan was promoted to Sergeant. He took part in the European Championships at Stockholm in 1934, becoming very aware of the growing militancy of the German team and convinced that war was coming.

In a letter to the 'Police Review' Colonel C. E. Vaughan wrote on the birth of the

Self Defence Inctructor, Metropolitan Police, 1930s

Sergt. S. J. BISSELL
(Self Defence Instructor Metro. Police.)
National C. as C. C. Champion.
Middleweight 1930-34. Lightheavy 1934. Heavyweight 1932-33.
Runner up British Empire Games 1930-34 (Canada and Wembley.)
Represented England European Championships
Brussels, Stockholm, Paris.
Metro. Police Champion. Heavy 1935. Middle 1936.
P.A.A. Heavyweight Champion 1936.
Judo (Black Belt. 1st Dan.) Captain Baron Matsui Cup Team 1936.
Metropolitan Challenge Shield 1934.

Sergt. S. J. BISSELL
(Self Defence Instructor Metro. Police.)
National C. as C. C. Champion.
Middleweight 1930-34. Lightheavy 1934. Heavyweight 1932-33.
Runner up British Empire Games 1930-34 (Canada and Wembley.)
Represented England European Championships
Brussels, Stockholm, Paris.
Metro. Police Champion. Heavy 1935. Middle 1936.
P.A.A. Heavyweight Champion 1936.
Judo (Black Belt. 1st Dan.) Captain Baron Matsui Cup Team 1936.
Metropolitan Challenge Shield 1934.

Winning streak, 1930s

ASHDOWN ATHLETIC CLUB

Affiliated to the National Amateur Wrestling Association and Middlesex
County Amateur Wrestling Association.

— IN CONNECTION —

ALL SAINTS' MISSION, 90, White Lion Street, Angel, Pentonville, London, N.1

Chairman - Rev. A. LLEWELLYN-DAVIES

The following Catch-as-Catch-Can

WRESTLING COMPETITIONS

OPEN TO ALL AMATEURS

will be held at Headquarters on

TUESDAY, FEBRUARY 21st, 1933

Novices 9st. 7lbs. **Open 10st.**

ENTRY FEES—**2/-** each event;

Two Prizes in each event in which SIX compete

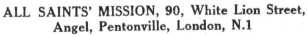 *Entries close first post Thursday, February 16th, 1933*

SPECIAL MATCH best two of three falls.

S. J. BISSELL v. R. COOK,

(P. Div. Metropolitan Police)	(Ashdown Athletic Club)
Middle-Weight Champion 1930.	Light Heavy-Weight Champion 1931-32
Runner-up British Empire Games 1930	Olympic Representative Amsterdam 1928
Represented Great Britain in European	Welter-Weight Champion 1928
Championship	International v. France & Belgium

SPECIAL NOTES TO COMPETITORS:—

Entries will not be accepted after the time stated above.
Entries will not be accepted without fees.
Competitors will only be allowed to compete in the weights
for which they have entered.
Competitors not answering their names at the times advised
for weighing in will be scratched.
The right is reserved to postpone or cancel any event that
may be found necessary.

Reserved Seat, 10/6 & 5/-; Unreserved, **2/4 & 1/6** (inclusive)

(THE RIGHT OF ADMISSION RESERVED)

Tickets, Entry Forms and full particulars from

Hon. Sec.: GEO. MACKENZIE, 60, Calabria Road, Highbury, N.5.

Doors open 7 p.m. Commence 7.30 prompt.

LADIES SPECIALLY INVITED.

PLEASE NOTE:—The National Championships, all weights,
will be held at Lambeth Baths, on SATURDAY, MARCH 18th 1933.

RANKIN & SON, Printers (T.U.), 370, Upper Street, N.1

Ashdown Athletic Club programme, February 21st, 1933

Police Commandos, reprinted later in the WALK TALL column. "It was early in 1942 that Brigadier Charles Haydon, who was then in command of the Commandos, met the Metropolitan Police Commissioner, Sir Philip Game, in London, and asked whether the Police should be allowed to volunteer for a force which was something new to the Army; and well indeed did they respond to this appeal.

The spearhead of the volunteers was none other than a person named Sonnie Bissell-seven times national wrestling champion and Black Belt [1st Dan], physical training and self-defence instructor at the Metropolitan Police Training School. Well do I remember this chap. He reported to me at Achnacarry in a blue suit. Complete with his bowler hat and small case. My first impression of him caused his immediate promotion to Staff Sergeant instructor. Following on the heels of this forerunner, in the volunteers from the Police Force came: on 24th June 1942-68 volunteers; on 22nd July 1942-273 volunteers; and on 15th October 1942- 84 volunteers; making a total of 426 of the finest material that I ever had to deal with in all my soldiering."

Stan's police records show he joined HM Forces on 9th June 1942, re-joining the Metropolitan Police Force on 18th August 1945. It appears that during his period in the forces, on 30th May 1943 he was promoted to the rank of Station Sergeant.

For just over three years during World War II, after qualifying as an Army Physical Training Instructor at Aldershot, Stan taught the Commandos close combat fighting at Achnacarry in Scotland, which had been taken over for Commando Basic Training in 1942. Some of the best and the bravest men from regiments all across Britain were to join the elite regiment, these were young, supremely fit soldiers. Stan at thirty-five years old, in a wartime training film to encourage soldiers to join the Commandos, is seen moving like a great panther, unerringly dealing with attack from every side.

On 5th July 1993 while recovering from a stroke, Stan wrote a letter to David L. Kentner. "Police were protected until that time, at my age when I was allowed to volunteer. I was a Royal Fusilier for about one day when I asked to join the newly formed Commandos and was sent to the Commando Basic Training Centre [CBTC], Achnacarry, Invernesshire, near Fort William in Scotland. Here I met the Commander Charles Vaughan. He promoted me to Sgt. Instructor on the PT staff.

The CO told me that he had taken over the Commandos and that they were now Army Commandos with a new syllabus of training. He wanted me to look at the 'unarmed combat' being taught. I found this was mainly based on Fairbairn & Sykes book of self-defence. Reading it I decided it was too complicated to instil techniques of attack and defence into the minds of Commando recruits on a six-week training course. The CO agreed on the syllabus being changed. It was agreed in the time available complicated techniques could not be taught. I then set up a six week syllabus of what I termed 'direct attacks', these were simple and direct and ones that could be allied with normal training. Eventually this was called 'close combat.' One must realise that due to war conditions re: secrecy, very little was committed to paper and photos were out!

1943-44 I did go to the Army School of PT on a course. There I was asked to sit in on a meeting re: the self-defence syllabus with, I believe, the Chief Instructor and

Commando, 1942-1945

Army School of Physical Training, Aldershot, 1944. Stan is in the centre of the back row

Army School of Physical Training, Aldershot, 1944.

another to discuss our Commando 'close combat.' Various changes were made and 'unarmed combat' came into being. My memory is not what it was, and I hope this is right!"

Lt. Colonel [Retired] Alan Peckham, late Commando, vividly remembers his training with 'the master.' In a letter written shortly after Stan's death he says:

"I only knew Sonny for the duration of the six weeks Commando Course at Achnacarry in 1944. Although our meeting was brief he made a tremendous impact on me as he did on all the young officers on the course; and the 'impact' was in more ways than one. He was the unarmed combat instructor and from time to time one was given a bayonet, a rifle and bayonet or a pickaxe handle and invited to inflict as much damage as possible on a completely unarmed Sonny. Invariably, after charging at him, one finished up sailing through the air landing flat on one's back some yards away without being at all sure how one got there, with a beaming Sonny standing and looking at you and asking if you would care to have another try!

Although by then in his late thirties, he was supremely fit and marvellously well co-ordinated. He was a great man and it is my regret that I did not meet up with him after the war."

Stan took part in almost every sport; he was seven times National Free Style Wrestling Champion of Great Britain. He always felt that he was in peak condition for the 1936 Olympics at Munich, he beat both the medal winners before the Games, but had flu when the trials took place and so been unable to qualify. He was selected to compete in the middleweight Greco-Roman wrestling at the 1948 Wembley Olympics; he believed that although at forty-two he was physically very fit, he was past his best. His memories were of the good comradeship amongst the participants, and the fact there were no leotards at this time so wrestling costumes were worn, but little else.

He founded the Metropolitan Police Wrestling Club, was a runner who competed in the cross country, the half mile and the mile, and a long distance road race walker. As a boxer he took part in boxing finals at the Albert Hall, he was also a 2nd Dan Black Belt in Judo-the highest qualification outside Japan.

"In 1945 I returned from the commando camp at Achnacarry and helped to open up the recruit training school at Peel House. Having already passed my inspector rank examination and been promoted in my absence to station sergeant, it was not long [31st May 1948] before I was again promoted to the inspector grade in charge of the physical training and recreation at both Peel House and Hendon recruit training schools. It was at this time that a very strong liaison was formed with Major [Retd.] T.L. Fletcher. This liaison was carried on when Lieut. Colonel B.M. Consitt [Retd.] took over the secretary-ship of the APT Corps. Association, and happily it continued with Major D.B. McBain MBE"

Commando Memorial, 1997

Commando Special Services Brigade Chirstmas card

WHO'S WHO IN THE SHOW

JUDO

NO show of Physical Recreation is complete without a spot of fun, especially when there's a moral behind it. The demonstration to-day of Woman v. Bandit shows how the gentler sex skilled in the art of Judo can defend itself against attack. By kind permission of the Budokwai we present Cheerful **Ted Mossom,** one of the finest judo exponents in Europe.

The demure lady is played by **Mary Hobbs,** First Ruffian by **Stan Bissell** and **J. Robertson** provides the second assault. Stan is a Black Belt 1st Dan, International Wrestling Champion 1946, British Light-heavyweight Champion 1939. Jack is a Brown Belt holder.

Picture shows Ted Mossom throwing Stan Bissell in one of the many delightful and instructive exhibitions given recently.

Olympic display programme, London Palladium, 29th May, 1948

Metropolitan Police Officer

201

In a letter dated 21st July 1953 Stan writes: "You have probably heard from Leah that I was in this years Coronation Honours List, being awarded the BEM. I am enclosing a cutting from the Police Review. You may not recognise my photo, as it was taken some years ago. I have been 'ribbed' enough about it all the time at the school."

Stan retired on 30th November 1955 at the age of forty-nine having served for twenty-nine years and nine months. His monthly pay as an Inspector on retirement was £74. 11s. 4d. When he retired from the Police Force in George Whiting's column of the of December 3rd 1955 Evening Standard headlined:

LONDON LOSES ITS TOUGHEST POLICEMAN.
ATHLETE, WRESTLER, CYCLIST, CRICKETER,
ANGLER, BOXER, FOOTBALLER, CLIMBER.

London's toughest policeman handed in his warrant card and ceremonial helmet this week. Inspector Stanley J. Bissell, having preached the gospel of sport to generations of policemen, Commandos and juvenile delinquents for nearly a quarter of a century, has packed his wife, younger son, gum boots and presentation oil lamp into the family motorcycle combination and hit the road for cabbages and cricket in Stourton Caundle, Dorset. Grey-eyed, close-cropped "Sonny" Bissell has ended his 29 years of constabulary service and his 24 years as officer-in-charge of physical recreation at the police training schools at Hendon and Peel House, Westminster.

Game to the last. With every adjacent policeman from Commissioner to constable popping in to wish him a rosy retirement at 49, Bissell spent his last working hours answering telephone calls about the amateur status of a wrestler, the whereabouts of somebody's soccer boots, and the health of a Divisional rugby pack.

Known to sport as a seven-times national wrestling champion, Bissell has taught, trained, organised and competed against the top men of nearly every game in the calendar. It was with the considerable respect of an all time rabbit, therefore, that I listened to his opinions of the present scene of athletic endeavour in these tight little islands. "The way things are going," said this sporting Pooh Bah, "there will soon be no real amateur sport left in this country-only big business. Give me champions if you like, but not automatons. For my money, a hundred men running a mile in five minutes is a darn sight healthier than than one man running it in four.

There is too much pot hunting and job-hunting in amateur sport these days, mores the pity. I sometimes think we are tending to professionalise our games for the sake of the result. We British used to be recognised as the kind of sportsmen who played for the sake of the game and had a good laugh afterwards. If ever we lose that reputation, then we have lost everything."

Pious clap-trap? Not at all. This Bissell man has every right to talk any way he pleases when it comes to sport. Raised in Dulwich by a widowed mother on

National Assistance, he could probably have become a professional at any one of at least a dozen games. Instead he began his working life helping to cut up bodies in the post-mortem department at Bromham Hospital, and joined the police in 1926 as the only conceivable means of enjoying sport without jeopardising the well being of either his mother or his sister.

At the hawk-eyed age of ten, Bissell saw a bunch of gymnasts doing handsprings in a park in Peckham, demanded instruction, decided on the spot that anything they could do he could do better- and has been proving it ever since. At wrestling, in addition to his seven titles, he performed as a middle-weight for England in two Empire Games finals, turned reluctantly from free-style to Graeco-Roman in the 1948 Olympics, and wrestled in international matches in nearly every country in Europe.

"Never had a scratch" says Bissell "except when I got thrown on my head and nearly broke my neck at Lambeth Baths. Funny thing, I went on to the final and won the competition without remembering a thing about it. Concussion, they said."

Mention any sport and you will find that ex-Inspector Bissell has participated with serious intent and considerable distinction since he won his first silver medal for a five-minute mile at Herne Hill. After gymnastics and athletics, came long distance cycling, then the wrestling which was to make him a known and respected opponent on the mats of half the world.

He has walked from London to Brighton twice and from Barking to Southend ten times. Taken three wickets for eight runs with his medium-paced off-breaks at the Oval. Propped up the hooker in many a rugby scrum for the Commandos. Boxed for a coveted Lafone trophy as a cruiserweight. Played badminton in the Middlesex League. Performed with represen-tative match distinction at lawn tennis, table tennis, soccer [right-back], billiards, basket-ball [top scorer for his side only a day or two ago], and hockey [outside-right]. Beagled with the South Herts. Achieved his Black Belt at Judo and his life-saving medallion at swimming. Climbed Ben Nevis.

Southend walk, 1st September, 1955

Caught salmon in and sailed a boat on the Scottish Lochs. Camped, motored and motor cycled in most of the counties of Britain.

Add three years of rope climbing, unarmed combat, bayonet drill and militarily legalised mayhem as a staff-sergeant instructor of Commandos during the war…then concede that Stanley Bissell has put up a pretty good show of sporting versatility.

Yet it is not as a practitioner that this tough-fibred but soft-voiced London bobby would wish to be known. Nor does he particularly like to be reminded of the time he brought in three belligerent and slightly tipsy Irishmen who thought it was fun to roughhouse a Home Guard during a wartime black-out.

No Sonny Bissell, up to his knees in Dorset mud from now on, would sooner we remember him as a pioneer, a teacher, an organiser, and an unashamed protagonist of sport for sports sake. It was for such endeavours that they gave him the British Empire Medal two years ago.

If there are any non-sporting policemen, any un-neighbourly villagers, or juvenile delinquents in Stourton Caundle, they had best look out. Ex-Inspector Bissell will have them carrying the Olympic torch come lambing time.

Dorset was unable to contain Stan for very long- the wide-open spaces and fresh challenges tempted him to leave England. Stan, Helen and Denis were at Stourton Caundle for about six months, while Geoff was in his last year at Southampton. Geoff recalls that the offer of a position came through Fred Oberlander, a Jewish businessman and wrestler who had known Stan for many years. "Dad and I went out first and then as far as I recall Helen and Denis followed later. We went to Montreal in July 1956, I remember the ship stopping in the St Lawrence at Quebec City just past midnight and having enough time to climb up the famous Heights of Abraham, walk along the boardwalk and have an ice cream. After a year Mum and Denis went back to England, Dad stayed on another couple of years and I went off to Vancouver."

Stan takes up the story, "Canada beckoned in the shape of the offer of a post with the Young Men & Young Women's Hebrew Association as an Assistant Director of PE at their headquarters in Montreal. During the time I was there it was possible for me to build up various sections, including wrestling, boxing, judo, golf, tennis, and athletics. The most popular activities that I was able to develop were in the keep-fit area for both sexes and all ages. The Free movement exercises were held to piano music. There were morning, afternoon and evening classes for men, women and teenagers. Children's classes were usually held on Sunday mornings or afternoons. The 'Y' had a very large membership of families so that one became quite deeply involved. Housewives attended gymnasium during the mornings and afternoons. Husbands, who were mainly professional engineers, architects and businessmen, attended each afternoon. On selected evenings classes were organised for teenagers who were also very much concerned with fitness and dance movement. Numbers in the classes varied from 30-80, and every effort was made to encourage them to undertake a games activity such as badminton or volleyball. Softball, skating, tennis and golf were very popular.

During the time I was in Montreal I was able to stimulate a Mountain Activities group for hill walking/ scrambling and camping in the Laurentians and Adirondaks. Regular cross-country runs were held over the Mont of Montreal [Mount Royal]. Gymnastics and athletics were not very popular activities at the 'Y', but one must remember there was ample scope for skiing and skating in the Canadian winter. The health club, sauna/steam and swimming facilities were exceptional. Also whilst in Canada I became a member of the Canadian Black Belt Association as 2nd Dan and competed for the Seido Khan Judo Club."

On his return to England in 1960 he became the first Director for the newly established Police Cadets at Hendon College. A report from the *Daily Mirror* dated 17th June 1960 headlined THEY'RE TOUGH AT THE TOP announces his latest challenge:

Two remarkable men will get together next month to organise the new police cadet school due to open at Hendon in October. They are the "headmaster," Colonel N. A. C. Croft, DSO, MA, and his chief assistant, ex-police inspector Stanley Bissell. Col Croft commanded the 'Balaclava Mission,' a wartime undercover group that operated on the French Island of Corsica. His task was to land Allied agents in France and Italy, and then to get them safely out. The determination and strength of Colonel Croft was a byword with his men. He has also taken part in many expeditions to the Arctic.

"Stan" Bissell served thirty years in the Metropolitan Police, and for most of that time he taught unarmed combat and was in charge of physical education. He was a champion wrestler and has represented Britain in the Olympics and two Empire Games.

This combination of leadership and fitness should produce some superb new policemen.

One of these young men was Denis Garvey. "One of Stan's main sporting events was wrestling, it was also mine, which I continued to do on joining the police in 1958. He was also Director of PE for cadets at Hendon in the early 60's and I joined his staff in 1964. In those days our wrestling practice took place at Elliot House, just off Edgeware Road, London where other well-known characters attended, Tommy Baldwin, Alf Jacobs, Frank Dodds etc. I didn't have a car then so Stan would take me in his. Although I was much younger, stronger and maybe fitter than he was, we used to wrestle and it was always difficult to 'pin' him to the ground. He had a way of interlocking his legs around his opponent and was difficult to shake off.

Because of my job at Hendon Stan sent me on a PE course for three months with the Army at Aldershot for which I was always grateful, it stood me in good stead and was useful to me throughout the rest of my service. During the course at Aldershot he would come and pick me up and drive me home at weekends.

Cadets also had to attend weekend, and at times a fortnights camp involving outdoor activity such as assault course, rope climbing etc. Stan could always demonstrate what

Police cadets, Devizes to Westminster Canoe Race, 1960s. Stan centre of back row.

With Stewart Granger in Gainsborough 'Caravan', 1946

the technique of a particular subject was!"

"The cadets joined at 16 plus and remained in a boarding school type of establishment until they were 19 years of age. They were then eligible to join the regular force after undergoing a further three months of adult training."

Stan was responsible for the next five years for 40% of the cadet training, as well as self-defence he led canoeing expeditions, and introduced mountain climbing to the curriculum, establishing two mountain climbing centres in Wales.

His expertise was such that it was even sought by Hollywood stars. He coached Michael Rennie, Stewart Granger and Katherine Hepburn among others the correct way to throw their opponents in the movies. He showed Stewart Granger how to throw a villain off a cliff for the Gainsborough production of 'Caravan' and responded to Miss Hepburn's frantic phone call for help while she was filming 'The Millionairess.' En route to a formal dinner engagement, Stan arrived in his tuxedo and spent part of his evening being held in a stranglehold and thrown across the room by the glamorous actress until she was confident of her role as a judo expert.

The decision to buy a home in Codford was due to local and distant family connections. The Cole family settled in Codford in 1919, Harry and Lillian Cole were Londoners; Harry arrived in the area in the Great War, building pumping stations for the Army camps. The relationship is tenuous, a shared ancestor Hugh Fraser known as Tom, married twice. Leah Bissell's husband was Tom's grandson, his mother was Emma Fraser, the eldest of three children from the first marriage; Lillian Cole was one of the seven children of Tom's second marriage. Stan's brother-in-law's grandfather was Lillian Coles father, making the Coles and the Bissell's cousins by marriage. The families were close and visited often; no doubt it was local knowledge that discovered that the cottage by the Chitterne Brook owned by Mrs Lock was up for sale. Denis says when the family arrived in 1964 they immediately built an extension, adding a kitchen and bathroom at the northern end nearest the Ron Sutton's cottage. Ron and Stan's friendship remained to the end of Stan's life. Until Stan eventually retired the family lived in London during the week, returning to Codford at weekends.

The Bissell family moved around a great deal during Stan's varied career opportunities. Denis explained the chronology of his early years. "When I was born in 1948 we lived in police accommodation at Peel House, the original training centre in Westminster that preceded Hendon training school. In 1956 when he retired with thirty years service we moved to a farm in Tarrant Gunville, Dorset, we lived in a bungalow that had no electricity, hence my collection of Tilley lamps in the garage. I remember we kept chickens and bantams, and I was allowed to choose my first and only dog from a litter of pups. I chose the one I liked the look of, the farmer said he was the runt of the litter but I did not change my mind. We quickly became very attached to 'Toby.'

My father got itchy feet and had the offer to go to Canada, the YMHA in Montreal was a very big site, not at all like the small YMCA in the UK. He and Geoff went out first to establish a base and get settled in an apartment, Mum and I moved in about September 1957, I think Geoff moved to Vancouver just before we got there. Mum couldn't settle, missed her family and didn't like the intensely cold winter. She and I came back in about September 1957 and stayed, I think, with Godfrey Cole until Mum got a job and cottage in Tarrant Gunville, near Blandford. We stayed until June 1958 when we went back to give it another try in Canada. All the journeys at this time to Canada of course were by ship and that meant lots of adventures for me. Liverpool via Greenock across the Atlantic and up the St Lawrence River to Montreal.

After another ten months, in May 1959, we all came home together, dad got a job as an entertainments manager in a Cornish holiday camp, after seeing the job advertised in the Times while travelling back from Liverpool. This lasted the season then we came to Codford when Dad got a job running three youth clubs, at Amesbury, Durrington and Shrewton, for Wiltshire County Council. We then moved in the spring of 1960 to a house we rented in the New Forest at Hale Green. When the job as Director of Physical Education in the newly formed Police Cadet Corps came up we moved to Hendon in about August 1960 into a police house on the site. It was here I spent the longest period of childhood, up to the age of sixteen. From being born in Westminster in 1948 I attended ten schools, Westminster, Stourton Caudle, Montreal, Tarrant Gunville, Montreal, Downderry, Warminster [approx August 1959-March 1960], Fordingbridge and Hendon. I seem to have spent most of the late 1960's travelling to Codford each weekend."

In 1975 when Stan retired again, after forty-five years in the Met, he moving permanently to rural Wiltshire, settling in Codford and becoming actively involved in village life. His cottage garden led down to the chalk water stream, the Chitterne Brook. "The Brook carried a large number of trout, and a favourite practice was that of tickling trout underneath the bank and scooping it out. In my early days in Codford and rather naïve, I was instrumental in what I later found out to be poaching. A certain person had constructed a very large barrel of chicken wire that had one closed and one open end. A further barrel was made which rotated inside the original, but was not fully circular. Being half the diameter it was made to circulate, when worked by hand it trapped any fish that swam into it. The trap was fixed across the Brook, a fact I was unaware of until many months later.

My part in the affair was that occasionally I was asked to walk up the stream; some excuse was made which I can't remember. The whole point was that walking in the middle of the stream drove the trout up into the trap. As they swam into the chicken wire trap the rotating part would be pulled round thus preventing the trout from escaping. Anything up to a dozen trout could be caught in this way."

It was in the mid to late 1970's that I first met Stan who lived across the road and down the lane from the Police Station. He was supposedly in his old age, certainly seventy but still fitter than many a youth, a tall, upright crew-cutted figure striding or cycling on his way. He very much approved of my husband, John, a serving police officer who had been a police cadet and was a life long Scout working with the teenage Venture Units. He and I also became good friends- Stan reminded me of my beloved grandfather; he was seven years younger but the same generation, very much a man's man, someone who respected people who stood their ground. He had a wide circle of friends all across the world, and I was frequently summoned to meet visitors and take

Cross country in the 1960s

Royal Visit to Hendon Gymnasium, late 1960s. Photo
Hendon Times

20-mile hike, 10th July, 1971

them to see the local sites. I was adopted into the Bissell circle, meeting the family members, his niece Linda, who lived in Canada, with her children Christopher & Colleen, and his two sons, London based Denis and Geoff, with his wife Shirley and daughter Karen from Auckland, New Zealand.

Stan's thirst for life and passionate interest in everything and everyone around him never faltered. He cycled and taught tennis to the local youngsters. After the death of his wife Helen in 1988 he continued to support local activities, which included theatre visits, coach trips, gardening club outings, attending Evergreen Club meetings, and, almost to the end of his life he went on day trips with a group of male friends-usually Ron Sutton, Jim Hunter and the Reverend John Tipping, very much 'Last of the Summer Wine.' John Tipping explains " It all started at the Codford Evergreen Club in March 1994. Danny Howell the local historian had come to give a talk and spoke in glowing terms about the County Records Office in Trowbridge. He told us it would be well worth a visit. The outcome of this was to see Ron, Jim, Stan and myself all in Jim's car going one March morning to Trowbridge where we spent a couple of hours in the Records Office, and a fascinating place it was. As we came away we were drawn to have lunch at the Lamb, which was very near the Office. As I recall there was a special offer for Old Age Pensioners- so we all had fish and chips-a menu that was to feature prominently in our subsequent outings. We enjoyed the meal and I was expecting that we would return home. The suggestion was made that we go for a ride – on we went I can't remember exactly where, except that we ended up for tea at Lacock, with some lovely fruitcake in a café that had an affinity for cats.- ornamental or real, I can't remember. I do remember the village was rather crowded as a big funeral was taking place! Even after this we didn't go home- I have recollections of going through Calne and Devizes. We got home about 4.50pm with a strong desire to do this sort of thing again- so was born the idea that reminded us of the TV programme 'Last of the Summer Wine' and even associated our different members with the TV personalities!"

Stan's with Reverend John Tipping at his 90th birthday party

The nucleus of the group was Stan Bissell, John Tipping and Jim Hunter, with Ron's place occasionally being taken by Ken from Warminster and once by Norman Bennett. The groups adventures took them to the Cotswolds, the seaside and the Isle of Wight, they visited military museums, abbeys and railways. There was a thirst for new experience and an appetite for wholesome food.

Stan was a keen photographer, mastered the intricacies of microwave cookery, wrote long letters to friends and newspapers on his typewriter, and at eighty-nine he enrolled in a beginners French class, [where he quickly became the 'teacher's pet'] so as to be able to converse with his adored tri-lingual grand daughter Karen who was living in Paris.

At the age of eighty-five Stan was among 860 British Olympians to receive a special Olympic Badge as part of Manchester 2000 for taking part in the 1948 London Games. In 1995 he proudly wore his dark green beret in the street parade to mark Codford' celebration of fiftieth anniversary of V.E. Day.

Stan exercised every day of his life, until his stroke in his mid-eighties he was still doing 100 push-ups each morning. As his health deteriorated he continued to work out as much as possible, buying himself a walking and a rowing machine and strengthening his upper body by chair push-ups. He was fiercely independent; attempting to garden despite the fact his legs were no longer able to hold him without support.

Scotland, 1997

Before he died Stan took a camper van trip with his son Denis and granddaughter Karen to visit his old wartime haunts in Scotland, the Great Glen, Spean Bridge and Achnacarry. He lived his life to the full, to quote from Tennyson's 'Ulysses': "I cannot rest from travel: I will drink life to the lees: All times I have enjoyed greatly: Both with those that loved me, and alone: I am a part of all that I have met; Yet all experience is an arch wherethro' Gleams that untravell'd world, whose margins fade for ever and ever when I move."

His philosophy was that a man should be given the opportunity to take part in a variety of sporting activities. He did not set out to produce champions but to help each man find himself and discover his potential and his weaknesses.

Stan died in Salisbury General Hospital on 2nd January 1999 aged ninety-two. At his funeral there were five life members of the Metropolitan Police Athletic Association, an honour given to those who had given a lifetime of outstanding service to sport and the Association. Among this elite company was Stanley [Sonny] John Bissell. At the beginning of 1999 only 20 of 56 members granted life membership were still living.

His good friend and fellow adventurer on the village outings former Rector, the Reverend John Tipping summed up the man when he quoted:

> Youth is not a time of life...it is a state of mind.
> Nobody grows old by merely living a number of years;
> People grow old only by deserting their ideals.

Stan never deserted his ideals, never gave up believing in possibilities and refused to succumb to the limitations of old age. In his lifetime he had followed his dreams, served his country, helped generations of young people and made a difference – a fitting epitaph for a remarkable man.

Note

I have used 'Sonnie' and 'Sonny' throughout the text as required. To his family and intimates the spelling was always 'Sonnie', to others who knew him briefly it was spelt as it sounded, 'Sonny.'

Sources

Stan, Geoff and Denis Bissell, Lt. Col. [retired] Alan Peckham, Denis Garvey, Maurice Cole, Reverend John Tipping.

Col. C. E. Vaughn letter to *Police Review*; George Whiting's column, December 3rd 1955, *Evening Standard*; 'Crime Page by Tom Tullett' in *Daily Mirror* June 17th 1960; Metropolitan Police Central Record of Service; *Codford Tales of the Chitterne Brook* by Romy Wyeth [1994].

Bibliography

A Wylye Valley Childhood published by The Wiltshire Life Society. Now out of print the copyright is now with The Lackham Museum of Agriculture & Rural Life Trust.

The Highland Light Infantry Magazine: *The Outpost*

Hornchurch During the Great War: an illustrated account of local activities and experiences by Charles Thomas Perfect published in 1920.

New Zealand Medical Services in the Great War 1914-18

Official History of the War, Diseases of the War, Volume 1

Eyre & Lowe 'Prophylactic Vaccines against Catarrhal Infections', *Lancet* 1918, Vol. 2

The War Dead of the Commonwealth: Wiltshire Section, published by the Commonwealth War Graves Commission, London 1961

Wiltshire & the Great War by Terry Crawford

For Your Tomorrows by E. Martin

Warriors For the Working Day: Codford During Two World Wars by Romy Wyeth published 2002 by Hobnob Press, Salisbury, Wilts.

6th Guards Tank Brigade: The Story of Guardsmen in Churchill Tanks by Patrick Forbes published by Sampson, Low, Marston & Co Ltd. London

Battalion War Diaries 1939-1945 of the Welsh Guards

'Excavation of Spitfire BM540, East Farm, Knook, Wilts September 2005' compiled for the Marches Aviation Society by Ian Hodgkiss MA, Beng, PGCE